THE CONSTITUTION OF ISRAEL

This book presents the main features of the Israeli constitutional system and a topical discussion of Israel's basic laws. It focuses on constitutional history and the peculiar decision to frame a constitution 'by stages'. Following its British heritage and the lack of a formal constitution, Israel's democracy grew for more than four decades on the principle of parliamentary supremacy. Introducing a constitutional model and the concept of judicial review of laws, the 'constitutional revolution' of the 1990s started a new era in Israel's constitutional history. The book's main themes include: constitutional principles; the legislature and the electoral system; the executive; the protection of fundamental rights and the crucial role of the Supreme Court in Israel's constitutional discourse. It further presents Israel's unique aspects as a Jewish and democratic state, and its ongoing search for the right balance between human rights and national security. Finally, the book offers a critical discussion of the development of Israel's constitution and local projects aimed at enacting a single and comprehensive text.

Constitutional Systems of the World
General Editors: Peter Leyland and Andrew Harding
Associate Editors: Benjamin L Berger and Grégoire Webber

In the era of globalisation, issues of constitutional law and good governance are being seen increasingly as vital issues in all types of society. Since the end of the Cold War, there have been dramatic developments in democratic and legal reform, and post-conflict societies are also in the throes of reconstructing their governance systems. Even societies already firmly based on constitutional governance and the rule of law have undergone constitutional change and experimentation with new forms of governance; and their constitutional systems are increasingly subjected to comparative analysis and transplantation. Constitutional texts for practically every country in the world are now easily available on the internet. However, texts which enable one to understand the true context, purposes, interpretation and incidents of a constitutional system are much harder to locate, and are often extremely detailed and descriptive. This series seeks to provide scholars and students with accessible introductions to the constitutional systems of the world, supplying both a road map for the novice and, at the same time, a deeper understanding of the key historical, political and legal events which have shaped the constitutional landscape of each country. Each book in this series deals with a single country, or a group of countries with a common constitutional history, and each author is an expert in their field.

Published volumes

The Constitution of the United Kingdom; The Constitution of the United States; The Constitution of Vietnam; The Constitution of South Africa; The Constitution of Japan; The Constitution of Germany; The Constitution of Finland; The Constitution of Australia; The Constitution of the Republic of Austria; The Constitution of the Russian Federation; The Constitutional System of Thailand; The Constitution of Malaysia; The Constitution of China; The Constitution of Indonesia; The Constitution of France; The Constitution of Spain; The Constitution of Mexico

Link to series website
http://www.hartpub.co.uk/series/csw

The Constitution of Israel

A Contextual Analysis

Suzie Navot

·HART·
PUBLISHING
OXFORD AND PORTLAND, OREGON
2014

Hart Publishing
An imprint of Bloomsbury Publishing Plc

Hart Publishing Ltd
Kemp House
Chawley Park
Cumnor Hill
Oxford OX2 9PH
UK

Bloomsbury Publishing Plc
50 Bedford Square
London
WC1B 3DP
UK

www.hartpub.co.uk
www.bloomsbury.com

Published in North America (US and Canada) by
Hart Publishing
c/o International Specialized Book Services
920 NE 58th Avenue, Suite 300
Portland, OR 97213-3786
USA

www.isbs.com

**HART PUBLISHING, the Hart/Stag logo, BLOOMSBURY and the
Diana logo are trademarks of Bloomsbury Publishing Plc**

British Library Cataloguing-in-Publication Data
A catalogue record for this book is available from the British Library.

ISBN: 978-1-84113-835-0

Typeset by Hope Services Ltd, Abingdon
Printed and bound in Great Britain by
Lightning Source UK Ltd

To find out more about our authors and books visit www.hartpublishing.co.uk. Here you will
find extracts, author information, details of forthcoming events and the option to sign up for our
newsletters.

In memory of my parents,
Bela and Naftali Eisenberg

Preface

> We hereby declare the establishment of a Jewish State in *Eretz-Israel*, to
> be known as the State of Israel.[1]

The Land of Israel is the birthplace of the Jewish nation, where its
national identity was developed over the ages and its right to self-
determination was realised in 1948. On 29 November 1947, the United
Nations (UN) General Assembly endorsed the Partition Plan, which
represented the basis for the establishment of a Jewish State on Palestine
soil, then a territory under the British Mandate. The Holocaust expe-
dited the implementation of the decision to grant the Jews a national
homeland, as presented by the British government in the Balfour
Declaration of 1917.

According to the Partition Plan, as confirmed in UN Resolution 181,
three independent entities were to be established: a Jewish state, an Arab
state and another entity under a UN-governed international regime in
Jerusalem. While the leadership of the Jewish settlement in Palestine
accepted the Resolution, the Arab countries rejected the legitimacy of a
new Jewish state and launched a comprehensive attack against the
Jewish settlement, comprising some 600,000 people, starting what Israel
has since called the War of Independence. The Jews saw the creation of
Israel as the embodiment of their long-held aspiration for a land of
their own, but for Palestinians, the loss of their homes and land in 1948
became known as the '*Nakba*' or 'the catastrophe'. Some 700,000
Palestinians left what had been British-controlled Palestine, becoming
refugees in neighbouring countries.

The UN Resolution ordered Great Britain to evacuate the land and the
British Parliament decided that the Crown rule of Palestine would end on
15 May 1948. In view of the ensuing power vacuum, the local Jewish population decided to establish initial governing bodies for the future Jewish
state. On 14 May 1948, the leaders of the Jewish organisations, known as

---

[1] The Declaration of the Establishment of the State of Israel, 14 May 1948. For
the English version, see: http://mfa.gov.il/MFA/AboutIsrael/State/Pages/A%20
Free%20People%20in%20Our%20Land-%20Declaration%20of%20
Independence.aspx.

the National Council, gathered in a special session in Tel Aviv and declared the establishment of the State of Israel, publishing a document that was later known as the Declaration of the Establishment of the State of Israel, or the Declaration of Independence. This document was ratified by the National Council and was personally signed by each member. It was based on the UN Partition Plan and treated that Plan as the legal foundation for the Jewish nation's right to establish its state. David Ben-Gurion, soon to be Israel's first Prime Minister, opened his declaration speech by saying:

> Accordingly, we, the members of the National Council, representing the Jewish people in Palestine and the Zionist movement of the world, met together in solemn assembly today, the day of the termination of the British Mandate in Palestine, and by virtue of the natural and historic right of the Jewish Nation and of the Resolution of the General Assembly of the United Nations, hereby proclaim the establishment of the Jewish State in Palestine, to be called the State of Israel.[2]

The Declaration stated that once the Mandate ended and until regular and elected government bodies started functioning, the National Council would serve as the state's Constituent Assembly. It further stated that the 'setting up of the duly elected bodies of the State' would be done 'in accordance with a Constitution, to be drawn up by a Constituent Assembly no later than the first day of October 1948'.

The Provisional National Council's first legislative act was the enactment of the Law and Administration Ordinance 1948, which partially arranged the distribution of powers in the new state and the transition from the Mandate to the new government. This volume will elaborate upon the history of those first days, because decisions made then are still of crucial and constitutional importance today. The Declaration of Independence stated that Israel would elect a constituent assembly that would draft a constitution for the State of Israel that would guide the establishment and activities of the elected authorities. The constitution of which the founding fathers dreamt was, however, never written.

The Israeli Constituent Assembly was indeed elected and even discussed the future constitution, but never truly used its constituent power. The discussions ended in deadlock. The Constituent Assembly (which renamed itself the First Knesset) reached a compromise (known as the Harari Resolution) that is unique and unusual in terms of comparative

---

[2] Ruth Lapidoth and Moshe Hirsch (eds), *The Arab-Israel Conflict and its Resolution: Selected Documents* (Dordrecht, Martinus Nijhoff Publishers , 1992).

constitutional law. Israel would enact a constitution 'in stages': the constitution would be composed of chapters, each of which would stand as an independent basic law, each chapter would be endorsed by the Knesset and, after this, the chapters would form the Israeli constitution.

Following this Resolution, the First Knesset, Israel's constituent power, eventually dispersed, transferring its powers to the next and all subsequent Knessets. In theory, this meant that Israel's *pouvoir constituant* ceased to exist and its powers expired. Some believe that this move severed the constitutional chain that started when the state was founded. Others argue that the constituent power is alive and 'belongs' to the parliament; thus, every elected Knesset holds that constituent power and may endorse a constitution whenever it sees fit.

In any event, Israel started out without a constitution or a bill of human rights, based on the British tradition of parliamentary sovereignty. In the early years, the prevailing concept was that the Knesset was legislatively sovereign and 'omnipotent', and that the Supreme Court was not competent to review its legislative acts. Attempts made over the years to convince the Supreme Court that, in the absence of a constitution, the Declaration of Independence is the fundamental Israeli legal norm have failed.

The first chapter of this book outlines Israel's unique constitutional history and deals with the basic laws that were enacted over the years and were meant to comprise Israel's constitution. In 1992, two basic laws on human rights were introduced that limited the legislative power to infringe human rights. These laws were the focal point of a crucial Supreme Court ruling in 1995 that fundamentally changed Israel's constitutional nature. The monumental *Bank Hamizrahi* ruling marked the climax of what became known as the 'constitutional revolution'. In it, the Supreme Court declared the supremacy of the basic laws and their constitutional status. Overnight, the basic laws became 'constitutional' and all regular laws became subordinate to them. The sovereignty of the Knesset was thus declared to be limited by norms that the Knesset itself established in its 'constituent' capacity. At the same time, the Supreme Court recognised its power to judicially review laws.

As a result, the State of Israel underwent a constitutional metamorphosis from a state based on the British model of parliamentary sovereignty to a constitutional state. Furthermore, the Supreme Court's generous interpretations of those basic laws introduced significant constitutional concepts.

The status of the basic laws will be extensively discussed in this book. Presently, the basic laws together form the Israeli constitution, which is written but is still being formed. It is a limited constitution, and the Israeli constitutional arrangement is a unique and incomplete project. Chapter two shall discuss the sources of Israel's constitution. Many argue that Israel has a 'judicial' constitution that lacks many elements that characterise more complete constitutions found in other countries. For example, some of the basic rights are not entrenched in basic laws, but were created by the Supreme Court. Some of the requirements of the basic laws are rigid, while others can be modified by an ordinary Knesset majority. Some of the provisions were written in flowery and festive language, offering general and very brief instructions, while others are too detailed and cumbersome. Certain fundamental constitutional issues do not appear in Israel's basic laws and their legal status remains unclear. Yet, though the constitution is incomplete, the Israeli courts have acknowledged certain principles that may not be modified – primarily the constitutional principle that refers to the Jewish and democratic nature of the State of Israel.

The Declaration of Independence singled out some of the basic principles of the new state. It stated that the Jewish state established in Israel 'will be based on freedom, justice, and peace as envisaged by the prophets of Israel; it will ensure complete equality of social and political rights to all its inhabitants irrespective of religion, race or sex'. Thus, it was founded as a 'Jewish and democratic' state. These fundamental principles will be discussed in chapter three. The Jewish nature of the state is a fundamental characteristic that was determined by the international community in the 1947 UN Partition Plan before the State of Israel was established. It was further explicitly stated in the Declaration of Independence and subsequently in a long series of practical arrangements by which Israelis live.

Israel is a Jewish state in the sense that it is the nation in which the Jews realised their right to self-determination. A Jewish state has constitutional consequences: it serves as the basis for arrangements such as the Law of Return, according to which all Jews – and only Jews – may become Israeli citizens automatically upon immigration. Although the Jewish religion is not a state law, as we shall see, the state may impose restrictions on individual liberties when seeking to promote and preserve the Jewish heritage and nature of public life.

Potential tensions exist between the basic Jewish and democratic tenets of Israel. As will become clear, Israel's commitment to the basic values of democracy – primarily the acknowledgement that all people were created equal and have a right to dignity – leads to the conclusion that it is a Jewish nation state only so long as this does not impair the fundamental principles of democracy, namely, the rule of law, the separation of powers and the protection of acknowledged human rights.

Chapter four is dedicated to the Israeli parliament, the Knesset. This single-chamber house serves as the constituent power that is authorised to enact and amend basic laws. The Israeli parliamentary system follows the British model, in which the government must have the confidence of the House of Parliament. The Knesset supervises the executive and the state budget. Focusing on the Knesset and its role in the Israeli constitutional set-up, this chapter opens with a discussion of the Israeli election method, which is unique in comparative law terms. Israel is a single, undivided constituency that elects 120 representatives as Members of the Knesset. In the 1990s, the State of Israel experimented with a special arrangement that combined the presidential and parliamentary methods: the Prime Minister was elected personally and did not require the confidence of the Knesset. This method failed and, less than a decade later, Israel returned to the parliamentary method with slight modifications. This chapter will also examine the activities of the Knesset and the various political parties, focusing on unique issues such as the status of political parties and the disqualification of anti-democratic parties.

Chapter five addresses the government and the executive in Israel. In the first part of this chapter, we will present a brief overview of the presidency, its status and the (mostly symbolic) roles of the state's President. Further on, we discuss the election and composition of the government, and focus on the new system for the election of the Prime Minister, the reasons that prompted it and why it failed. Here, a special discussion is devoted to the nature of government performance, the rules of responsibility and accountability, and the role of the military in the constitutional context. Finally, we will present Israel's civil service, which serves any government in power, and the local government powers.

Chapter six reviews Israel's supervising bodies such as the State Comptroller, commissions of inquiry and the Attorney General. The latter holds one of the most powerful public positions in Israel, but is not mentioned in any constitutional text. It is surprising that no basic law applies to the Attorney General and that the powers enjoyed by that office are not even gathered under a single law. The Attorney General is the chief prosecutor and has the power to order criminal prosecutions, represents the state in the courts, offers legal advice to the government and is the government's official interpreter of the law. Furthermore, the Attorney General's legal opinions are binding on the government. This chapter will also discuss the special role of non-governmental organisations and the media in Israeli society.

Chapter seven addresses the judiciary, focusing on the Supreme Court, which serves as the High Court of Justice (HCJ), as court of appeals, and as Israel's constitutional court. It is impossible to describe the development of the Israeli constitution without considering the role of the Supreme Court sitting as the HCJ. The HCJ's impact on constitutional law is crucial, as is its influence on Israeli society. Despite the fact that the HCJ did not have powers to oversee all government and legislative decisions granted by the constitution, the public has used the Court to obtain public policy decisions that could not be obtained through any other means. This phenomenon gradually enhanced and strengthened the Court's position as a key political player which may be seen to have resulted in a new balance of power between the branches of government. Until the 1980s, the HCJ set a threshold requirement of standing as a precondition for hearing petitions, and many issues were treated as unjusticiable. Following various political and social changes in the 1980s, the HCJ dropped these justiciability barriers, thereby becoming an influential – even dominant – force in shaping the Israeli constitutional system. The Court's activist adjudication on political, military and security issues, coupled with its criticism of government powers, is famous worldwide. Presently, it plays the most significant role in shaping Israel as a democratic society, as we shall see in this contextual analysis.

The last chapter of this book deals with human rights. The public debate over human rights is particularly complicated for several reasons. Israel does not have a complete constitutional text that defends human rights. A political compromise in 1992 allowed the Knesset to agree on and vote for the constitutional entrenchment of a few particular human rights on which consensus has been reached, leaving the discussion of 'problematic' rights such as equality and freedom of religion, speech and conscience pending. These human rights are not anchored in Israeli basic laws and a single comprehensive basic law on human rights has not yet been written.

Furthermore, since its establishment, Israel has been in a state of war and in extended periods of emergency. War and terror acts have resulted in an almost daily examination of restrictions of human rights, pressing the need to find the right balance between defending those rights and protecting national security. A special part in this chapter will deal with security cases. One-fifth of Israel's citizens are Arab nationals (Palestinian Israelis) who wish to preserve their culture, religion and language, while sympathising with the Palestinian nation and the Arab world, with which the State of Israel is in a state of ongoing belligerency. This unique relationship between majority and minority populations is particularly important and shall be discussed within the principle of equality. Furthermore, in the 1967 war, Israel occupied populated territories, which created serious debate about the civil status and general fate of the Palestinian population of the West Bank and the Gaza Strip. The Supreme Court allowed these Palestinians to appeal against decisions made by the military commanders of the occupied regions, sharply defending the need to protect human rights even in times of emergency. The unresolved conflict between Israel and the Palestinians presented the Supreme Court with problematic questions which will be discussed, such as the legality of the Security Fence and pre-emptive killings. The challenges that Israel has faced and will face in this context are central in this final chapter.

Acknowledgments

I would like to thank Peter Leyland, Andrew Harding and Benjamin Berger for their challenging invitation to partake in this essential project of reviewing the constitutions of the world. They made countless and invaluable comments, remarks and suggestions to the first draft of the book, and I am most thankful to them.

Thanks to my colleagues at the Striks Law School for their help and support, and to my research assistants Matan Spector, Yehonatan Prusak, Rosa Feldman, Noam Avital and Moran Kandelstein-Hainne for their valuable research. I wish to thank Professor Claude Klein, teacher and mentor, for his advice all along. Special thanks to Baruch Gefen and Breony Allen for their impressive, intelligent and meticulous editorial work.

Thanks to Richard Hart, who made this project possible, and special thanks to Putachad Leyland for the wonderful book cover she designed that perfectly reflects Israel's colourful complexity.

Last, but not least: thank you, Yoram, love of my life, always by my side. This book would never have been completed without you, our daughters and the rest of our wonderful and supporting family.

Suzie Navot
Israel, 2013

Contents

Table of Cases

United States

Table of Legislation

International

1

Israel's Constitutional History

Part I: History – The Establishment of a 'Jewish State' – The Declaration of Independence

Part II: From Parliamentary Sovereignty to a Limited Legislature – The Declaration of Independence as a Constitutional Norm – The Status of Basic Laws before 1992

Part III: The Constitutional Revolution – Basic Laws on Human Rights – The *Bank Hamizrahi* Decision: A 'Judge Made' Constitution? – Unresolved Constitutional Questions – Conclusion: Does Israel Have a Written Constitution?

PART I: HISTORY

THE ESTABLISHMENT OF A 'JEWISH STATE'

THE BIRTH OF Israel as the 'Jewish State' – the nation-state of a people, the majority of whom did not reside within its territory – was an exceptional event, explicable only within its particular historical context. Towards the end of the nineteenth century, Zionist movements that emerged in Europe stressed that it was imperative for the Jewish people to return to Zion and establish a Jewish state. In 1896, Theodor Herzl, known as 'the Visionary of the Jewish State', published *The Jewish State*, a book in which he outlined the justifications and reasons for the establishment of a state for the Jewish people. The publication coincided with the 1897 convention of the First World Zionist Congress in Basel, Switzerland. Among other things, the Congress recommended that Jews settle in Palestine, which was then under the rule of the Ottoman Empire. The subsequent development of the Zionist movement led to the establishment of small Jewish colonies in the Land of Israel even before the First World War.

The Allied victory in the First World War was followed by the downfall of the Ottoman Empire and the British conquest of Palestine in 1917. Published on 2 November 1917, the Balfour Declaration expressed the British government's commitment to the idea of establishing a Jewish home in Palestine. The Declaration stated: 'His Majesty's government view with favour the establishment in Palestine of a national home for the Jewish people, and will use their best endeavours to facilitate the achievement of this object, it being clearly understood that nothing shall be done which may prejudice the civil and religious rights of existing non-Jewish communities in Palestine, or the rights and political status enjoyed by Jews in any other country.'[1]

In 1922, the League of Nations entrusted the area of Palestine to Great Britain as Mandated territory.[2] According to the Mandate for Palestine, the British government was charged with creating the political, administrative and economic conditions required for the establishment of the Jewish National Home, as anticipated by the Balfour Declaration.

Under British rule, Jews in Palestine experienced accelerated economic and demographic growth that resulted, to a large extent, from the massive influx of Jewish capital and immigrants. Between 1922 and 1944, the country's population grew from 750,000 to some 1,700,000 and the Jewish population grew from about 83,000 to about 530,000 (increasing from 10 to 30 per cent of the population).[3]

In 'Mandate Palestine', the British encountered a legal system unlike their own. The law of the pre-Mandate land was Ottoman, originating from Islamic religious law, and developed over the years to regulate many other areas of law, inter alia, evidentiary, land and civil laws. The hegemony of the Ottoman law ended at the turn of the twentieth century when a legal reform heralded the incorporation of European

---

[1] The Balfour Declaration (dated 2 November 1917) was a letter from the UK's Foreign Secretary Arthur James Balfour to Baron Rothschild, a leader of the British Jewish community. The text was later incorporated into the Mandate for Palestine.

[2] Section 22 of the Covenant of the League of Nations.

[3] Assaf Likhovski, *Law and Identity in Mandate Palestine* (University of North Carolina Press, 2006) 21.

norms into the Ottoman legal system.[4] The Ottoman system was characterised by autonomous judicial courts that addressed issues of personal status. This meant that clerical courts of religious communities were granted exclusive jurisdiction over matrimonial issues.

Some three weeks after the League of Nations approved the British Mandate over Palestine, the King's Order in Council for Palestine of 1922 was issued. This was a foundational document, tantamount to a constitution, and formed the basis of the regime in Palestine. The Order in Council extended British legislative authority to the foreign territory. The Mandate charter itself was regarded as a political document, whereas legislation and local administrative practices drew their powers from Great Britain by force of section 46 of the King's Order in Council, which referred to English law for resolving lacunae. Thus, Ottoman law remained in effect for as long as it was not revoked by a mandatory provision, but the local courts were at liberty to apply English law in cases of lacunae. The British therefore left the indigenous law nominally intact, but changed the nature of the law as actually applied in Palestine. Indeed, British influence greatly impacted on Israeli law in general and on Israeli constitutional law in particular.

The British streamlined law enforcement, adopted the principle of stare decisis and introduced the adversarial system, but not a jury system. They also created an Official Gazette for the publication of laws and ordinances, replaced the Ottoman Criminal Code, consolidated the rules of civil and criminal procedure, and changed some of the laws of evidence. Having recourse to section 46 of the Order in Council, the British government was able to introduce numerous areas of common law into the Mandate legal system, including the English principles of equity and tort law. As a result, the country's legal system underwent a partial metamorphosis during the Mandate. The British expanded the jurisdiction of state courts and strengthened state control over religious courts and other informal tribunals. In a process often called anglicisation, the country's legal system, which had been based on Islamic and French norms and procedures, was thus remodelled with significant common law elements. The ultimate result of that anglicisation was a mosaic system made up of many legal pebbles: Ottoman, Muslim, French, Jewish and, above all, English.[5]

---

[4] Assaf Likhovski, 'In Our Image: Colonial Discourse and the Anglicization of the Law of Mandatory Palestine' (1995) 29 *Israel Law Review* 291.

[5] Likhovski (n 3) 23.

The unique combination of Ottoman, British and Mandate law was retained even after the establishment of the State of Israel in 1948. The newly formed Israeli government prevented a legal vacuum by applying the same technique that the Mandate government had used, leaving the entire existing legal system in place. Its first legislative act was therefore the enactment of the Law and Administration Ordinance (1948), which provided: 'The law which existed in Palestine on 5th Iyar, 5708 (14 May 1948) shall remain in force insofar as there is nothing therein repugnant to this Ordinance or to the other laws which may be enacted by or on behalf of the Provisional Council of State, and subject to such modifications as may result from the establishment of the State and its authorities.'

Referring to the authority of the courts, the Ordinance further stated that 'so long as no new law concerning courts of law has been enacted, the courts that exist in the territory of the State shall continue to function within the scope of the powers conferred upon them by law.' The Ordinance therefore established the continuity of the British legal system. Though the enactment of original Israeli legislation proceeded apace following the establishment of the state, the nexus to English law as a binding legal source was retained, as will be discussed later on.

THE DECLARATION OF INDEPENDENCE

On 29 November 1947, the UN General Assembly voted for the establishment of a Jewish state on the territory known as Palestine or the Land of Israel. At the time, the territory of the Land of Israel was a narrow strip of land on the eastern shores of the Mediterranean Sea, with a population of some 70,000 Jews and some 200,000 Arabs. UN Resolution 181 adopted the Partition Plan,[6] according to which three political entities would be established in Palestine: a Jewish state, an Arab state and a special international regime for Jerusalem, to be administered by the UN.

The UN General Assembly intended to establish an executive commission[7] which, upon the termination of the British Mandate, would

[6] The text of the decision appears in Ruth Lapidoth and Moshe Hirsch (eds), *The Arab-Israel Conflict and its Resolution – Selected Documents* (Dordrecht, Martinus Nijhoff Publishers, 1992) 33.

[7] Yoram Shachar, 'The Early Drafts of the Declaration of Independence' (2003) 26 *Tel-Aviv Law Studies* 523, 539–40.

operate in Palestine and would prepare the provisional institutions of self-government ahead of the establishment of the two states. The Jewish and the Arab states were to be based on a constitution, the main elements of which were dictated in that resolution: 'The Constituent Assembly of each State shall draft a democratic constitution for its State and choose a provisional government to succeed the Provisional Council of Government appointed by the Commission.'

The decision of the UN General Assembly was accepted by the national leadership of the Jewish *Yishuv*[8] in Palestine at the time, but the Arabs rejected the legitimacy of a new Jewish state and launched a comprehensive offensive against the Jewish entity. Under the terms of the General Assembly resolution, Britain, the mandatory power, was called upon to withdraw its armed forces from Palestine. The British government permitted the entry of the UN Executive Commission to Palestine shortly before the Mandate ended and withdrew its forces without any formal and orderly transfer of power to a local independent government (Arab or Jewish). On 29 April 1948, the British Parliament enacted the Palestine Act, in which it determined that the jurisdiction of the Crown in Palestine would be terminated on 15 May 1948. This confluence of circumstances forced the Jewish leadership to prevent a political and legal vacuum and, taking the initiative, decided to establish preliminary governmental institutions for the nascent Jewish state.

The Declaration of Independence of the State of Israel was drafted in three weeks, beginning on 20 April 1948. It was a ceremonial document such as the historic American Declaration of Independence or the French Declaration of the Rights of Man and of the Citizen. The Israeli Declaration of Independence purported to present the credo of the new state while establishing legal facts to suit a state created *ex nihilo*.[9]

On Friday 14 May 1948, one day before the termination of the British Mandate, a festive gathering of the members of the People's Council[10]

---

[8] Pre-state Jewish settlement.

[9] Pnina Lahav, 'A Jewish State to be Known as the State of Israel: Notes on the Israeli Legal Historiography' (2001) 19 *Law and History Review* 387; Elyakim Rubinstein, 'The Declaration of Independence as a Basic Document of the State of Israel' (1998) 3(1) *Israeli Studies* 195; Tuvia Friling and S Ilan Troen, 'Proclaiming Independence: Five Days in May from Ben-Gurion`s Diary' (1998) 3(1) *Israel Studies* 170, 172.

[10] The leaders of the Jewish settlement decided to establish a Provisional Government for the Jewish state in March 1948. It was later renamed the People's Council. It consisted of 37 members who appropriately represented the range of

was held in Tel Aviv. Serving as the parliamentary body of the nascent state, the Council issued the Declaration of the Establishment of the State of Israel. This document was published, confirmed and signed by all the members of the People's Council, who then became the Provisional Council of State.

The Declaration is based upon, and views, the UN Partition Decision as the key international reference for the Jewish people's right to establish its state. After outlining the historical aspects of that right, David Ben-Gurion, later the first Prime Minister of the State of Israel, stated:

> Accordingly, we, members of the People's Council, representatives of the Jewish community of *Eretz-Israel*[11] and of the Zionist movement, are here assembled on the day of the termination of the British mandate over *Eretz-Israel* and, by virtue of our natural and historic right and the strength of the resolution of the United Nations General Assembly, hereby declare the establishment of a Jewish State in *Eretz-Israel*, to be known as the State of Israel.[12]

The Declaration determined the mechanism for electing the principal organs of the state. As for the constitution, the Declaration stated that the People's Council would operate as a Provisional Council of State between the termination of the Mandate and the establishment of regular, elected state authorities. It further stated that the establishment of those regular, elected authorities would be done in accordance with a constitution that was to be adopted by the Elected Constituent Assembly no later than 1 October 1948. The first legislative act of the Provisional Council of State was the enactment of the Law and Administration Ordinance, which partially regulated the distribution of power and authority in the new state, and the transition from the Mandatory government to the new government. The Ordinance further stated, inter alia, that 'The Provisional Council of State is the legislative authority' and, accordingly, the Provisional Council of State established the Constituent Assembly Elections Ordinance.

---

political persuasions within the *Yishuv* and elected the People's Administration that operated as an executive arm from among its members.

[11] *Eretz-Israel* is the Jewish/Israeli Hebrew equivalent of Palestine as a geographical unit (*Eretz* = land).

[12] Lapidoth and Hirsch (n 6).

The Provisional Council of State appointed a Constitution Committee and instructed it to collect and coordinate proposals and materials relating to the constitution, as well as to author a draft constitution that was to be submitted to the Constituent Assembly along with the opinions and reservations of the committee members. The Constitution Committee was presented with several draft constitutions and its deliberations focused primarily on institutional matters pertaining to the structure of the government, the electoral method and the legal system. In late 1948, however, even before the election of the Constituent Assembly, members of both the Provisional Council of State and the Constitution Committee of the State's Provisional Council expressed their opposition to a written constitution, some arguing that the state was only in the very early stages of its formation, while others cited ideological reasons.

The elections for the Constituent Assembly were held on 25 January 1949, after which a Constituent Committee was ordered to draft a constitution for the state, pursuant to the Declaration of Independence.

The original plan was that, following the election of the Constituent Assembly, the Provisional Council of State and the Constituent Assembly would coexist as two separate bodies with different compositions and tasks. The Constituent Assembly – which was the constituent authority – was to function alongside the Provisional Council of State, and because it was elected in general elections by all the members of Israeli society, it was assigned the unique task of formulating a constitution.

The two bodies, however, did not function as separate entities. Following the elections and upon the establishment of the Constituent Assembly, the Provisional Council of State dispersed and it was made clear that the Constituent Assembly would handle both ongoing legislative and constitutional matters. This was the unequivocal message of the election campaigns at the time, as expressed in the parties' platforms that addressed all national issues, not only constitutional matters. The Israeli residents who voted in the elections for the Constituent Assembly knew that they were voting for a body that would have both constituent and legislative powers.

The Constituent Assembly was thus elected in January 1949 as both a constituent and a legislative body, meaning that it could draft the constitution and act as the legislative power. Immediately upon its establishment, the Constituent Assembly enacted the Transition Law 1949, which provided that: 'The legislature of the State of Israel will be known as the Knesset. This Constituent Assembly will be known as the First Knesset.'

Though prima facie the Constituent Assembly merely renamed itself, it seems that the renaming procedure was politically motivated. Its purpose was to bury the subject of the constituent authority altogether and perhaps even to abandon the notion of the written constitution, to which then Prime Minister David Ben-Gurion was opposed. The Prime Minister's opposition to a written constitution was meant to prevent struggle and debates between political parties and social segments, which threatened the country's ability to establish new national institutions. Just as dismantling underground military groups was a condition for the establishment of a national army, so too was the prevention of an ideological debate and a cultural war that threatened to follow the enactment of a written constitution. To Ben-Gurion, this was a preventive step allowing the establishment of the military, government, law and administrative systems based on the principles of the rule of law rather than on sectarian ideologies.[13]

The First Knesset deliberated on the principal question of whether it was even desirable to frame a written constitution. A stormy debate was conducted in the Knesset as opponents felt that Israel should defer the adoption of a constitution for a few years and first regulate the functioning of the institutions of state using primary legislation.[14] In the absence of a consensus on the need for a constitution, its content and form, constitutional deliberations reached a deadlock. Opponents of the constitution argued that it was undesirable to establish rigid constitutional principles when the majority of the nation had yet to immigrate, that framing a constitution at this time was liable to lead to a cultural war among the various sectors of the nation and that the State of Israel was still in a dynamic flux of crystallisation. These factors, they argued, were antithetical to the concept of a rigid constitution. It is also worth noting that the religious Members of the Knesset (MKs) were also opposed to formulating a constitution, arguing that the *Torah* (Old Testament) was their only and exclusive constitution. Prime Minister Ben-Gurion, who was also the head of the largest political party, opposed the adoption of a constitution with normative supremacy, as already mentioned. Evidently, Ben-Gurion's opposition proved

---

[13] Nir Kedar, *Ben-Gurion and the Constitution: On Constitutionalism, Democracy and Law in David Ben-Gurion's Policy* (Bar-Ilan University Press and Zmora, Bitan, Dvir Press, 2014) (Hebrew).

[14] Ruth Gavison, 'The Controversy over Israel's Bill of Rights' (1985) 15 *Israel Yearbook of Human Rights* 113.

decisive,[15] though the Israeli public generally came to believe over the years that it was the opposition of the religious parties that eventually tipped the scales against framing a constitution. Recently, it has become increasingly clear that the supposed opposition of the religious parties was a mere smokescreen that Ben-Gurion and his party employed to avoid the fulfilment of their obligation to frame a constitution.[16]

Ultimately, the Knesset adopted a compromise that, in terms of comparative constitutional law, was unique: Israel would introduce a constitution 'in stages'. Thus, the Knesset completed its constitutional deliberations by endorsing what became known as the Harari Resolution (named after MK Harari who proposed it), according to which: 'The First Knesset charges the Constitution, Law, and Justice Committee with the preparation of a proposed constitution for the State. The constitution will be composed of chapters, each comprising a single Basic Law unto itself. The chapters will be brought before the Knesset and . . . together will constitute the Constitution of the State.'

The First Knesset (or Constituent Assembly) ultimately dispersed without having prepared so much as a 'draft constitution for the state', nor did it adopt a single basic law. Upon its dissolution, the First Knesset enacted the Transition (Second Knesset) Law 1951, which provided that 'The Second Knesset . . . shall have all the powers . . . that the First Knesset and its members had' and that this provision would also apply 'to the Third Knesset and every subsequent Knesset'. This meant that, prima facie, the Constituent Assembly disappeared along with its constituent powers. Thus, it may be argued that any future attempt to frame a constitution would require either new elections for a constituent assembly or a national referendum.

From an historical perspective, there are some who believe that when the First Knesset abandoned its duty to frame a constitution, it sowed

---

[15] Michael Mandel, 'Democracy and New Constitutionalism in Israel' (1999) 33 *Israel Law Review* 259, 274: 'The hegemony of Labour at the helm of a strong state . . . seems to me the most convincing explanation for the lack of a constitutional Bill of Rights in the first generation of the State's existence.'

[16] Yehoshua Segev, 'Why Israel Does Not and Will Not Have a Constitution?' (2006) 5 *Netanya Academic College Law Review* 125, 131, note 14 (Hebrew) and in the accompanying text; Giora Goldberg, 'Religious Zionism and the Framing of Constitution for Israel' (1998) 3(1) *Israel Studies* 211, 212; Philippa Strum, 'The Road Not Taken: Constitutional Non-Decision Making in 1948–1950 and its Impact on Civil Liberties' in Ilan Troen and Noah Lucas (eds) *The Political Culture in Israel: The First Decade of Independence* (Albany, NY, SUNY Press, 1995) 83, 87.

the first seeds of a fundamental characteristic of the Israeli regime – the government's inability to govern. Deferring a decision on the constitution, the Knesset essentially 'decided not to decide', a tactic that has characterised Israel's constitutional law from the First Knesset to this very day.[17]

Being a political compromise, the Harari Resolution left many questions unresolved. Perhaps the simplest of those was how much time the Knesset would allocate to complete the process of enacting the basic laws and consolidating them into a single constitution. In fact, eight years would pass between the adoption of the Harari Resolution and the Knesset's endorsement of the first basic law, and even after that, the process of enacting basic laws proceeded at a snail's pace. Can a constitutional project stretch over dozens of years – an internationally unparalleled phenomenon? The Harari Resolution did not specify a timeframe for drafting a constitution.

Another question that the Harari Resolution left open concerns the status of the basic laws to be enacted and their status vis-a-vis 'regular' laws that the Knesset enacts as the legislative authority.[18] Do basic laws enjoy 'constitutional' status even before the completion of the constitution? In other words, the questions of the constitution's rigidity and supremacy remained unanswered.

This brings us to the question of *pouvoir constituant* (constituent power). Is it even possible to create a constitutional text if the body that creates it is devoid of *pouvoir constituant*? Was this power transferred from the First Knesset – which, as noted above, was the Constituent Assembly – to all of the subsequent Knessets? Perhaps only the Constituent Assembly, elected in 1949, was authorised to adopt a constitution for Israel. If so: 'This trust, placed by the people in the Constituent Assembly, was not transferable to anyone else inasmuch as the people did not authorise it to transfer its authority to anyone else.'[19] This conundrum attracted the title of 'the problem of constituent continuity'[20] and

---

[17] Segev (n 16) 127.

[18] Segev (n 16) 139–40. See also Eliahu Likhovski, 'Can the Knesset Adopt a Constitution that Will Be the Supreme Law of the Land?' (1969) 4 *Israel Law Review* 61, 63–64.

[19] Justice Cheshin, in the *Bank Hamizrahi* case, CA 6821/93 *United Hamizrahi Bank v Migdal Cooperative Village* 49(4) PD 221 (1995) (hereinafter *Bank Hamizrahi*) 489.

[20] Melville B Nimmer, 'The Uses of Judicial Review in Israel's Quest for a Constitution' (1970) 70 *Columbia Law Review* 1217, 1239 (1970); Eliahu Likhovski, 'The

was discussed at length in the *Bank Hamizrahi* judgment, which will be addressed later on.

Many of the questions that the Harari Resolution left open have been addressed in Israel's constitutional law today, but most of the answers concerning the status of basic laws were actually provided by the Supreme Court rather than the Knesset, as might have been expected. As we shall see, the prevailing view today is that the basic laws constitute the 'constitution' of the State of Israel. In other words, they enjoy normative supremacy over regular Knesset legislation and restrict the legislative authority.

In many respects, the failure to frame a constitution upon the establishment of the state was the result of disputes among the various political parties. In addition to disagreements as to the content of the constitution, political factions were divided over the nature of constitutional arrangements and desirable state institutions. While the consensus was that the regime of the nascent state must be democratic, certain factions advocated democracy in the 'narrow' sense and even argued that choosing this kind of regime was the product of utilitarian political considerations.[21] Given that many who disputed the content of the constitution are still with us today, the ongoing struggle between secular and religious factions over issues such as human rights, the status and rights of minorities in Israel, the basic principles that should be anchored in the constitution and who should safeguard them, as well as the issue of judicial review, are not just legacies of the past – they remain topical issues today. Thus, in the second decade of the twenty-first century, the completion of the Israeli constitution still seems unrealistic. Despite the important constitutional move of 1992 and the transition from a Knesset with unlimited parliamentary sovereignty to a constitutional regime, the constitutionalisation of human rights is still plagued by the 'decision not to decide'. This being the case, as discussed below, the Supreme Court's influence over constitutional trends turns out to be decisive.

Courts and the Legislative Supremacy of the Knesset' (1968) 3 *Israel Law Review* 345, 358; Dalia Dorner, 'Does Israel Have a Constitution?' 43 *St Louis Law Journal* 1325, 1333.

[21] Dan Horowitz and Moshe Lissack, *Trouble in Utopia: The Overburdened Policy of Israel* (Albany, NY, SUNY Press, 1989). Daphna Sharfman, 'Living without a Constitution' (1993) *Civil Rights in Israel* 33.

PART II: FROM PARLIAMENTARY SOVEREIGNTY TO A LIMITED
LEGISLATURE

THE DECLARATION OF INDEPENDENCE AS A
CONSTITUTIONAL NORM

The result of the Constituent Assembly's dissolution and the decision
not to frame a written constitution was that Israeli constitutional law
developed along the lines of the British model. Israel lacked a written
constitution, but, in a similar fashion to the English 'mother' constitution, it had an unwritten constitution: a set of fundamental principles,
coupled with a list of bodies authorised to exercise sovereign powers,
and specific election procedures for them.

Even in the early days of the state, an attempt was made to convince
the Supreme Court, sitting as the High Court of Justice (HCJ), that the
Declaration of Independence was in fact the 'constitution' – a document
of supreme normative status that authorised the Court to review and
even annul legislative acts. Certainly, the Declaration of Independence
possessed at least some of the hallmarks of a constitution, having been
written by the *pouvoir constituant* and being perhaps the closest document
to an Israeli constitution at the time. Even though the Declaration of
Independence was not written as a constitution, the notion of its trans-
formation into a binding legal document might have been supported by
the UN Partition Plan. The Plan stipulated a number of provisions that
each of the states was obligated to include in their independence declarations, explicitly stating that terms set by the respective declarations would
enjoy the status of basic laws of the state, to be neither contradicted nor
violated by any other law, regulation or official act.[22] Israel's Declaration
of Independence was apparently drafted with the intention of complying
with the conditions set forth in the UN Resolution, but the question of its

---

[22] 'A declaration shall be made to the United Nations by the Provisional
Government of each proposed State before independence. It shall contain, inter alia,
the following clauses . . . The stipulations contained in the Declaration are recognized
as fundamental laws of the State and no law, regulation, or official action shall conflict or interfere with these stipulations, nor shall any law, regulation, or official action
prevail over them.' The intention was to guarantee the safety of and access to the holy
sites, the maintenance of religious and minorities' rights, and outline terms pertaining
to citizenship, international contracts and financial undertakings.

legal standing from the perspective of Israeli law remained open and became increasingly important as time passed and no constitution was framed. The Supreme Court addressed the status of the Declaration of Independence in the *Ziv* case in 1948, shortly after the establishment of the state. The petitioner attempted to rely on the Declaration as grounds for annulling an order that condemned his property. His petition was actually a request to annul Knesset legislation, referring to the status of the Declaration as the basic, constitutional norm that enabled judicial review of legislation that conflicted with its content. The petitioner argued that the ordinance (bearing the normative status of a regular law), by the power of which the condemnation order was issued, contradicted a provision in the Declaration according to which: 'The State of Israel . . . will be based on freedom, justice, and peace as envisaged by the prophets of Israel.' Sitting as the HCJ, the Supreme Court dismissed the claim and refused to confer the Declaration with a 'constitutional' status that would enable the annulment of legislative acts: 'The only object of the Declaration was to affirm the fact of the foundation and establishment of the State for the purpose of its recognition by international law. It expresses the vision and credo of the nation, but contains no element of constitutional law which determines the validity or repeal of various ordinances and laws. The body temporarily empowered to enact statutes was the Provisional Council of State, which was established with the Declaration of the State.'[23]

Why did the Supreme Court refuse to ascribe constitutional status to the Declaration? Israeli legal literature concerning the status of the constitution offers various explanations. One is that the Court presumed that the Knesset would enact a constitution that would incorporate and anchor the principles of the Declaration. From that perspective, the fact that the Knesset abdicated its role as drafter of the constitution was referred to as 'a missed historic opportunity'.[24] Others opined that 'had

---

[23] HCJ 10/48 *Ziv v Gubernik, District Commissioner, Urban District of Tel Aviv* ver 1, 85 (1948), 89.

[24] For example, Professor Aharon Barak, former President of the Supreme Court, wrote in his book *Interpretation in Law: The General Theory of Interpretation* (Jerusalem, Nevo, 1992) 632 (Hebrew): 'Conceivably, upon the creation of the State, within the framework of the general social consensus in Israel, it might have been possible to reach a different result; an historic opportunity may have been then . . . Today, this path is closed to the judiciary. Were a judge to rule that the Declaration of Independence is a "Supreme Law", such an act would be regarded by the legal

the court attempted to unilaterally impose a constitution upon the state, it would have been morally inappropriate and politically mistaken'.[25] Either way, the Supreme Court clarified its position soon after the state was established, asserting that the Declaration of Independence is not a binding legal document and does not enjoy the status of a constitution.

The Supreme Court adhered to this position for decades. A key ruling on the status of Israel's Declaration of Independence was handed down in 1970 in the *Rogozinsky* case.[26] At issue was the Rabbinical Courts' Jurisdiction Law (Marriage and Divorce), which provided that all marriages and divorces by Jews in Israel are to be subject to *Din Torah* (Jewish religious law) and that Rabbinical courts possessed exclusive jurisdiction to adjudicate in these matters. This meant that, by law, Israeli Jews could not choose the manner in which they marry or divorce because their only option was pursuant to Jewish religious law.

The case concerned a couple who had been married in a civil ceremony and requested that their marriage be recognised by the state. They claimed that the Rabbinical Courts' Jurisdiction Law conflicted with the values anchored in the Declaration of Independence, which promised freedom of religion and conscience. The Supreme Court rejected the claim, ruling unequivocally that the Declaration of Independence 'is not to be regarded as a constitution to which all of the laws of state are subordinate, nor should it affect the validity or invalidity of a state law'.[27] Hence, the Declaration of Independence expresses the 'the vision and credo of the people',[28] but does not have the status of a state law. The Court stressed that whenever the Knesset legislation is clear, explicit and unequivocal, it must be followed even if it is inconsistent with one of the principles of the Declaration of Independence.

Though years went by and the adoption of a constitution 'chapter by chapter' became an increasingly protracted project, the Supreme Court remained steadfast in its refusal to recognise its authority to nullify laws

---

community as illegitimate.' Moshe Negbi too opined in a similar vein in his book on the rule of law in Israel: Moshe Negbi, *Above the Law: The Constitutional Crisis in Israel* (Tel Aviv, Am Oved, 1987) 27 (Hebrew).

[25] This is the view of Professor Gideon Sapir in his book *The Constitutional Revolution in Israel: Past, Present & Future* (Ramat Gan, Miskal, Yedihot Haharonot and Hemed, 2010) 33 (Hebrew).

[26] CA 450/70 *Rogozinsky v State of Israel*, ver 26(1), 129, 29 (1970).

[27] ibid 135.

[28] ibid.

that contradicted or conflicted with the principles set forth in the Declaration of Independence. This position remains unchanged. This, however, is not to say that the Declaration has no 'legal' standing at all. Though lacking the status of a formal constitution, it serves as a powerful tool for legislative interpretation, particularly because it explicitly refers to the democratic nature of the state. The Court has relied on the Declaration in its legislative interpretation, curtailing the powers of the executive and recognising fundamental human rights. The preamble of the Declaration, which outlines the historical source of the Jewish nation's right to self-determination, provided the basis for the judicial finding that the state is both democratic and Jewish in nature. The Declaration itself used the term 'Jewish state', and the State of Israel was the framework within which the Jewish people, as a national group, realised their right to self-determination. This is the fundamental importance of the State of Israel being a 'Jewish state'. The Court further ascribed special importance to the Declaration as an expression of the 'credo'[29] of the Jewish people.

An interesting example of the Court's treatment of the Declaration as a 'given constitutional fact of the state' addresses the question of disqualifying political parties in Israel. In 1965, the Supreme Court refused to allow a party that denied the existence of the State of Israel to run in the Knesset elections, despite the fact that, by law, the party was entitled to run.[30] President Shimon Agranat ruled that the authority of the Central Elections Committee to prevent a list of candidates from participating in the elections should not be determined solely on the basis of explicit statutory provisions:

> To define the [Central Elections] Committee's authority, we must first consider constitutional 'facts' that pertain to this question. Thereupon, we find that there can be no doubt whatsoever – as clearly stated when the Declaration of Independence was made – that not only is Israel a sovereign, independent, and peace-seeking state, characterised by its popular regime, but that it was also established as 'a Jewish State in the Land of Israel' primarily on the basis of

---

[29] The original wording in Hebrew is '*Ani Ma'amin*' or 'I believe'. The meaning is similar to the word 'creed', from the Latin 'credo', ie, all the features that define the identity of the people living in Israel. *cf* Samuel P Huntington's writings on the American creed in *Who are We? The Challenges to America's National Identity* (New York, Simon and Schuster, 2004) .

[30] EA 1/65 *Yardor v Chairman of Knesset Elections Committee*, ver 19(3), 365, 390 (1965).

'the Jewish People's natural and historical right to live as any other nation, independent in its own sovereign state'. These words reflect the vision of the nation and its credo. The continuity . . . of the State of Israel is a basic constitutional fact, which no authority of the State may deny while exercising any of its powers.[31]

In keeping with these remarks, the majority in the *Yardor* case held that the Central Elections Committee was authorised to prevent a candidate list who denied the existence of Israel as a Jewish state from participating in the elections, even though the law did not explicitly authorise the Committee to consider a party's platform when deciding to disqualify it as a candidate. This ruling was viewed as exceptional because it conflicted with the explicit wording of the law. However, the Declaration of Independence provided the justification (in President Agranat's opinion) for the Court's decision.

As we shall see in the next part of this chapter, the enactment of basic laws in 1992, namely Basic Law: Human Dignity and Liberty and Basic Law: Freedom of Occupation, for the first time included in Israeli legislation reference to the provisions of the Declaration of Independence. The opening section of Basic Law: Human Dignity and Liberty states: 'Fundamental human rights in Israel . . . shall be upheld in the spirit of the principles set forth in the Declaration of the establishment of the State of Israel.'

An interesting question that remains open is whether the inclusion of the Declaration of Independence in basic laws altered the status of the Declaration, particularly after the constitutional revolution, which elevated the basic laws to a constitutional level. Supreme Court Justice Levin opined that the inclusion of the Declaration of Independence in the text of basic laws led to 'a dramatic change in the status of the Declaration of Independence: It is no longer a mere source of interpretation, but has become an independent source of human rights'.[32] This, however, was a minority view that was not repeated in later case law. The prevailing view is, as stated, that reference to the provisions of the Declaration in Basic Law: Human Dignity and Liberty does not alter their legal status. Essentially, this Basic Law refers to 'the principles set forth in the Declaration', which explicitly anchors the Declaration's status as an interpretative source. It does not constitute an independent

---

[31] ibid 386.
[32] HCJ 726/94 *Clal Insurance Co Ltd v Minister of Finance*, ver 48(5), 441 (1994), 465.

source of basic rights, nor does it constitute an independent source for judicial review of legislation.

In Israeli constitutional law today, the Declaration of Independence is considered to be primarily declarative. It expresses the *Grundnorm*[33] of Israeli law and the credo of the nation. As such, it delineates the defining characteristics of Israel as a Jewish and democratic state. Indeed, in the absence of a complete constitution, the Declaration has remained relevant in recent years as a document that can bridge the divides in Israeli society.[34]

THE STATUS OF BASIC LAWS BEFORE 1992

During the first 20 years following the establishment of the state, the Knesset was generally regarded as an equivalent of the British Parliament. This approach gradually changed, however, and was finally overturned in the *Bank Hamizrahi* judgment – the most important constitutional decision in Israeli history.

The concept of the Knesset's sovereignty – the local version of the British notion of parliamentary sovereignty – was first articulated in case law relating to the Court's inability to judicially review Knesset legislation. In that sense, the historical discussion of the Knesset's sovereignty was actually a discussion of the Knesset's supremacy and the implications of the absence of a constitutional norm to serve as a benchmark for examining Knesset legislation. Only later did legal discussions begin to focus on a new and important issue – the Knesset's ability to restrict its own legislative powers.

The *Rogozinsky* judgment clearly expressed the Court's view that it lacked the authority to judicially review Knesset legislation even when the laws infringed human rights. As mentioned earlier, this judgment dealt with the status of the Declaration of Independence in relation to the Rabbinical Courts' Jurisdiction Law (Marriage and Divorce). Indeed, the Court often stated that: 'The Knesset is sovereign in the enactment of laws. It is at liberty to choose both the subject and contents of any law, and any law emanating from it should be conferred validity. That

---

[33] I use the term 'Grundnorm' in the sense intended by Hans Kelsen in *The Pure Theory Of Law* 8, 193 (Berkley, University of California Press, 1967).

[34] Amnon Rubinstein and Barak Medina, *The Constitutional Law of the State of Israel* 6th edn (Jerusalem/Tel Aviv, Shoken, 2005) 49 (Hebrew).

the Court is not authorised to question . . . the validity of a law or the correctness of its contents is common knowledge.'[35]

This perception of the status of the Knesset and its legislation was based on the way in which the Supreme Court perceived Israel's constitutional structure at the time.[36] Similarly, the question of the Knesset's ability to limit its own legislative powers was widely accepted in the history of Israeli law, which led to the constitutional revolution. 'Knesset sovereignty' can be understood as referring to the unlimited legislative power of the Knesset, even to the extent that the Knesset was incapable of limiting its own powers. This understanding relates to the Knesset as the legislative authority, although this approach gave rise to exceptions and qualifications governed by manner and form provisions that are not always entirely clear.[37] In Israel, however, the doctrine of Knesset sovereignty was tempered by the parallel recognition of the Knesset's power of self-limitation. This stemmed from the fact that the first self-limiting provisions – which were essentially procedural, addressing the requisite majority for amending a law – appeared in basic laws and not in regular legislation. Later on, this discrepancy allowed for a distinction to be drawn between regular legislation and basic laws, and led to the ruling that the Knesset's power of self-limitation is rooted in the fact that, by imposing basic laws, the Knesset was functioning as a constituent authority.

The Harari Resolution did not clarify the status of the basic laws before they were consolidated in a single document. This issue was discussed extensively in academic circles over the years until it was finally resolved by the Supreme Court. The Constituent Assembly (or the First Knesset) did not explicitly state that successive Knessets would have constituent powers, but its decision to frame a constitution in stages indicates that it intended for the constitution to be framed in an ongoing process and that the Knesset was to be charged with its implementation. Accordingly, the Second Knesset prepared the first chapter of the con-

---

[35] HCJ 188/63 *Batzul v Minister of the Interior*, ver 19(1), 337, 349.

[36] In the sense of a 'rule of recognition' according to Hart. See HLA Hart, *The Concept of Law*, 2nd edn (Oxford, Claredon Press, 1994).

[37] See, for example, Robin Elliot, 'Rethinking Manner and Form: From Parliamentary Sovereignty to Constitutional Values' (1991) 29 *Osgoode Hall Law Journal* 215. On the discussion of this subject in Australia, see Jeffrey Goldsworthy, 'Manner and Form in the Australian States' (1987) 16 *Melbourne University Law Review* 403.

stitution in Basic Law: The Knesset, which was enacted by the Third Knesset. Subsequent Knessets continued the project of enacting basic laws – ultimately enacting 12.[38]

The 12 basic laws share several features. Unlike regular laws, the year of their enactment is not part of their name, and they are generally couched in briefer and more concise terms than regular laws, which is typical of constitutions. Similarly, like a constitution, they often articulate general principles, leaving the completion of details to regular legislation. For the most part, they address subjects generally treated in constitutions, namely, the institutions of the state and their powers. On the other hand, in terms of their format, some are far more detailed than others. Only a few sections in one of the basic laws were formally entrenched, meaning that a special majority of MKs is required to amend them. The Knesset may have been expected to guarantee the entrenchment of all basic laws even before the completion of the constitution in a manner that would prevent the adoption of amendments or contradictory legislation by any regular Knesset majority. Despite these expectations, none of the basic laws adopted until 1992 were entrenched by the Knesset, which means that the Knesset did not view basic laws as having special status or as being normatively superior to regular legislation. One of the central hallmarks of a constitution is stability and rigidity, specifically, the difficulty of amending its provisions. This feature is absent from Israel's basic laws. The title 'basic law' may indicate that once all basic laws are introduced, they will become the building blocks that form a constitution, but as long as the constitutional project is incomplete, a basic law is no different from regular legislation in terms of its vulnerability to amendment. In operative terms,

---

[38] Basic Law: The Knesset (1958); Basic Law: Israel Lands (1960); Basic Law: The President of the State (1964); Basic Law: The Government (1968); (Amendment – adoption of a mixed electoral system – 1992; Return to system of proportional elections – 2001); Basic Law: The State Economy (1975); Basic Law: The Military, (following the Agranat Commission of Inquiry, established in the wake of the Yom Kippur War of October 1973); Basic Law: Jerusalem Capital of Israel (1980); Basic Law: The Judiciary (1984); Basic Law: The State Comptroller (1988). In 1992, two basic laws pertaining to human rights were enacted: Basic Law: Freedom of Occupation and Basic Law: Human Dignity and Liberty. In 2011, a basic law was enacted by way of a temporary provision in order to determine that the state budget would become a biannual judgment: Basic Law: State Budget (Special Provisions) (Temporary Provision) (Amendment 2011). Further discussion is devoted to this special legislation below.

this means that a regular law enacted by a regular majority of Knesset members (Israel does not have a quorum requirement for legislation) can change, revoke or override the provisions of a basic law.

The Supreme Court's rulings regarding the early basic laws indicated that the mere fact that a law was enacted as a basic law did not infuse it with any special legal significance, and the Knesset could revoke any provision that was not entrenched. As mentioned above, only three of the provisions of the basic laws were entrenched before 1992, which meant that the Knesset was able to repeal the provisions of other basic laws, directly or indirectly, and all such cases would be governed by the rule of *lex posterior derogat priori*.

The basic laws as a whole lacked superior normative status, but the fate of the three entrenched provisions was ultimately determined by an unexpected judicial development. Basic Law: The Knesset was enacted in 1958 and included three entrenched provisions whose amendment required a special majority (a vote of 61 of the 120 MKs). The enactment of entrenched provisions that imposed limitations upon future Knesset legislation was not regarded as problematic and the MKs viewed themselves as being authorised to entrench sections in the framework of basic laws should they so desire. This may have stemmed from the perception of basic laws as the building blocks of the future Israeli constitution. The unexpected development came in the form of an exceptional Supreme Court ruling on one of the entrenched sections. Section 4 of Basic Law: The Knesset reads: 'The Knesset shall be elected by general, nationwide, direct, equal, secret, and proportional elections, in accordance with the Knesset Elections Law; this section shall not be amended, save by a majority of the members of the Knesset.' This section defends the Israeli electoral system with a minimalist legislative entrenchment so that at least 61 positive votes out of 120 are required to amend it.[39] In 1969, the Supreme Court had to address the status of this entrenched section in view of a regular law that apparently contradicted its provisions. Before the Knesset elections of 1969, the Knesset adopted a law allowing parties to draw on public funds to finance their campaigns. Fund allocation was based on parties' representation in the outgoing Knesset, which meant that new parties would be deprived of any funding under the law. The law was passed by a regular majority. The petitioner, Dr Bergman, questioned

---

[39] Today Israel has two completely entrenched basic laws: Basic Law: The Government and Basic Law: Freedom of Occupation.

the compliance of the new law with the entrenched section according to which the Knesset is to be elected in equal elections, arguing that the Party Financing Law violated the principle of equality in the election's process.[40] The first question addressed by the Supreme Court was whether it was in fact authorised to examine the legality of a Knesset law. Justice Landau began his judgment by stating that the petition raised 'potentially weighty preliminary questions of a constitutional nature, relating to the status of basic laws, and to the justiciability of the Knesset's actual compliance with self-imposed limitations'.[41] Nevertheless, he decided to avoid these questions and went on to discuss the issue on its merits: did the Party Financing Law substantially violate the principle of equal opportunity for the various parties to be elected? He ruled the law invalid because it was not adopted by the required special majority of 61 MKs.

The *Bergman* decision, a notably slim judgment of just a few pages, took the Israeli legal community by surprise. In many ways, it changed the prevailing rule that the Court does not have the power to judicially review laws. *Bergman* was the first time since the establishment of the state that a law passed by the Knesset was later invalidated by the Court. Yet, perhaps the most surprising element of the ruling was the fact that the Court chose not to address the most important questions in the case, namely, the status of basic laws and the Court's power to judicially review a regular law that it viewed as contravening a basic law.

Furthermore, the ruling failed to address other questions. For example, can the Knesset enact legislative provisions that limit its own future legislative powers? Will such limitations be restricted to procedure or may they also address substantive issues? Must such limitations be enacted in the framework of a basic law or may they be enacted by way of regular legislation? What is the theoretical basis for the possibility of self-imposed limitation? This was the first time that a Knesset law was annulled because it conflicted with the entrenchment provision of a basic law. Notably, the Court did not rely upon any judicial or constitutional theory to justify its ruling that the Minister of Finance was not authorised to distribute funds to parties under the law so long as the law had not been amended. Thus, the law had to either be reworded

---

[40] HCJ 98/69 *Bergman v Minister of Finance*, ver 23(1), 693 (1969). For an English translation of the *Bergman* case, see (1969) 4 *Israel Law Review* 559. See also: http://elyon1.court.gov.il/files_eng/69/980/000/Z01/69000980.z01.pdf.
[41] ibid *Bergman* 696.

in a manner that would remove the inequality contained therein or re-enacted by a majority of 61 MKs, meaning that from the Court's perspective, it was just a 'procedural' ruling.

The *Bergman* decision preoccupied the legal community in subsequent years. Constitutional experts believed it indirectly acknowledged the special normative status of basic laws and the Knesset's ability to limit its legislative power in basic laws. Yet, despite this ruling, the Court refused to acknowledge the normative supremacy of basic laws until 1995. For example, in the *Negev*[42] case, the Court ruled that the Standards Law was not to be invalidated under the pretext that it conflicted with Basic Law: The Government because the latter was not entrenched (at the time). Justice Berenzon even ruled that the basic law had no special status and added that, in fact, it was quite the opposite: the Standards Law was *lex specialis* and thus was distinct from Basic Law: The Government, which is a general law. According to the rule of statutory interpretation, specific laws prevail over general laws. Thus, it emerged from the *Negev* ruling that basic laws have no special normative status and are not superior to regular legislation or at the peak of the Kelsenian pyramid of norms. Accordingly, if a contradiction between norms can be resolved by the rule of *lex specialis*, it means that when considering their normative status, the norms are on an equal footing in the Court's eyes.

At the same time, where a general law conflicts with an 'entrenched provision' of a basic law, the *Bergman* ruling indicates that the Court is entitled to judicially review the legislation and declare it invalid. Thus, in the *Laor* judgment, the Court wrote:

A Knesset law, regular or basic, that purports to alter an 'entrenched' provision (the special majority requirement – i.e., formal entrenchment) without attaining a majority of the Knesset contradicts the entrenchment provision of the basic law. The 'entrenched provision' takes precedence due to its legal status. Normal rules according to which a posterior law supersedes earlier laws do not apply where there is a conflict between an entrenched provision and a provision purporting to alter it without having attained the required majority. This conflict is governed by the principle of the normative supremacy of the entrenched basic law.[43]

However, at this time, this doctrine of judicial review of legislation had

[42] HCJ 107/73 *Negev Automobile Service Station Ltd. v State of Israel*, ver 28(1), 640 (1973).
[43] HCJ 142/89 *Laor Movement v the Knesset Speaker*, ver 44(3), 529 (1989), 539.

yet to be adjudicated and provided with a sound foundation in Israeli law. In the *Bergman* case, the Financing Law was invalidated without any theoretical basis or justification. Justice Landau, who wrote the judgment, expressly stated that he was not discussing constitutional issues raised by the judgment, such as the possibility of declaring the invalidity of a statute and the Court's power to do so.

In fact, despite the supposed normative supremacy of the entrenched section, the Knesset could quite easily overcome the special majority requirement. All it needed to do was to pass a law imposing electoral inequality by a majority of 61 votes. In such a case, the Supreme Court would be powerless to declare that law invalid.

This was the scenario faced by the Court in the *Kaniel* case of 1973, which was heard a few years after *Bergman*. In this case, Kaniel filed a petition against the Knesset Elections Law that established arrangements for the distribution of surplus votes. He claimed that the law gave the large factions an advantage at the expense of the smaller factions and, in so doing, violated the principle of equality guaranteed by section 4 of Basic Law: The Knesset. Though the Knesset Elections Law was adopted by a majority of more than 61 MKs, the petitioners argued that it should be invalidated nonetheless because it was not named 'Basic Law'. Furthermore, the petitioners argued that if basic laws normatively enjoy special and superior status, any changes made to them must follow the same norm. The claim was interesting and potentially presented the Supreme Court with the opportunity to recognise the normative supremacy of basic laws. However, the Court rejected Kaniel's claim, explaining that nothing in the language of the basic law indicated that it could only be changed by another basic law. This meant that such changes could even be effected by means of regular Knesset legislation when supported by a majority of 61 MKs.[44]

An examination of the Supreme Court case law indicates that, before the enactment of the basic laws on human rights in 1992, the Court had already recognised its authority to judicially review laws concerning

---

[44] In fact, several laws concerning the principle of equality in elections were passed by a majority of 61 MKs, clearly reflecting the Knesset's intention to infringe on the principle of equality – for example, the amendment of Basic Law: The Knesset, which permits the disqualification of parties in view of the contents of their platform. This amendment was passed by a majority of 61 MKs; the assumption was that denying a party's candidacy violates the principle of equality in elections as guaranteed by s 4 of Basic Law: The Knesset.

the entrenched provision of section 4 of Basic Law: The Knesset. The rule which emerged from case law concerning the status of basic laws was that, on the whole, unentrenched provisions of basic laws enjoy the same normative status as provisions of 'regular' legislation. 'Supremacy' was (normatively) granted only to a few particular provisions of basic laws that were 'entrenched' and included instructions that explicitly limited the Knesset's authority to change, amend or infringe upon them.

A distinction was thus made between two categories of provisions of basic laws: 'unentrenched' provisions from which the legislature may deviate, just as it may deviate from or contradict other laws; and entrenched provisions, in relation to which any deviation must meet specific terms (usually the requirement of a special majority). The Court thus recognised the Knesset's authority to entrench basic laws against the possibility of amendment and to impose 'formal' or 'structural' limitations (such as a requirement of a majority of 61 votes of 120) on its legislative power. Moreover, the judgments indicate that the Court recognised the normative superiority of entrenched provisions of the basic laws. On the other hand, Supreme Court rulings relating to section 4 did not provide a theoretical basis for its authority to conduct judicial review, nor was there any reliance on the rhetoric of 'constituent authority'.

The upshot of this case law was that the Court substantiated its authority to engage in judicial review. In the first stage, it relied upon the doctrine of judicial review only when examining the validity of legislative provisions that contravened the requirement established in section 4 of Basic Law: The Knesset. Indeed, it avoided unequivocally ruling on its own authority to judicially review all laws, relying instead on the consent of the state – as the respondent in the petition – to have the validity of laws examined in these types of cases. This authority to engage in judicial review was exercised in extremely specific circumstances. This prevented a swell of public debate concerning weighty and loaded constitutional questions. Consequently, the Court provided the government with a convenient way of realising its goal, despite the invalidation of the law, by either amending the law or by re-enacting it with a majority of 61 MKs.

The Knesset did not consider that these rulings seriously impaired its sovereignty and did not regard itself as 'limited' in the wake of the invalidation of its legislation. One Justice in the *Bank Hamizrahi* case stated: 'The *Bergman* decision provides additional proof of the famous statement of Justice Holmes that a page of history is worth a volume of logic.'[45] The *Bergman* case was revolutionary – both in terms of the possibility of judicial review of laws and in terms of its recognition of the Knesset's authority for self-limitation – and in many ways paved the way for the real 'constitutional revolution', staged with the enactment of basic laws on human rights, discussed in the following part.

PART III: THE CONSTITUTIONAL REVOLUTION

BASIC LAWS ON HUMAN RIGHTS

Between the establishment of the state and the early 1990s, the State of Israel did not have a written bill of human rights. During that period, however, the Knesset completed the enactment of almost all of the institutional basic laws of Israel. Basic laws creating sovereign authorities such as the Knesset, the government and the judiciary joined other basic laws concerning the president, the army and the state comptroller. Even Jerusalem as the capital of Israel was granted a special basic law. Still missing, however, was the Basic Law: Legislature, which would regulate the legislative proceedings for regular and basic laws and, in addition, establish the supreme normative status of basic laws and the Supreme Court's authority to judicially review legislation.

Though the Knesset managed to introduce basic laws concerning state authorities and structural issues, it failed to introduce a basic law that would anchor a bill of human rights. Clearly, in the absence of such a formal charter, the Supreme Court's ability to protect human rights was limited, due to its inability to invalidate primary legislation that infringed human rights. Still, all attempts to enact legislation of this nature have failed.

The proposal to draft a basic law on human rights was first submitted to a special Knesset committee a few years after the establishment of the State of Israel. Upon enacting Basic Law: The Knesset in 1958, the Constitution and Law Committee announced that the next basic law should address human rights. However, this intention was not fulfilled and the first comprehensive bill of human rights was not tabled until

---

[45] Justice Zamir in *Bank Hamizrahi* (n 19).

1964. Though several draft proposals were submitted between then and the 1990s, none of them successfully traversed all the legislative stages. The reasons for this varied and resembled the reasons that dictated the fate of preliminary discussions concerning the constitution. The most prominent of these reasons derived from the perennial dispute over the Jewish nature of the State of Israel, which invariably came to the fore in discussions concerning freedom of religion and conscience. Thus, repeated efforts by successive Knessets to confer statutory status upon human rights have all failed.

During the first years of the State, the opposition stemmed from Mapai, Prime Minister Ben-Gurion's ruling party, which considered the entrenchment of human rights unimportant, given that this kind of entrenchment was non-existent even in Britain, which served as an appropriate constitutional model. In 1977, the largest opposition party at the time, the Likud Party, came to power under Menachem Begin, who supported the entrenchment of human rights. This time, however, the religious parties' block – headed by the ultra-Orthodox (who since 1977 have had the power to tip the scale in the composition of any government) – vetoed the idea. Being entirely dependent upon the ultra-Orthodox, the new Likud-led government had no choice but to succumb to their dictates.

In the early 1990s, then Justice Minister Dan Meridor (an attorney by trade) presented the government with a draft proposal for Basic Law: Human Rights. However, this proposal was not adopted due to the opposition of the Prime Minister and the religious parties. Other MKs tabled their own draft proposals. MK Amnon Rubinstein (a leading professor of constitutional law in Israel) endorsed the proposal of the Justice Minister and tabled a draft proposal known as Basic Law: Human and Citizen Rights that included both 'formal' entrenchment (prescribing that a basic law could only be amended by a special majority) and 'substantive' entrenchment (restricting the Knesset's ability to infringe rights protected in a basic law).

Aware of just how difficult it would be to introduce such a bill in this original format, MK Amnon Rubinstein sought to promote the vote on that basic law in a manner that would circumvent the minefields that destroyed its precursors. Accordingly, he selected several less controversial rights from the original proposal and submitted them for a preliminary reading as separate basic laws. Among others, he tabled draft proposals for Basic Law: Freedom of Occupation and Basic Law:

Human Dignity and Liberty. Both bills passed all the legislative stages. The ramifications and the deep constitutional changes that these new basic laws created were never really discussed and there is no evidence of any deep public debate or real understanding of that truly historical moment. Commenting on the lack of public attention and debate, Professor Rubinstein wrote a few years later: 'Most of the print media failed to even report on the legislative process, and the TV totally ignored it.'

The success of the 1992 change may be explained by the fact that its initiators adopted a modus operandi similar to the one employed in the introduction of the Harari Resolution. This Resolution represented an attempt to overcome the obstacles that prevented the framing of a constitution by dividing the constitutional project into stages. The initiators of the human rights bills adopted a similar tactic. MK Rubinstein avoided attempting to introduce a complete bill of rights, which had been under discussion for years but was never enacted. Employing an approach that was later known as 'atomisation' or 'division into components', the authors of the bill decided to promote a 'compromise', whereby the framework for human rights would also be enacted in stages. In the first stage, they chose to anchor rights that had achieved consensus and to defer the completion of the chapter on human rights to a later stage.[46] This meant that disputed rights – such as freedom of expression, the principle of equality, and freedom of religion and conscience – were not included in the basic law. The rights that were included in the framework of Basic Law: Human Liberty and Dignity were the rights to human dignity, liberty, privacy and property, while freedom of occupation was the subject of the other draft proposal, Basic Law: Freedom of Occupation.

---

[46] Yehudit Karp, 'Basic Law: Human Dignity and Liberty – Biography of a Power Struggle' (1993) 1 *Law and Government* 323 (Hebrew). Referring to the move he initiated, Professor Rubinstein wrote the following: 'My idea was to divide the draft bill of the basic law into four separate laws: the two basic laws that were enacted, and another two basic laws concerning freedom of speech and freedom of association that only passed the preliminary reading. My aim was first and foremost to eliminate the religious opposition or, alternatively, to place the Likud-led coalition in a difficult position from a public perspective. Yet, the idea of splitting the laws up was also based on another intention: to tackle easier parts first, before dealing with the more difficult ones so as to introduce the laws that would, at least, entrench rights to which opposition was minimal.' Amnon Rubinstein, 'The Knesset and Basic Laws on Human Rights' (2000) 5 *Law and Government* 339, 340 (Hebrew).

Opposition to the enactment of a bill of rights came primarily from the religious sector, which had reservations with respect to constitutional initiatives concerning religion and state. A key factor in allaying their fears and accommodating greater flexibility, which finally led to the religious parties' consent to the enactment of the basic law, was that the basic law also offered to anchor the Jewish nature of the state. The text of the proposed two basic laws on human rights opens with the dual characterisation of the State of Israel as 'Jewish and democratic', which the religious parties viewed as an achievement.[47]

Thus, in March 1992, the Knesset adopted these two basic laws that in time would trigger the constitutional revolution, though they were endorsed by slightly more than 20 MKs voting in their favour.[48] The normative status of these basic laws should not have been different from other basic laws. The Supreme Court had already ruled that when a regular law and an unentrenched basic law were in conflict, the basic law per se would not take precedence. Thus, and on the face of it, the principle of parliamentary sovereignty remained intact and in force. It seems that, as former President of the Supreme Court Aharon Barak wrote: 'The constitutional revolution took place quietly, almost clandestinely.'[49]

The enactment of the basic laws on human rights in 1992, however, significantly changed the meaning of 'constitutional entrenchment'. Until then, 'entrenchment' meant 'structural' or 'formal' entrenchment. Accordingly, even an entrenched section of a law – such as section 4 of Basic Law: The Knesset – could be amended if the formal conditions for the amendment were satisfied. The entrenched provision of this section, which guaranteed equality in elections, could therefore be changed or even annulled by another law, provided that the latter was adopted by a majority of 61 MKs.

Basic Law: Freedom of Occupation reiterated this idea when it included a section that entrenched – for the first time – the entire law, stating that this basic law may only be amended by another basic law that should be endorsed by an absolute majority of at least 61 MKs.

---

[47] Sapir (n 25) 69.

[48] Referring to this point, Professor Rubinstein (n 46) 349 wrote: 'The truth is that no parliament has ever adopted a constitution in this manner – in the face of opposition from the government and the prime minister, by way of a private member's bill, in an atmosphere of strange media indifference, and despite the intentional non-participation of the opposition.'

[49] Aharon Barak, 'Basic Law: Freedom of Occupation' (1994) 1 *Law and Government* 1995 at 217.

Basic Law: Human Dignity and Liberty was also to include a section providing for formal entrenchment, but no majority was found for the entrenchment section in the final voting process. This means that of the two basic laws on human rights, only the one concerning a relatively 'minor' right was actually entrenched. It seems that, according to the traditional approach, only Basic Law: Freedom of Occupation had a 'constitutional status' that made it a foundation for judicial review, as demonstrated in the *Bergman* case. The view at the time was that basic laws do not enjoy normative supremacy; only their entrenched components do.

Nevertheless, the formal requirement of a majority to amend the new basic law on occupation was not the only 'entrenchment'. Both basic laws on human rights include the notion of the non-absolute status of human rights, allowing an infringement of human rights only when this serves worthy causes and complies with other requirements, as stipulated in the basic laws themselves.

Though they seemed to preserve the Knesset's sovereignty to enact laws that conflict with human rights, the passage of these two new basic laws actually marked the first time in the history of the State of Israel that the Knesset's ability to infringe human rights was legally restricted.

The legislation adopted a criterion similar to that prescribed by the Canadian Charter[50] and called it the 'limitation clause'. According to this clause, a 'regular' law that 'violates' a human right expressly stipulated in a basic law is valid only if it satisfies the cumulative conditions of the limitations clause: 'There shall be no infringement of rights under this Basic Law except by a law befitting the values of the State of Israel, enacted for a proper purpose, and to an extent no greater than is required.'[51]

This clause defines the conditions under which infringements of the rights to human dignity, liberty and freedom of occupation would be permitted. It also introduced an innovation in Israeli legislation, establishing a 'substantive entrenchment' or 'substantive limitation' – not just a formal 'majority' entrenchment – of the Knesset's power to enact a law that contradicts a basic law. Therefore, a restriction of the human rights protected by the basic laws may only be imposed for worthy purposes and only if it

---

[50] See the Limitation Clause in s 1 of the Canadian Charter of Rights and Freedoms. The limitation clause will be further discussed in ch 8 below.

[51] Section 8 of Basic Law: Human Dignity and Liberty. A similar provision appears in Basic Law: Freedom of Occupation.

satisfies the principle of proportionality. The real meaning of this provision, however, still remained to be seen.

One of the first scholarly articles to appear after the enactment of these basic laws was written by Justice Aharon Barak, who was already on the Supreme Court bench. In an article entitled 'The Constitutional Revolution: Protected Human Rights',[52] Barak argued as follows:

> Fundamental human rights . . . were transformed into constitutional rules . . . The legislature itself is now bound by fundamental human rights. No longer can it be claimed that Israel has no (formal and rigid) 'written constitution' regarding human rights. The new legislation has taken Israel out of its isolation and placed it in the large community of nations in which human rights are anchored in a 'written and rigid' constitution, or in other words, in a document of normative supremacy or normative superiority. Indeed, a 'regular' law of the Knesset can no longer unlawfully infringe on the freedom of occupation.[53]

Evidently, some of the Knesset members who voted in favour of the basic laws had not been aware of the matters to which Justice Barak was referring. Knesset debates on the basic law reflected no awareness on the part of the MKs that they were actually participating in a constitutional revolution. Many MKs voted with their feet and were absent at the time of voting.

Yet the development of Israeli constitutional law was to be deeply influenced by the enactment of these two basic laws – Basic Law: Human Dignity and Liberty and Basic Law: Freedom of Occupation. Both include a substantive limitation allowing the legislator to infringe a human right, but only in accordance with a proportionality test. As such, the very structure of these basic laws created a kind of entrenchment by putting the merits of substantive laws up for debate as 'justified' or not, rather than simply requiring a formal majority. This new concept would allow the courts to intervene and review Knesset legislation.

Both basic laws provided the political support and normative framework required for instituting judicial review of Knesset legislation and brought the discourse of constituent authority back to the heart of the legal arena. The Supreme Court's willingness to add the missing link of judicial review and to confer upon it its full constitutional weight was a

---

[52] Aharon Barak, 'The Constitutional Revolution: Protected Human Rights' (1992) 1 *Law and Government* 9 (Hebrew).
[53] ibid 12–13.

natural and perhaps even necessary development of the Court's case law[54] – a development that remains controversial to this day. This entire development became known as 'the constitutional revolution'.

THE *BANK HAMIZRAHI* DECISION: A 'JUDGE MADE' CONSTITUTION?

March 1992 was a turning point in Israeli constitutional law as two basic laws came into force, defining and providing a constitutional basis for human rights in Israel. As Justice Aharon Barak wrote, this time as the incoming President on the Supreme Court: 'In March 1992, the Knesset enacted *Basic Law: Freedom of Occupation* and *Basic Law: Human Dignity and Liberty*. The enactment of these two basic laws effected a substantive change in the status of human rights under Israeli law . . . The constitutional revolution occurred in the Knesset in March 1992. The Knesset endowed the State of Israel with a constitutional bill of rights.'[55]

Prior to the enactment of these basic laws and until the *Bank Hamizrahi* judgment was handed down in 1995, the prevailing view was that Israel had no formal, written constitution. Until then, it was seen as having only a material constitution – a collection of binding principles and arrangements that reflected the prevailing laws and social reality, as well as values enshrined in the Declaration of Independence. The transition from a substantive to a formal constitution was based on limitation clauses in both human rights basic laws. The *Bank Hamizrahi* judgment determined that the limitation clause was intended to limit the Knesset's legislative power and that despite the absence of a formal entrenchment provision in Basic Law: Human Dignity and Liberty, Israel had a 'formal' constitution.

In this far-reaching decision, the Supreme Court justices ruled that if a law infringed any of the fundamental rights contained in a basic law

---

[54] David Kretzmer, 'From Bergman and Kol Haam to Bank Hamizrahi: The Path to Judicial Review of Laws Limiting Human Rights' (1997) 28 *Mishpatim* 359, 363–69 (Hebrew).

[55] *Hamizrahi Bank* (n 19). For an English translation of the entire judgment, see *Israel Law Reports* 1995(2) – Special Volume, and http://elyon1.court.gov.il/files_eng/93/210/068/z01/93068210.z01.pdf. For an English translation of certain paragraphs, see *Hamizrahi Bank v Migdal* (the Gal Amendment), translated extracts with commentary in (1997) 31 *Israel Law Review* 754. Page numbers relate to the Hebrew version of the judgment.

and failed to meet the conditions of its limitations clause, that law would be invalid regardless of the Knesset majority that enacted it. In so ruling, the Supreme Court for the first time recognised that it has a right to judicially review Knesset legislation, not only in the formal sense of ascertaining that it was enacted by the requisite majority,[56] but also in the substantive sense of having the right to invalidate a law that violates basic terms prescribed by a basic law. Often referred to as heralding the 'constitutional revolution', the *Bank Hamizrahi* judgment laid down not only the normative supremacy of basic laws according to the doctrine of constituent authority, but also the principle of a limited legislative authority as well as the concept of judicial review. As a result, Israel became a constitutional democracy.

The question presented to the Supreme Court in the *Bank Hamizrahi* case concerned the validity of a law enacted after the introduction of the basic laws of 1992. The facts of the case are incidental and were not the main focus of the Court's deliberations. Of relevance was the fact that petitioners argued that a new law infringed their right to property as guaranteed by Basic Law: Human Dignity and Liberty and failed to meet the conditions of its limitations clause. It was the relationship between the allegedly infringing law and the basic law that raised a host of constitutional questions.

Deviating from its approach in the *Bergman* case, the Supreme Court decided to take the bull by the horns and address the full scope of constitutional issues raised by the *Bank Hamizrahi* petition, even if this was not required for deciding the case at hand. Accordingly, a special nine-judge panel broached the broader issue of the normative status of basic laws in Israel and the impact of the new basic laws upon the legal system. The judgment was published in a separate volume, comprising 419 pages, dedicated primarily to the status of basic laws in general – both the new ones, enacted in 1992, and those concerning the various state institutions, enacted earlier.[57]

---

[56] The rule established in *Bergman v Finance Minister* (n 40) presented the possibility of judicial review of Knesset legislation on a formal level by examining the requisite majority, ie, a violation of the formal entrenchment appearing in art 4 of Basic Law: The Knesset. Under the *Bergman* ruling, a violation of the principle of equality is only permitted within the context of elections and provided that the formal entrenchment requirement was complied with. Accordingly, it has been claimed that the constitutional revolution actually began with the handing down of the *Bergman* judgment.

[57] Most of the judgment is *obiter dictum* because, as stated above, there was no need to hold a constitutional discussion on the basic laws to solve the case at hand.

President Aharon Barak wrote the majority opinion. The judgment focused on the constituent authority of the Knesset or, in other words, its authority to endow Israel with a constitution. President Barak stated that the Knesset dons 'two hats', serving as both a legislature and a constituent authority. As a constituent authority, the Knesset formulates 'basic laws' that serve as 'constitutional' norms at the pinnacle of the Kelsenian pyramid. Acting as a legislature, the Knesset formulates 'regular' laws that are normatively subordinate to basic laws. The Knesset's legislative power is limited by the norms that it establishes in its constituent capacity. The scenario of a legislature that has constituent power is by no means exceptional, particularly where it concerns the authority to amend the constitution. The novelty of the *Bank Hamizrahi* decision lies in its notion of a permanent, ongoing constituent authority.

In ruling that the Knesset has constituent power, the Court relied on three legal models. First, the 'constitutional continuity model', which is an historical model based on the idea that the Knesset was assigned constituent authority upon the establishment of the State of Israel, and that authority devolved to all subsequent Knessets. Significant portions of the opinions of President Barak and Justice Cheshin are devoted to the question of *pouvoir constituant*. According to President Barak, this authority 'passed' regularly from the Constituent Assembly to the First Knesset and on to all the subsequent Knessets.[58] Therefore, the Knesset continues to hold *pouvoir constituant*. Nonetheless, something appears to be lacking in this formal justification of constituent authority based on its having been transferred to every subsequent Knesset. The authority to grant a constitution cannot be based exclusively on the Second Knesset (Transition) Law. Accordingly, President Barak clarified that his view that the Second Knesset and every ensuing Knesset held constituent authority expresses the 'underlying beliefs of the Israeli society . . . as to the enactment of a constitution and the power of the Knesset to adopt a constitution for Israel'.[59]

The second model is based on Hart's rule of recognition, according to which the Knesset's constituent authority derives from the public perception of the Knesset as having that authority. The rule of recognition is determined by the court, which expresses society's views as to

---

[58] Justice Cheshin remained in the minority on this issue. His view was that the First Knesset did not intend to transfer constituent powers to the subsequent Knessets and was not authorised to do so in any event.

[59] *Bank Hamizrahi* (n 19) 367.

how norms (including constitutional norms) are created. Does Israeli law recognise the authority of the Knesset to frame a constitution for Israel? Responding affirmatively, President Barak relied on an evaluation of facts and an appreciation of societal views drawn from extensive citations of statements by Knesset members over the years. Thus, the Court appears to be writing the constitutional history of Israel, employing its interpretation of Knesset proceedings as the foundation of its conclusions regarding the Knesset's constituent power.

The third model for determining the Knesset's constituent authority employed in the decision is the empirical model. Based on the writings of Ronald Dworkin[60] – quoted in the decision – this model attempts to identify the best and most coherent explanation for the entire legal and social history of a given system at a particular point in time. President Barak writes as follows: 'Indeed, the most fitting interpretation of the entire socio-legal history of the State of Israel is that the perception that the Knesset is empowered to adopt a constitution for Israel is deeply ingrained in the social and legal consciousness of the Israeli community. This is part of our political culture and the most befitting interpretation of our social and legal history, from the establishment of the State to this day.'[61]

President Meir Shamgar's conclusion was similar to President Barak's.[62] He too found that the Knesset had the power to limit itself and enact norms of constitutional character and status. His approach, however, was not based on the Knesset's constituent power, but rather on recognising its power of self-limitation. According to him, the Knesset's power of self-limitation is not contingent upon its constituent power; rather, the Knesset enjoys unlimited sovereignty and therefore can enact both regular and constitutional legislation. Because its sovereignty is unlimited, the Knesset is also empowered to impose limitations upon its own legislative authority.

---

[60] Ronald Dworkin, *Law's Empire* (Cambridge, MA, Harvard University Press, 1986); Ronald Dworkin, *A Bill of Rights for Britain* (London, Chatto and Windus, 1990).

[61] *Bank Hamizrahi* (n 19) 358.

[62] There were actually two 'Presidents of the Supreme Court' for this judgment. President Shamgar was actually a retired justice of the Supreme Court who had completed his term, and President Barak replaced him. In accordance with existing arrangements, a judge who completes his term has 90 days within which to complete the writing of judgments he adjudicated. The *Bank Hamizrahi* judgment was published within that 90-day period.

This approach creates a problem because the source of the Knesset's power to limit itself is not clear. In the English model, an acting Parliament cannot bind its successors, except in matters of procedural 'manner and form'. Therefore, the power of the Knesset to restrict itself is particularly problematic as it enables the current Knesset majority to limit the power of a future Knesset majority. This problem is aggravated by the fact that presently – at least until Basic Law: Legislation (regulating the manner of adopting basic laws and the required majority) is enacted – the Knesset could adopt entrenchment provisions with a simple majority vote.[63] It should be noted that President Shamgar's view of the Knesset's unlimited sovereignty has not been cited in later opinions and therefore remains a 'minority' view.

Throughout his opinion, Justice Cheshin expressed his unequivocal dissent from the constitutional view of his colleagues. In a long, emphatic and carefully reasoned opinion, he explained why he would not side with the majority. According to him, the Knesset does not have *pouvoir constituant*. This power was a unique, one-time phenomenon that ended when the First Knesset dispersed. Today, the Knesset is exclusively a legislative authority, and should it choose to frame a constitution for Israel, it would have to ask the nation to grant it constituent authority. It would seem, however, that from the array of arguments in his opinion, the thrust of Cheshin's critique lies in what he views as an attempt to frame a constitution by way of case law. As he put it: 'Yet, with all my might I will oppose our recognition of the Knesset's authority to enact a constitution by force of a judicial ruling via a legal analysis of a document dating back 47 years, while relying on disputed concepts that have no firm roots in Israeli society. And where are the people? Should we not ask their opinion?'[64]

Cheshin's opposition to conferring constitutional status upon basic laws notwithstanding, he agreed that the Knesset was entitled to impose different kinds of limitations on its legislative power. As we shall see, in case law following the *Bank Hamizrahi* decision, Justice Cheshin actually concurred with the majority opinion in cases involving judicial review of legislation in the wake of the constitutional revolution.

---

[63] Rubinstein and Medina (n 34) 74.
[64] *Bank Hamizrahi* (n 19) 358, Justice Cheshin's decision at [63].

UNRESOLVED CONSTITUTIONAL QUESTIONS

The process orchestrated by the majority ruling in *Bank Hamizrahi* was primarily based on foundations already established by the Knesset. It is doubtful that the *Bank Hamizrahi* judgment could have been written had the Knesset not first enacted two basic laws that included limitations and an entrenchment clause. The Supreme Court, however, went a few steps further. In ruling that the Knesset has constituent authority and that it exercises that authority whenever it enacts a basic law, it recognised the supreme constitutional status of all basic laws, which at once became Israel's constitution. The Court thus became a partner in the process of writing the constitution.

In the wake of the *Bank Hamizrahi* judgment, the currently accepted approach is that the Knesset indeed dons two hats, functioning as both a legislature and a constituent authority. Norms established by the Knesset exercising its constituent power (basic laws) have constitutional status and are at the top of the pyramid of norms. Norms established by the Knesset exercising its legislative power (regular laws) are subordinate to and limited by the norms established by it as the constituent authority.[65]

This conclusion has ramifications for the judicial review of laws that infringe basic laws. The Court's endorsement of judicial review is based upon the American tradition that does not premise the Court's authority to engage in judicial review upon explicit constitutional authorisation. In the famous *Marbury v Madison* case,[66] the US Supreme Court recognised its authority to judicially review laws enacted by Congress despite the absence of any authorisation to do so in the Constitution. The Israeli Supreme Court has followed the same course.

The most concise expression of the upheaval in Israeli constitutional law wrought by the *Bank Hamizrahi* case appears in the following paragraph from the judgment: 'The Knesset is endowed with constituent authority. With that authority, the Knesset enacted a constitution for

---

[65]   Professor Klein wrote that, theoretically, it actually holds three roles: it is the original constituent authority; the authority able to amend the constitution by force of 'derivative constituent authority'; and the legislative authority. For a comprehensive discussion of constituent authority, see Claude Klein, *Théorie et Pratique du Pouvoir Constituant* (Paris, Presses universitaires de France, 1996).

[66]   *Marbury v Madison* 5 US 137 (1803).

Israel. It did so chapter by chapter in accordance with the Harari Resolution. Each of the basic laws constitutes a chapter in the constitution of the State of Israel. Each chapter stands at the head of the normative pyramid. Thus, the State of Israel has a constitution – the basic laws.[67]

Notably, the constituent act is described in the past tense. According to the Court, the Knesset had already 'enacted a constitution for Israel' – it was a fait accompli. Thus, the *Bank Hamizrahi* judgment retroactively changed the normative status of all basic laws – whether or not they were (formally or substantively) entrenched. According to the judgment, all basic laws, the designated 'chapters' of the future constitution, have a constitutional status from the date of their enactment, even before being consolidated into a state constitution under the Harari Resolution. This recognition of the status of basic laws had two main results: first, the recognition of the normative primacy of arrangements prescribed in basic laws over regular legislation (the idea of supremacy); and, second, the recognition of the validity of the entrenchment provisions included in basic laws (the idea of rigidity). Since the *Bank Hamizrahi* judgment, the accepted view is that a legislative provision that purports to limit the power of the Knesset is valid only if the 'limiting' provision is the product of the Knesset exercising its 'constituent authority'. The Knesset may 'as a legislative authority, enact any law without being limited by a previous Knesset' and 'if it seeks to limit its power by a later law, it must do so by exercising its constituent authority'.[68]

Given the ease with which changes can be made to basic laws, the special standing of basic laws differs from the standing generally conferred on a constitution. Most basic laws are not entrenched, which means that the Knesset can alter a basic law by a regular majority. The only proviso is that in doing so, it must exercise its constituent authority. In the 'formal' sense, this means that it must employ the term 'basic law' in the title of the proposed law. The Supreme Court reiterated this position in several judgments, stating that a basic law may only be changed by another basic law.

Apparently, the recognition of the Knesset's constituent power is not the final word. In the judgment, the Court sought ways to identify a constitutional norm. Is a basic law norm necessarily a constitutional

---

[67] *Bank Hamizrahi* (n 19) 389.
[68] ibid 568–69.

norm, granting it supremacy? What rule concerning constitutional provisions appears in regular laws? In the *Bank Hamizrahi* judgment, it was decided that constitutional norms would be identified formally. The Knesset exercises its constituent authority when it expresses its intention by referring to the norm as a basic law. Such an approach, however, is rather problematic. The contents of the basic laws enacted to date do not necessarily indicate that the Knesset intended them to be included in a future constitution. While anchoring several fundamental principles, Israel's basic laws also include a series of specific arrangements. Often, the term 'basic law' is used even when the law does not substantively warrant inclusion as a chapter of the constitution.[69] For example, Basic Law: Israel Lands states that: 'The ownership of Israel lands – whether they belong to the State of Israel, the Development Authority, or the *Keren Kayemet Le-Israel* – shall not be transferred by sale or in any other manner.'

Furthermore, under certain compositions and coalitions, the Knesset might even abuse its constituent authority. Nonetheless, despite these difficulties, the Supreme Court chose to recognise all of the provisions of the basic laws as the product of the Knesset as a constituent authority, and not only those that include a limitation clause and/or an entrenchment clause. This approach is based on the concept that certainty and stability require a simple test for the identification of 'constitutional provisions'.

From a practical perspective, the recognition of the constitutional status of basic laws means that an arrangement prescribed in a basic law can only be changed by another basic law. No special procedure is required for the enactment of a basic law and, as stated above, all that is required for its amendment is the enactment of another law entitled basic law.

In addition, the formal nature of the test for identifying the product of a constituent authority precludes conferring constitutional status upon a number of laws that express the fundamental principles of the State of Israel, including the Law of Return (1950), which entitles every Jew to immigrate to Israel and obtain citizenship, and the Women's Equal Rights Law (1951).

---

[69] See Basic Law: Jerusalem: The Capital of Israel and Basic Law: Israel Lands.

Despite the broad scope of the *Bank Hamizrahi* judgment, many questions remained unanswered,[70] presumably not by accident. The *Bank Hamizrahi* judgment can be viewed as an attempt by the Supreme Court to initiate a constitutional process and possibly an attempt to 'shake up' the legislature following a long hiatus in the constitutional project. This may have been a judicial attempt to restart the stalled constitutional engine and to spur the legislature into completing the task of enacting a constitution. It would seem that the Supreme Court did not feel authorised to fill in the blanks, which must ultimately be addressed in a future basic law on the legislature.

The *Bank Hamizrahi* decision was a turning point in Israeli constitutional law. The constitutional revolution impacted on the political as well as on the legal spheres in several ways. On the one hand, the years following this ruling were characterised by politicians' increasing awareness and understanding of the special status attached to the enactment of basic laws. Accepting the concept of judicial review of legislation, the Knesset actually pledged to verify the compliance of Knesset legislation with the provisions of the basic laws and to examine their constitutionality in accordance with them. Judicial review has been conducted with circumspection and restraint, but even so, the Supreme Court has consistently ruled that there is judicial review in Israel, which is a position that follows from the supremacy of the basic laws. On the other hand, the Knesset, which was supposed to resolve the pending questions in the *Bank Hamizrahi* case, has in fact completely abandoned the task of completing the constitution – apparently in response to the constitutional revolution.

CONCLUSION: DOES ISRAEL HAVE A WRITTEN CONSTITUTION?

The opportunity to frame a constitution at the 'revolutionary moment' of the State of Israel's establishment was missed, but the constitutional significance of the *Bank Hamizrahi* judgment still reverberates in Israel. Enacting a basic law is not a matter of 'everyday, mundane politics'.[71]

---

[70] Questions such as: how are basic laws enacted?; what is the majority required?; who has the authority to judicially review legislation?; which rules apply to laws of a constitutional nature that are not basic laws?; and can regular laws be entrenched too?.

[71] Rubinstein and Medina (n 34) 74.

The supremacy and constitutional status of basic laws is expressed through both the judicial review of laws and the Knesset's legislative procedures of the past decades. It would seem, however, that the Knesset has not yet fully grasped the procedure of endorsement and amendment of the basic laws. Though formally, basic law votes follow the same procedure as any other regular legislation, it could have been assumed that, in the wake of the *Bank Hamizrahi* case, the introduction and/or amendment of basic laws would not be a routine act and would instead require broad public consensus. In many ways, the situation is quite paradoxical. On the one hand, the Knesset and the Israeli public have become increasingly aware of the unique status of basic laws over the past several years. Throughout the legislative stages, the Knesset examines the constitutionality of tabled bills that conflict with basic laws. Discussions held in the Knesset plenum or in various Knesset committees indicate that the MKs are aware of the constitutional status of basic laws and of legislative restrictions that follow from their supremacy.[72]

In addition, public criticism was often levelled at amendments of basic laws that were introduced to promote narrow and even personal interests. For example, the public criticised the 1999 amendment of Basic Law: The Government, which followed the establishment of a new Cabinet and eliminated the legal restriction on the number of Cabinet members so as to allow the nomination of more government ministers than the basic law permitted.[73] Furthermore, almost all of the coalition agreements signed when governments are established have included a clause according to which basic laws would not be amended without the consent of all the

---

[72] See, for example, the memorandum on Basic Law: State Budget for 2009 and 2010 (Special Instructions) (Temporary Provision) (Amendment), where p 4 reads: 'Given the governmental, social, and economic significance of the budget allocation process, it is important that the process of formulating and legislating a permanent arrangement in this matter be conducted in an educated and orderly manner, based on most of the accumulated information, and through an appropriate public broaching of the issue, all the while being aware of the need to only moderately amend basic laws.'

[73] Section 33(a) of Basic Law: The Government (Direct Election Act 1992) stated that: 'The number of cabinet members, including the prime minister, shall not exceed eighteen.' On 1 August 1999, a Knesset majority was obtained throughout the legislation stages in voting on Basic Law: The Government (Amendment 9) that nullified the restriction as stated in s 33(a), and further nullified s 37(a) of the basic (government) law, which restricted the number of deputy ministers to no more than six.

coalition members. These facts indicate that basic laws have taken hold in Israel's judicial culture, and politicians and the public normatively view them as parts of the state's 'constitution'.

On the other hand, the fact that it is rather easy to amend Israel's basic laws contradicts their status as a 'formal' constitution. Supreme Court President Dorit Beinisch asserted that a constitution needs some stability: 'A constitution presents society with a normative standard. The complex process of amending a constitution keeps this standard solid and stable even at times of social turmoil and alternating regimes. The situation in Israel is not like that. Most of its basic laws are not entrenched and thus may be amended by a regular majority of the Knesset members and through routine legislative processes.'[74] It appears, therefore, that Israel is still far from having a stable constitutional situation.

Since 1992, the Knesset quite easily passed a growing number of amendments to basic laws, sometimes for very specific needs. For example, Basic Law: The Knesset was enacted in 1958 and until 1992 – some 34 years – was amended 15 times, whereas from 1992 onwards – it was amended another 24 times. Similarly, Basic Law: The President of the State was enacted in 1964 and until 1992 – over 28 years – was amended twice, and between 1992 and 2011 – some 18 years – it was amended on five additional occasions.[75]

The judicial process that allowed for the constitutional revolution – called by Justice Cheshin a 'judge made constitution' and also criticised by academia[76] – had a great influence on the political discourse of the Israeli constitution.

Since the *Bank Hamizrahi* case, the Knesset has stopped the constitutional process. Though the Harari Resolution spoke about framing a constitution in stages, not a single basic law has been introduced between 1992 and today.[77]

---

[74] HCJ 4908/10 *Bar-On, MK v The Knesset* (rendered on April 2011), President Beinisch's opinion at [21].

[75] Suzie Navot, 'Israel' in D Oliver and C Fusaro (eds) *How Constitutions Change* (Oxford, Hart Publishing, 2011) 191, 200.

[76] Moshe Landau, 'Bestowing a Constitution upon Israel by Way of Adjudication, CA 6821/93 Bank Hamizrahi et. al v Migdal Communal Village et al' (1993) 3 *Law and Government* 697 (Hebrew); Ruth Gavison, *The Constitutional Revolution: Description of Reality or Self-Fulfilling Prophecy?* (Jerusalem, The Israel Democracy Institute, 1998) (Hebrew); Sapir (n 25).

[77] Nevertheless, during the Tenth Knesset (elected in 2006), the Constitution, Law and Justice Committee held intensive discussions on introducing a constitution based

Moreover, it has been argued[78] that the emerging constitution is an enterprise promoted mainly by the secular Jewish majority in Israel, which is culturally and politically associated with Western culture and ideals, and does not address the aspirations of large minority groups in Israeli society. The religious parties argued that they failed to comprehend the meaning of the 1992 basic laws and resented the Supreme Court's judicial review prerogative. It was not long before their opposition to the constitutional revolution turned into an open struggle against the Supreme Court, which, religious parties claimed, 'assumed' the power to judicially review laws without being explicitly authorised to do so by the Knesset. Apparently, these parties realised, somewhat belatedly, that the power of a constitution lies in its interpretation, not in the wording of its actual text.

Ever since the constitutional revolution started, the religious parties have been opposed to the constitutional process and thus – because they were members of every coalition since then – the process has stopped. The strong sentiment of the Knesset's religious sector was expressed through an assertion that 'even if the Knesset should decide to add the Ten Commandments to the constitution, we [the religious parties] would still oppose that because they would still be subject to the Supreme Court's interpretation.'[79] The Court was presented by the Orthodox media as the 'public enemy'.[80] The culmination of this campaign was a giant demonstration, attended by some half a million ultra-Orthodox Jews and staged on 14 February 1999, against the Supreme Court and 'the dictatorship of the liberal ideology' that they believed was imposed on Israel.[81]

Furthermore, it turned out that Justice Cheshin's worries were not unfounded: authorising the Knesset to entrench itself by exercising its constituent authority, he feared, might allow the majority to abuse its power. Frequent amendments of basic laws are not the only signs of

on a broad consensus. It held weekly meetings, deliberating the laws by chapter and clause, and even inspected several wording options for the comprehensive constitution. Attendance was full at first, but over time, the number of MKs declined and even constitutional law professors stopped attending. The meetings eventually ended without leaving a trace, except for a brochure that summed up the discussions.

[78]   By Professor Sapir, for example: Sapir (n 25).
[79]   This statement is attributed to MK Arie Deri.
[80]   Claude Klein, *La Democracie d'Israel* (Paris, Seuil, 1997) 148.
[81]   Claude Klein, 'La Cour suprême d'Israël: un îlot dans la tourmente' (2003) 70 *Cahiers de l'Orient* 497.

their weakness. Another inadequacy of the Israeli constitution may be discerned from the *Bar-On* case of 2011. In this case, the Supreme Court was asked to annul and judicially review a 'provisional' basic law (or *pouvoir constituant*) or, rather, a new basic law that 'amends' Basic Law: The State's Economy, but does so 'temporarily'. Each year, as in many other states, Israel regularly introduces an Annual State Budget Act,[82] but in 2009, the Knesset decided to irregularly introduce a two-year budget, which it then decided to anchor in a provisional order of a basic law. A year after this provisional basic law was enacted, the government decided that the biennial budget was preferable and decided to extend the Act by another two years to cover 2011 and 2012. This amendment was unique because it was an extension of a provisional measure that was meant to be 'temporary' in nature.

Addressing a petition against this 'provisional constitutional amendment', the Supreme Court was faced with numerous constitutional issues. A seven-judge panel unanimously rejected a petition that challenged the constitutionality of amending a basic law. Their ruling, however, contained harsh remarks about the procedure chosen by the Knesset for this move. President Beinisch repeatedly stated that such legislation evokes serious difficulties. Nevertheless, the Court was not convinced that this was the case in which the Supreme Court should intervene in the Knesset's basic law-making as a constituent authority. This was probably not the time for the Court to employ the 'unconventional weapon' of nullifying a basic law in Israel – particularly because the constituent authority theory, which served as the foundation for judicial review laws, does not necessarily permit the placing of basic laws under judicial review as well. Beinisch stressed that even in an ideal world, where states have special rules for amending their constitutions, it is not certain that a constitution can be amended temporarily.[83] The situation in Israel is not ideal and therefore a basic law cannot be nullified only because it was introduced as a provisional instruction.

---

[82] By the power of the instruction contained in s 3(a) of Basic Law: The State's Economy, s 3(a)(1) states that 'the state budget shall be anchored in a law' and s 3(a)(2) reads: 'The budget will be marked for one year and present expected and planned government expenditures.'

[83] 'Even in an ideal state of affairs, where there exists an orderly and rigid apparatus for amending and correcting a constitution, there is doubt that amending a constitution by way of a provisional instruction is even possible.' President Beinisch in *Bar-On* (n 74) [24].

Another interesting argument made in the *Bar-On* petition refers to the boundaries of judicial review and the option of revoking a constitutional amendment. The petitioners argued that the amendment impairs a constitutional principle because, in Israel's parliamentary regime, the annual state budget is one of the tools that the Knesset uses to supervise government actions. In this respect, the Supreme Court addressed – for the first time in the history of Israel's constitutional adjudication – the unconstitutional constitutional amendment doctrine and its potential application to Israeli law. The Supreme Court established that the question of whether a basic law may be disqualified for conflicting with the fundamental principles of a regime is a rather complicated issue that addresses the very legitimacy of the constituent authority and the root of the Court's authority to judicially review laws. In this case, the judges held that the fact that the biennial state budget impaired the Knesset's ability to monitor government expenses was not so grave as to justify the annulment of a basic law.[84]

The verdict eventually called on the Knesset to complete the constitutional process and legally anchor procedures for endorsing and amending basic laws, but it is not at all certain that this call will be heeded. Professor Ruth Gavison believes that as long as there is no sense of crisis or urgency that imposes a need to make compromises and mutual concessions that would yield an honest arrangement, a constitution cannot be framed.[85]

In summary, one may say that Israel presently has a formal constitution. Though it is neither complete nor perfect, its 'chapters' – that is, basic laws – address a substantial number of the issues covered by formal constitutions of other democratic states. Furthermore, though this formal constitution is weak, limited and even 'crippled', it is nonetheless a constitution that defends the most important human rights through restrained but effective judicial review.

---

[84] President Beinisch's opinion (ibid [34]) reads: 'Indeed, I too believe that there are fundamental principles supporting our existence as a state and society which, if harmed, might raise serious questions about authority, including doubts of whether we are looking at an amended constitution or the enactment of a new constitution. In such a case – which should never happen – the court will have to decide whether the Knesset violated its constituent authority and harmed the basic foundations of Israel as a Jewish and democratic state. This is not the case before us.'

[85] Gavison (n 76) 95.

The *Bank Hamizrahi* verdict mainly established that effective judicial review exists in Israel, but that the constitution itself contains numerous flaws. It actually resembles a selection of institutional rules of procedure, which is a 'slim' constitution that is not necessarily valid as a real statement of coexistence or national credo. It lacks many characteristics that exist in constitutional states. Some of the rights are missing; certain instructions are entrenched, while others are not; some are worded in a festive language, while others are long and cumbersome; and, above all, a basic law that arranges the process of identification and enactment of basic laws is clearly missing, which is why basic laws can be introduced or amended by any Knesset majority. It is the 'unbearable lightness with which changes can be made in basic laws'[86] that actually impairs their status. Israel's constitution is unstable; it is still a constitution in the making.

The appropriate way to advance and complete the constitutional process remains an unresolved question. It is not at all certain that a comprehensive arrangement of introducing a constitution is even possible in ordinary times and, as noted above, all the attempts to do so have thus far failed. On the one hand, the Knesset acts as a constituent authority; on the other, it makes no use of that authority to complete the constitutional process. It has been suggested that the process should be completed through a plebiscite, which should grant it true legitimacy, but the plebiscite issue is greatly disputed in Israel, where it is not a prevailing custom. Since the State of Israel was established, the Knesset has raised the plebiscite option on numerous occasions, seeking ways to let 'the people' decide on controversial issues, but these ideas were rejected even before they turned into bills. The heterogeneous nature of Israeli society does not lend itself to the generation of clear-cut decisions by popular majority. In recent years, discussions of the plebiscite issue were mainly associated with the notion of ceding territories in the framework of peace arrangements.

Plebiscites have advantages and disadvantages, but introducing them would mean a constitutional change of the government system. Thus, when in 1999 the plebiscite issue was first mentioned in a legislative context, the Knesset was fully aware of the need to enact a basic law that would dictate the manner in which plebiscites are to be held in

---

[86] Ariel Bendor, 'Flaws in the Enactment of Basic Laws' (1985) 2 *Law and Government* 443 (Hebrew).

Israel, should the Knesset so decide.[87] Nevertheless, the fact is that the constitutional process and the political refusal to introduce basic laws of any kind impacted on the plebiscite issue as well.

In 2010, the Knesset did enact a plebiscite law as an 'ordinary' act and a majority of the MKs supported it, but the Knesset refused to make use of its constituent authority in this case. A petition that was filed against this law is still pending before the Supreme Court,[88] which will have to address yet another product of Israel's weak constitution. It will have to decide whether certain issues must only be provided for in the framework of a basic law, whether the power of the Knesset as a legislative branch is limited and thus whether regime changes must be made only by the 'constituent' authority. In 2013, a bill for a new basic law on plebiscites was tabled and voted on (at the first reading stage). This bill, if passed, will allow the Court to dismiss the case without dealing with the constitutional question.

Unlike most Western democracies, Israel has never formed a national consensus on fundamental issues and has failed to introduce a separate and distinct procedure for the establishment of constitutional arrangements. The original tactic of 'doing nothing' that served the founding fathers when they reached the Harari compromise remains latent in the Israeli constitutional discourse. Present-day Israel lacks a broad consensus on numerous arrangements, particularly those that pertain to state and religious issues. It seems that for as long as central and fundamental issues are not resolved, it would be hard to complete the final stage of the constitutional process, namely, the completion and unification of basic laws, and their merger into a full, formal constitution.

---

[87] In 1999, the Knesset introduced what is commonly known as the Golan Act, stating that a government resolution on ceding territories to which the Israeli law applies (eg, the Golan Heights) must be approved by a Knesset majority and a plebiscite, which should be arranged by the power of a basic law. Already then, the Knesset was aware of the need to enact a basic law before introducing a plebiscite apparatus in Israel.

[88] HCJ 9149/10 *Dr Muhammad S Watad v The Knesset* (2010). An enlarged panel of judges has been appointed to deal with this issue.

FURTHER READING

Barak, Aharon, 'A Constitutional Revolution: Israel's Basic Laws' (1993) *Faculty Scholarship Series*. Paper 3697. Available at: http://digitalcommons. law.yale.edu/fss_papers/3697.

Barak-Erez, Daphne, 'From an Unwritten to a Written Constitution: The Israeli Challenge in American Perspective' (1995) 26 *Columbia Human Rights Law Review* 309.

Dorner, Dalia, 'Does Israel have a Constitution?' (1999) 43 *St Louise Law Journal* 1325.

Gavison, Ruth, 'Constitutions and Political Reconstruction?: Israel's Quest for a Constitution', in Saïd Amir Arjomand (ed) *Constitutionalism and Political Reconstruction* 69 (Leiden, BRILL, 2007).

Harris, Ron, Kedar, Alexandre (Sandy), Lahav, Pnina and Likhovski, Assaf, *Israeli Legal History: Past and Present: The History of Law in a Multi-Cultural Society: Israel, 1917–1967* (Aldershot, Ashgate Publishing, 2002).

Hofnung, Menachem, 'The Unintended Consequences of the Unplanned Legislative Reform – Constitutional Politics in Israel' (1996) 44 *American Journal of Comparative Law* 585.

Lahav, Pnina, 'A Jewish State to Be Known as the State of Isarel: Notes on the Israeli Legal Historiography' (2001) 19 *Law and History Review* 387.

Likhovski, Eliahu, 'The Courts and the Legislative Supremacy of the Knesset' (1968) 3 *Israel Law Review* 345.

Mautner, Menachem, *Law and the Culture of Israel* (Oxford, Oxford University Press, 2011).

Rabin, Yoram and Gutfeld, Arnon, 'Marbury V. Madison and its impact on Israeli constitutional law', 15 *U Miami Int'l & Comp L Rev* 303 (2007).

Rubinstein, Elyakim, 'The Declaration of Independence as a Basic Document of the State of Israel' (1998) 3(1) *Israeli Studies* 195.

Segev, Joshua, 'Who Needs a Constitution? In Defense of the Non-decision Constitution-Making Tactic in Israel' (2007) 70 *Albany Law Review* 409.

Shachar, Yoram, 'Jefferson Goes East: The American Origins of the Israeli Declaration of Independence' (2008) 10 *Theoretical Inquiries in Law* 589.

Shapira, Amos, 'Why Israel Has No Constitution' (1993) 37 *St Louis University Law Review* 283

Weill, Rivka, 'Sui Generis? The Hybrid Israeli Constitutional Experience' (8 May 2009), Working Paper, available at: http://papers.ssrn.com/sol3/papers.cfm?abstract_id=1401360.

Yonah, Yossi, 'Israel's "Constitutional Revolution": The Liberal–Communitarian Debate and Legitimate Stability' (2001) 27(4) *Philosophy Social Criticism* 41.

2

Sources of the Constitution

————

Introduction

Sources of the Constitution: Basic Laws and Legislation –
Interpretation – Case Law – International and Comparative Law

INTRODUCTION

U NTIL THE ENACTMENT of the basic laws on human rights
in 1992 and the *Bank Hamizrahi* judgment of 1995, it was common knowledge that the State of Israel did not have a 'written'
or formal constitution. At the same time, it clearly had an unwritten
constitution in the British sense – that is, a set of principles and basic
values, including principles that define government institutions and the
procedures of their election, as well as principles that acknowledge the
protection of human rights. Israeli legislation was primarily based on
European sources, mainly in the field of civil law, while American jurisprudence made a significant imprint in the area of constitutional law.
Today, after six decades of the State of Israel's existence, all of these are
well-entrenched cornerstones of Israeli law that interplay in the framework of the structural and cultural conditions of the State of Israel.

The nexus to English law as a binding source of law has progressively
weakened over the years and the Israeli legislature gradually replaced the
old, Mandatory arrangements. Until 1980, the year in which section 46
of the Order in Council – which referred to English law for resolving
lacunae – was finally repealed, there was a clear connection between
Israeli law and common law that imprinted some of the main features
of the latter on the former, primarily the concept of court rulings as a
binding source of law. Judges' authority to create law, or 'case law', and

thereby author legal norms, became part of the Israeli legal tradition. In addition, Israel drew upon common law principles of legal interpretation, the principle of *stare decisis*, the status of judges and the overall structure of the legal system. This common law conception of the judicial role was particularly significant for the development of constitutional law.

Despite the adoption of Continental law concepts in private law, the Anglo-American common law characteristics of Israeli law are prominent. Moreover, English-speaking countries remain the major source of comparative law since most members of the legal profession in Israel are not fluent in Continental languages, which makes it more difficult to follow developments in Continental law.

In this context, the constitutional history similarly evidences new influences upon Israeli constitutional law. A prime example of this can be found in the basic laws on human rights, which were heavily influenced by the Canadian model (mainly the idea of a 'limitation clause').

Since the 1980s, Israeli academia has also experienced an Americanisation process. Many Israeli students travel to the US for postgraduate studies and the majority of university researchers spend varying periods of time there. This phenomenon has left a mark on academic legal writing in Israel, which leans primarily towards US law, a trend that is also visible in the constitutional rulings of the Israeli Supreme Court. For example, an examination of the Israeli Supreme Court's use of foreign precedents in constitutional rulings reveals that, while during the first years of the State of Israel, references were primarily made to English law, US sources have gradually replaced them over the past two decades.[1]

Israeli constitutional law was framed in two main legislative stages, reflecting two historical periods. Chronologically, the first stage proceeded from the decision not to adopt a written constitution and to establish Israeli constitutional law on the basis of the British model of parliamentary supremacy. The Israeli system operated on the basis of that decision for more than 40 years, until 1992. In the absence of a written constitution, the Supreme Court stepped up and assumed the

---

[1] See Suzie Navot, 'Israel: Creating a Constitution' – The Use of Foreign Precedents by the Supreme Court (1994–2010)' in Tania Groppi and Marie-Claire Ponthoreau (eds), *The Use of Foreign Precedents by Constitutional Judges* (Oxford, Hart Publishing, 2013).

role of protector of human rights. In its capacity as the HCJ,[2] the crucial role that the Supreme Court played in formulating Israel's constitutional law runs parallel to the development of the Knesset as the legislature. Thus, since very early on, the Israeli constitutional system relied upon constitutional principles and constitutional interpretation mainly developed by the Supreme Court. Therefore, in this chapter, particular attention is devoted to discussing interpretation as a source of the constitution.

SOURCES OF THE CONSTITUTION

BASIC LAWS AND LEGISLATION

According to the HCJ ruling in the *Bank Hamizrahi* case, Israel's basic laws are now normatively superior to regular Knesset legislation and thus, when a regular law conflicts with a provision of a basic law, the latter takes precedence.

The constitutional revolution, however, has not yet been completed because the basic laws are still shrouded in uncertainty, as legal issues concerning their status have not yet been fully clarified. For example, certain basic laws include a formal entrenchment clause stating that they may only be amended by another basic law and a special Knesset majority; other basic laws contain mainly substantively entrenched clauses, but are not formally entrenched by that majority; and a third kind of basic laws are not entrenched at all and thus can be amended by a regular Knesset majority.

One thing all of the basic laws have in common is that they are formally titled 'Basic' laws. They are mentioned without reference to their enactment year (as is the case with other laws and acts). According to this view, a single, unique feature is enough to identify a law as basic. This 'morphological' characteristic means that a basic law is a law whose name bears the words 'Basic Law'. Otherwise, there is no explicit way to identify basic laws in Israel, since Basic Law: Legislation – proposed by

---

[2] Acting as the High Court of Justice, the Israeli Supreme Court addresses petitions by the state's citizens against the government and is authorised to issue a *mandamus* or writ of mandate for legal public bodies.

several Ministers of Justice over the years in different versions – which was to address the manner in which basic laws are to be enacted, has not yet been passed by the Knesset. Ruling on the *Biennial Budget* issue,[3] for example, Supreme Court President Beinisch established that 'over the years, the various Israeli Knessets and this court identified [basic laws] by their morphological characteristic' and that 'the morphological test was further validated by the *Bank Hamizrahi* judgment'. The majority of judges agreed that the morphological characteristic is the test by which basic laws are identified. At the same time, Beinisch argued that the morphological test is 'too simplistic'.

Indeed, advocates of the morphological test willingly admit that it is arbitrary, but feel it should still be used for the sake of legal certainty. This approach is based on the wording of some basic law instructions, which actually sound like constitutional texts; for example, Basic Law: The Knesset states that 'The MKs shall have [parliamentary] immunity. Details shall be determined by law' and 'The Knesset buildings shall be immune; the specifics of that immunity shall be determined by law'. The problem with the morphological approach is that, presently, a significant part of the basic laws is worded in terms that are generally more typical of ordinary legislation than of the general formulations of basic laws.

The *Bank Hamizrahi* judgment further suggested that the examination of basic laws should look beyond their actual phrasing and into their essence, namely, whether the particular basic law addresses constitutional issues as they are generally perceived. Thus, a law should be examined for its 'constitutional content' – whether it speaks of basic principles, government structure or human rights and so on. This characteristic, however, is no less problematic because it leaves much room for the courts to exercise discretion and might create legal uncertainty. Theoretically, a court may rule that an ordinary law is constitutional in essence and thus might be accorded a superior status.[4] Currently, in the absence of a basic law that defines legislative procedures, the question of whether a combined (morphological and essential) test should apply remains open.

---

[3] HCJ 4908/10 *Bar-On, MK v The Knesset* (rendered on July 4 2011), President Beinisch's opinion at [10].

[4] This approach has been hinted at in Supreme Court rulings on, for example, issues that pertain to the constitutional nature of the Law of Return and the Women's Equal Rights Law, where the question regarding the normative status of these laws was 'left to be seen'. See CA 6821/93 *United Hamizrahi Bank v Migdal Cooperative Village*, 49(4) PD 221 (1995), President Shamgar's judgment at [37].

Presently, the Supreme Court follows the morphological test, which means that the Knesset is required to exercise restraint because it now has the power to change the normative value of legislation by preceding any law with the phrase 'basic law' and omitting its enactment year. Thus, following the *Bank Hamizrahi* case, there was fear that the legislature might abuse its powers. In her decision on the *Biennial Budget* case, President Beinisch warned against the abuse of constituent power and voiced her fear that the phrase 'basic law' might be attached to legislation that should not be part of the constitution on its merits.[5]

Normatively, basic laws are the highest written legal norm in the State of Israel. Constitutional norms are at the top of the pyramid of norms, with ordinary laws below them, and secondary legislation is on the lowest tier. Of all the Israeli basic laws, only those that deal with human rights include a limitation clause. According to the *Bank Hamizrahi* precedent, the limitation clause is intended to authorise the enactment of ordinary laws that might impair on basic laws.

In that regard, Basic Law: Freedom of Occupation further includes a special instruction, known as 'the override clause',[6] whereby a law that restricts and/or violates the freedom of occupation shall be valid for a four-year period even if it does not comply with the limitation clause, provided that it was part of a law that a Knesset majority supported and explicitly stated that it is valid regardless of the text of the basic law. The 'override clause' is intended 'to allow the legislator to fulfil its political and social goals, even if they impair the freedom of occupation and do not follow the requirements of the limitation clause'.[7] Indeed, contrary to the limitation clause – which is democratic in both the formal and essential sense, reflecting a parity between the nation's sovereignty and individual rights – the 'override clause' is an expression of only the formal aspect of democracy, as it expresses the majority viewpoint. Since its enactment, the override clause has only been used once, in order to enact a law that prohibits the importation of frozen meat unless it is *Kosher*.[8] This law was part of a political agreement between members of

[5] *Bar-On* (n 3) [24].

[6] Section 8 of Basic Law: Human Dignity and Liberty.

[7] See HCJ 4676/94 *Mitral v The Knesset*, ver 54, 50(5), 15 (1996) 26; *cf* the instruction in art 33 of the Canadian Charter.

[8] In March 1994, the Knesset enacted the Importation of Frozen Meat Law (1994), which stated that 'notwithstanding the provisions of any law, a person shall not import meat unless he has received a certificate of *Kashrut* in relation to it, this

the coalition and illustrates the possible use of the override clause. Formally, the voting procedure for both basic laws and ordinary legislation is the same. Basic Law: Legislation, which was supposed to arrange special voting procedures for basic laws, has not yet been endorsed, which is why enacting basic laws requires no particular procedural arrangement.[9] In addition, amending or modifying the vast majority of basic laws requires no particular voting procedure and no special majority. To amend a non-entrenched basic law, the Knesset has to use the constituent authority it applied when enacting it. Thus, a basic law may only be amended by another basic law: 'The two new basic laws, introduced in 1992, fully express the normative constitutional hierarchy as it emerges from the Knesset intentions when it introduced basic laws . . . [and] it is from now on possible to follow a single legislative yardstick according to which all basic laws may only be amended by a basic law.'[10]

At the same time, given that most basic laws do not include entrenchment clauses or a majority requirement, it would seem that theoretically any non-entrenched basic law may be modified or even nullified by a majority of only two MKs. This, in fact, is the biggest weakness of the current Israeli constitutional structure: amendment of the basic laws requires no clear or special majority, so that a vote with just a few MKs present could modify or amend a basic law. Not only ordinary but also constitutional legislation is passed relatively easily. A case in point would be the amendment of a basic law by a temporary provision, as in the *Bar-On* case. In its decision, the Supreme Court actually allowed the use of the procedure of amending a basic law by a temporary provision, though it explicitly stated that this course of action may only be taken in extraordinary circumstances.

It seems that the 'decision not to decide', which the founding fathers adopted as their tactic when they made the Harari Resolution, climaxed with the verdict in the *Biennial Budget* case. The fact that the Knesset now abstains from passing basic laws further establishes another characteristic of the Israeli political process: the systematic and regular turning to

law shall be valid notwithstanding the provisions of Basic Law: Freedom of Occupation'. This Meat Law was passed by a majority of 65 MKs.

[9] The most recent bill, tabled in 2000, states (in cl 3): '(A) A basic law shall be endorsed by three Knesset plenum readings; (B) In the first reading, a basic law shall be endorsed by a majority of the voting MKs; abstainers shall not be counted; (C) In the second and third reading, a basic law shall be endorsed by at least 70 MKs'.

[10] *Bank Hamizrahi* (n 4) President Shamgar's opinion at [26].

the HCJ as the alternative decision-making establishment when matters are not addressed by the legislator.

In 2011, Supreme Court Justice Elyakim Rubinstein provided a fine description of the response of the Knesset to the constitutional revolution:

> The most recent basic laws were introduced in 1992, but the *Bank Hamizrahi* verdict that arranged the constitutional powers was handed down in 1995 and ever since then, [the Knesset has observed SN] an operative 'constitution silence' – which it did not in other legislative issues. It seems that certain parts of the Knesset are not too happy with the constitutional powers of this court and fear that additional constitutional texts might only empower it further. I shall merely venture to argue that not only does this court employ its power to judicially review laws cautiously and sparingly, but also that anyone who examines the instances in which that power was employed will find that it addressed issues that generally do not concern the troubled parties . . .
>
> Why do I believe it is important to complete the constitution when in fact we live under a semi-constitutional regime? We need it for educational reasons, to instil Israel's values as a Jewish and democratic state, to serve as a text to be studied, one that would serve as a flowing historic stream of human and national values . . . A complete constitution will promote and improve the education of generations to come, which is why it should materialize in this world.[11]

With respect to legislation, Israeli law is not a homogeneous system, but comprises several layers, dating back to the British Mandate. The legislation includes 'orders', a term that is a relic of the British Mandate and is meant to distinguish between two types of legislation: laws introduced by the empires that ruled over this region and later by the Provisional Council of State before the State of Israel was established; and laws introduced by Israel's elected, legislative authority – the Knesset. Normatively, old laws and orders that are still in effect are of equal legal status. Certain Israeli laws still include the word 'order' to make it clear that they were part of the Mandatory legislation even if that order has been modified since the State of Israel was established.[12]

---

[11] *Bar-On* (n 3) Justice Rubinstein's opinion at [8].

[12] Section 3 of the Interpretation Law (1981) states that an Order is 'an order issued before the state was established or by the Provisional Council of State' and that a Rule is: '(A)(1) legislation; (2) religious rule – oral or written – that is valid in Israel; (3) a British Parliamentary act, or a King's Statement in his Council, or one of the above, or regulations made according to them, and the rules of England's

Orders introduced by the Provisional Council of State are of the same status as Knesset legislation, meaning that Mandatory orders remained valid in Israel if they were not nullified or implicitly amended. It is worth mentioning that the Mandatory orders that remained valid were all originally written and enacted in English. The Minister of Justice is authorised to issue a new version of every law that had been valid before the State of Israel was established and subsequently remained valid. Presently, the Israeli legislation includes not only 'new versions' of Mandatory orders, but also 'combined versions' of laws or orders that legislators introduced or amended over the years and were subsequently combined, bringing together instructions that had for years been scattered in law books.

On a normatively lower level is secondary legislation. While the Israeli government is the executive authority, which follows the laws as outlined by the legislative authority, it is involved in secondary legislation (regulation). The government has direct control over the establishment of binding legal norms. The executive authorities extensively use their legislative power in two main areas:

1) the power to introduce secondary laws in accordance with authorisation clauses in the main legislation; and
2) the power to introduce emergency laws.

The Emergency Defense Regulations top the list of secondary laws because they are the only legislative acts that may alter, temporarily nullify or set terms for existing laws and may also be employed to impose or raise taxes or other mandatory payments. The normal rule is that only a Knesset law may alter another law, but an emergency regulation is not a Knesset law. Emergency orders are dubbed 'regulations' and not laws, since they contain the main characteristics of secondary legislation and may be legally sanctioned by bodies so empowered by law and for purposes stipulated by law. For example, government ministers may issue emergency regulations if the Provisional Council of State (or the Knesset) declares that Israel is in a state of emergency. Indeed, the Council declared a state of emergency in Israel on 19 May 1948, and this declaration is still valid today and enabled by Basic Law: The Government.

---

customary justice and principles of integrity that are valid in Israel; (B) an Ottoman rule that is valid in Israel'.

A law comes into effect once it is published in *Rashumot* (the State of Israel's official journal or gazette) unless the law states that it will become valid before or after its official publication.[13] The *Rashumot* publication is meant to ensure that the law becomes public knowledge, which is a basic precondition for its validity. Furthermore, to amend or nullify a law, the legislator must follow an orderly legislative process – the Knesset needs to introduce an amendment or nullification of a law in the same way as it introduces new laws, and a law remains valid until it is explicitly or implicitly nullified by the legislator. There are a few exceptions to this rule: for example, when the text of the law names its expiry date or assigns its validity for a particular period; when laws are introduced explicitly for an emergency period, and expire once that emergency period ends; and when the laws' validity is limited by specific dates or events.

In recent years, the Knesset has increasingly used 'temporary provisions'. For example, it may introduce temporary provisions that impair certain human rights for a specified period of time. It seems that in doing so, it attempts to show the HCJ that though this particular law infringes human rights, the fact that it is temporary makes it 'proportional' and thus the court should avoid nullifying it if petitioned to do so.

Time-restricted laws that impose certain limitations for a given period may survive the constitutionality test and judicial review, but history has shown that the validity of most of these laws is extended time and again. For example, an amendment to the Criminal Proceedings Law was introduced in 2006 by way of a temporary provision, stating that a judge may rule on the extension of detention of persons held on suspicion of security offences even if they are not presented before a judge. The validity of this amendment was extended as soon as it expired. In 2011, a nine-judge HCJ bench ruled that this amendment was unconstitutional because it conflicted with Basic Law: Human Dignity and Liberty.[14] The 2003 amendment of the Citizenship Law that bans family

---

[13] Section 10(1) of the original Government and Justice Arrangements Order (1948). Presently, the power to introduce emergency regulations is found in cl 39 of Basic Law: The Government.

[14] Deputy HCJ President Eliezer Rivlin stated that the legal proceeding does not address absentees, but only present individuals. One of the most basic foundations of criminal law is that a person should not be tried in absentia. Justice Rivlin stressed that the defendant's right to be present at his own trial is part of the right to honest

reunions between Israeli Arabs and Palestinians who reside in the Palestinian Authority (PA) territories was also introduced as a temporary provision, but its validity was extended on numerous occasions. In early 2012, the HCJ rejected yet another petition against this law by a majority of six of the 11 judges. Most of the judges maintained that even though it impairs the Israeli Arabs' basic right to maintain family life, it is 'proportional' due to issues of security and the fact that the reunion in question relates to residents of a hostile entity. In addition, the law that exempts *Yeshiva* students from military service (the *Tal* Law) was first introduced as a temporary provision because it seriously violates the equality principle, but has been extended periodically.[15] The same thing happened with the amendment of Basic Law: The Israeli Economy that established a biennial state budget with a temporary provision and was then extended again. The temporary provisions or even legislation for a specific period of time, which has been increasingly employed by the Knesset in recent years, may appear to be a political reaction to the 'constitutionalisation' of human rights and judicial review. Temporary legislation is part of the discourse between the Israeli Parliament and the Supreme Court. The Knesset often needs specific measures to fulfil political compromises (such as the exemption from military service granted to *Yeshiva* students). Provisional laws have become a 'tool' used by the Knesset to attempt to avoid judicial review, arguing that the problematic law is 'temporary' and therefore 'proportional'.

INTERPRETATION

Constitutional interpretation in Israel, as in many constitutional systems, is guided by purposive or 'objective' interpretation rather than by the intentions of the authors of the texts, so-called 'original intent'.[16]

---

proceedings, which is a basic premise of the law and a protected constitutional right. He deducted the importance of this principle from the habeas corpus doctrine; see CC 8823/07 *John Doe v The State of Israel*, Deputy President Rivlin's opinion at [20] (published by Nevo on 11 February 2010).

[15] For a discussion of this affair, see the next chapter on basic principles that includes a discussion of Israel as a Jewish state.

[16] Aharon Barak, *Interpretation in Law, Vol III – Constitutional Interpretation* (Jerusalem, Nevo, 1994) 285 (Hebrew).

The *Bank Hamizrahi* case is perhaps one of the most fascinating examples of the interpretation of the original intent of a text's authors. Stating that basic laws have constitutional status, the judges attempted to examine the intention of legislators who enacted the basic laws. In his opinion, President Barak wrote: 'It is a fundamental perception of the Israeli society today – expressing the entire national experience – that the Knesset is nationally viewed as the body authorised to hand down an Israeli constitution. That view, crystallised in the Declaration of Independence, is part of our social-judicial culture.'[17] Barak's position is based, among other things, on remarks that MKs made during the legislative process, citing the enactment procedure of *Basic Law: The Knesset* in 1958 where 'no one even considered the possibility that the Third Knesset was not authorized to introduce a constitution, and everyone viewed the Knesset as performing its role according to the Harari Resolution'.[18]

In addressing the legislators' subjective purpose, the *Bank Hamizrahi* judgment is an exception among other constitutional rulings. It is generally held that the interpretation of constitutional texts should follow the objective, purposive approach that is based on historic developments, on society's fundamental principles and primarily on the basic principles of the judicial system, such as the rule of law, the separation of powers and human rights.[19] The attempt to apply these interpretative rules to basic laws is obstructed by a fundamental problem: the basic laws are not yet joined together as a constitution, they are incoherent and, as noted above, they are based more on rules and less on principles. Furthermore, until the 'constitutional revolution', the HCJ viewed basic laws as regular laws.

Professor Aharon Barak clearly played a central role in forming the foundations of constitutional interpretation in Israel. Having served on the HCJ bench for nearly 30 years, Barak presented a comprehensive view of the rules of constitutional interpretation in his publications, especially in his book on constitutional interpretation that is frequently cited in HCJ rulings.[20] Rich in comparative law discussions, Barak's book states that a constitutional text should be interpreted with a broad

---

[17] *Bank Hamizrahi* (n 4) 357.
[18] ibid 370–72.
[19] Aharon Barak, 'The Role of the Supreme Court in a Democratic Society' (1995) 51 *Hapraklit* 5, 6 (Hebrew).
[20] Barak, Constitutional Interpretation (n 16).

perspective and 'generosity', It should not be approached 'legalistically' or 'pedantically', but rather should consider the nature of the text and the ways it establishes the Israeli way of life in the long run. The constitutional purpose needs to be based on the values and principles that the constitutional norm was meant to realise, and when these values and principles clash, judges must find the balance between them.

Israeli constitutional law acknowledges various formulae that can be used to balance out such conflicting values. For example, Israel adopted the test of 'imminent certainty' to examine restrictions on the freedom of expression. This resembles the US 'clear and present danger' test, but differs from it in its 'gravity of probability' test. According to Professor Barak, constitutional interpretation should follow the fundamental principles of the legal system: 'The constitutional purpose that is the core of the constitutional text comprises the goals, principles, policy, and social purposes and interests that the constitutional text was meant to realize.'[21]

Constitutional interpretation in Israel has been focused on the basic laws on human rights, mainly because they include fundamental principles and clauses referring to their purpose.[22]

The clause outlining the fundamental principles in these basic laws states as follows: 'Fundamental human rights in Israel are founded upon the recognition of the value of the human being, the sanctity of human life, and the principle that all persons are free; these rights shall be upheld in the spirit of the principles set forth in the Declaration of the Establishment of the State of Israel.'[23]

This clause set forth the fundamental guiding principles of human rights in Israel and plays an interpretative role in understanding the scope of those rights, helping to shape the content and meaning of the rights stipulated in each basic law. These two basic laws further include a clause that stipulates their purpose. The purpose of these basic laws is to anchor the values of the State of Israel as a Jewish and democratic state in basic laws. Thus, the basic assumption is that Israel's values are the values of a 'Jewish and democratic' state. Though this clause features only in basic laws on human rights, Professor Barak wrote: 'It is

---

[21] ibid 83.
[22] Referring to expressions such as 'Jewish and democratic state', 'human dignity' and 'the values of the State of Israel', to mention but a few.
[23] Section 1 of Basic Law: Freedom of Occupation; s 1 of Basic Law: Human Dignity and Liberty.

only natural to assume that the State of Israel's values as a Jewish and democratic state are not limited only to the basic laws on human rights . . . A purposeful constitutional interpretation views constitutional instructions as uniform . . . The State of Israel's values as a Jewish and democratic state apply even beyond the confines of these basic laws.'[24] Still, the expression 'human dignity and liberty' was and remains the key for addressing aspects of human rights not explicitly protected in the constitution.

Since the enactment of Basic Law: Human Dignity and Liberty, judgments have yielded expanding constitutional interpretations of the 'human dignity' phrase, acknowledging the constitutional status of rights that were not explicitly mentioned in this basic law, even if this acknowledgement is sometimes partial in the sense that only the aspects directly and practically associated with human dignity were accorded constitutional status in the framework of that right. The rights in question here include freedom of expression, freedom of faith and worship, various rights in criminal proceedings and certain aspects of the right to equality. Granting constitutional status to those rights substantially changed Israeli constitutional law because it meant that the Knesset was restricted in its power to infringe them with laws that do not meet the terms of the limitation clause.[25] Furthermore, acknowledging the constitutional status of rights that were not included in basic laws means that it is the HCJ's prerogative to judicially review laws enacted by the Knesset that allegedly violate those rights. The interpretative means by which rights that had not been explicitly listed are included in the human rights laws have been in effect for several years, although the Knesset has not yet openly addressed them. In practice, this means that the Israeli constitution is amended in a process that is mainly interpretative in nature.

One of the most fascinating examples of this process is the *Adalah* case.[26] The HCJ heard a petition against the constitutionality of the Citizenship and Entry to Israel Law (Temporary Provision) 2003, according to which the Interior Minister shall not accord Israeli citizenship or

[24] Barak (n 16) 309–10.

[25] See Hillel Somer, 'The Unlisted Rights: On the Extent of the Constitutional Revolution' (1997) 28 *Mishpatim* 257 (Hebrew).

[26] HCJ 7052/03 *Adalah v Interior Minister*, ver 51(2), 202 (2006). See the English version of the verdict at: http://elyon1.court.gov.il/files_eng/03/520/070/a47/03070520.a47.htm.

residency status to residents of Judea, Samaria and the Gaza Strip, banning them from residing in Israel. That instruction did not apply to Israelis who reside in those regions and so, in practice, it banned family reunions between Israeli Arabs and residents of the PA.

The main purpose of this law was based on security concerns, against the backdrop of a wave of grave terror attacks perpetrated by Palestinian terrorists against the Israeli population. Its chief purpose was to prevent Palestinian residents who were allowed to reside in Israel with their Israeli spouses from aiding persons involved in hostile or terrorist activities. One of the main claims against the law was that it illegally violated the right to equality, which is not included in Basic Law: Human Dignity and Liberty.

President Barak wrote:

> It has been established that the human dignity right contains the right to equality inasmuch as it is closely and matter-of-factly associated with human dignity . . . The equality right is an inseparable part of human dignity. The acknowledgement of the constitutional aspect of equality does not follow from a judicial act of completing what is 'missing' from Basic Law: Human Dignity and Liberty. The acknowledgement of the constitutional aspect of equality follows from the constitutional interpretation of the right to human dignity – which is explicitly acknowledged by the basic act. Nevertheless, some of the aspects of equality [it could have] had it been acknowledged as an independent, self-sufficient right are not included in the law on human dignity. Only the aspects of equality that are closely and practically associated with human dignity are included in the broad definition of the right to human dignity.[27]

Thus, President Barak stated that the right of an Israeli spouse to maintain a family in Israel is part of the human right to dignity. Although the right to equality is not explicit in the basic law, some aspects of equality are contained in the concept of human dignity and are therefore protected by the basic law.[28] Barak's statement on the *Adalah* case clearly demonstrates that the Supreme Court adopts a limited understanding of the right to equality within the larger concept of human dignity. Still, the fact that the legislator remained silent on the matter created a situation in which the

---

[27] ibid, President Barak's opinion at [30].

[28] President Barak's opinion was in the minority in the final verdict on the petition, where a majority of six judges ruled against a minority stand of five and stated that the amendment of the Citizenship Law shall not be nullified. In 2012, the Court again ruled in this matter. The affair will be discussed at greater length in ch 8.

slow development and introduction of new human rights – that are missing from the Israeli constitution – is mainly achieved through a process that is essentially interpretative and led by the HCJ.

CASE LAW

The absence of a constitutional text impacted on constitutional adjudication in two main ways. First, it tightened the link between the Israeli and the English laws: the former used the latter as a complementary judicial source, and the Israeli regime essentially followed the English one. In the early days of the State of Israel, Israeli judges developed much of the legal system through common law. Large segments of administrative law, rules of evidence, and laws specifying remedies and compensation were created this way. Furthermore, until 1980, Israeli courts were bound to follow English judge-made law. The British system continues to serve as the historical source of many arrangements in Israeli constitutional law. The structure and hierarchy of the judiciary, rules of evidence and procedure, and the status of judges all bear similarities to England and other common law countries. Second, the absence of a constitutional text also helped judges create laws and refer to foreign law since they were not obligated to interpret constitutional texts or to attempt to discern the original intention of the founding fathers. This interpretative flexibility had a great impact on the sources of constitutional law, particularly the application of foreign laws as part of local adjudication.

In addition, Israeli judges are obligated to follow the stare decisis principle. According to Basic Law: The Judiciary, decisions of the Supreme Court bind all lower courts, but not the Supreme Court itself, which may deviate from them. Still, though the Supreme Court is not obligated to adhere to its own rulings, it rarely deviates from its precedents because it holds judicial stability as a major value.

As we shall see below in chapter 7, constitutional adjudication by the HCJ was initially characterised by a formalistic approach, adhering to the wording of the law. Thus, until the 1980s,[29] the HCJ employed standing doctrines by which it did not acknowledge *actio popularis* motions in

---

[29] Menachem Mautner, 'The Decline of Formalism and the Rise of Values in Israeli Law' (1993) 17 *Iyunei Mishpat* 503 (Hebrew).

which the HCJ was asked to address issues with political implications, but chose to abstain. Furthermore, until the early 1980s, the HCJ employed the justiciability doctrine, according to which the Court should not address certain issues, which prevented the HCJ from discussing sensitive matters of a political nature.

The 1980s marked a turning point in this respect. First, after the HCJ moved away from its traditional justiciability and standing restrictions, it could address issues of political significance and petitions against government decisions. It became increasingly involved in Israel's public life and engaged in closer supervision of various administrative decisions, even to the point of intervening in parliamentary processes. This period is known as 'the transition from formalism to activism'.[30]

This intensified judicial activism was coupled with the constitutional changes of 1992 which, from the HCJ's point of view, climaxed with the *Bank Hamizrahi* case. The transition to judicial activism was accompanied by a modification of the Court's rules of interpretation and reasoning in verdicts, which became less formalistic and referred to new and different interpretative sources. These processes impacted on the scope and meaning of constitutional decisions. The transition from the formalistic approach, which characterised Israeli adjudication prior to the 1980s, to judicial activism further explains why English law was abandoned and new links were established with American law. The more the judiciary moves towards the role of shaping the law according to considerations of policy and justice, the more it is relevant for judges to look to a variety of sources that deal with similar policy or moral questions.[31]

Thus, it may be safely stated that key changes in Israel's constitutional regime were introduced by HCJ adjudication, and the *Bank Hamizrahi* case is a clear example of the Court's crucial contribution to Israel's constitutional law.

INTERNATIONAL AND COMPARATIVE LAW

In Israel, international law and domestic constitutional law operate in principle on two parallel levels, since Israel maintains a dual apparatus

[30] ibid.
[31] Iddo Porat, 'The Use of Foreign Law in Israeli Constitutional Adjudication' in Aharon Barak, Daphne Barak-Erez and Gideon Sapir (eds), *Israeli Constitutional Law in the Making* (Oxford, Hart Publishing, 2013) 151

of absorbing international justice norms.[32] For international norms to be implemented in the local justice system, they need to be introduced as laws by a legislative act, independently of and in addition to any endorsement of international treaties by the State of Israel. Thus, though the Fourth Geneva Convention was ratified by the Israeli government in 1951, it was never enacted by the Knesset. When the HCJ was asked to order its implementation, it refused, arguing that it is not part of Israel's domestic laws that the courts may enforce. Similarly, it refused to enforce an international agreement to which the State of Israel was party because it had not been adopted by the Knesset.[33]

The situation in the West Bank (Judea and Samaria) – and until 2005 also the Gaza Strip – that Israel has been holding since 1967 through belligerent occupation (referred to as the Territories) required special reference to international law. Almost every petition filed with the HCJ against the State of Israel's operations in the Territories invokes international law. As a result, and because the residents of the Territories have been given the right to appeal to the Israeli HCJ, the Court often and extensively discusses international law. This, however, does not mean that HCJ verdicts are based on international law, and when the Court resorted to ordering the State of Israel to change positions – such as in the case concerning the security wall on which we will elaborate below – in most cases it referred to Israeli law, not to international law. Nevertheless, rules drawn from international law feature in almost every HCJ verdict that addresses activities associated with the Territories. In the legal literature, attempts have been made to establish a thesis whereby the Fourth Geneva Convention is indeed binding on Israel and the Israeli courts should follow its instructions,[34] but all of these attempts were rejected by the HCJ during the first years of Territories-related adjudication. In the *Afo* case,[35] the HCJ judges failed to agree on

---

[32] Amihay Cohen, 'Unequal Partnership? The Introduction of International Law Rules into the Israeli Law by the HCJ: The Case of the Territories' (2007) 6 *Maazaney Mishpat* 157, 164 (Hebrew).

[33] CA 25/55, 145, 148 *Guardian of Absentee Property v Samara*, ver 10, 1825 (1956).

[34] Amnon Rubinstein, 'The Changing Status of the Occupied Territories: From a Held Deposit to a Judicial Hybrid' (1986) 11 *Iyuney Mishpat* 439 (Hebrew); see also Meron Theodor, *Human Rights and Humanitarian Norms as Customary Law* (Oxford, Claredon Press, 1989) 25–37.

[35] HCJ 785/87 *Afo v Commander of IDF Units in Judea and Samaria*, ver 42(2), 1 (1988).

the proper interpretation of Chapter 49 of the Geneva Convention, but they nevertheless agreed that the Court cannot impose the Convention's provisions in the Israeli cases.

At the same time, HCJ rulings greatly contributed to the use of international law in Israel, as they did with respect to other constitutional issues, and here too we can clearly discern different 'periods' in the HCJ adjudication practices. Like the constitutional revolution, here too the HCJ acted as 'a partner' of the legislator. It was adjudication that established that the humanitarian provisions of the Fourth Geneva Convention may be viewed as binding norms – if only partially – because they were part of the Israeli government's instructions to the local military commander. A large part of the international law that addresses the rules of war and occupation is customary and was absorbed into Israeli law without requiring domestic legislation,[36] while another part was ratified by the government alone.

While in the early years, discussions mainly addressed the application of international law, the prominent phenomenon in recent verdicts is that judges have increasingly relied upon international law norms without discussing the problem of their applicability to Israel. For example, President Barak's verdict in the *Ajuri* case[37] referred to the Geneva Conventions as binding international law. This was also the case in the *Beit Surik* case, which addressed the security fence;[38] the case of *Almadani v The Defense Minister;*[39] and the judgment examining the legality of 'targeted killings', in which the court cited the Fourth Geneva Convention verbatim, almost without explaining or justifying it.[40]

In all of the above cases, appellants cited international law as a means for the protection of Palestinian residents from Israeli Defense Forces (IDF) policies, and in all of those cases, the HCJ ruled that the IDF policy indeed harmed Palestinian rights that international law protects.

---

[36] The local relevance of the international law as habitual practice does not require the explicit consent of the state, but it can be discerned from its conduct; see Cohen (n 33); see also Yafa Zilbershatz, 'International Law in Constitutional Law' (1997) 4 *Mishpat uMimshal* 47, 57 (Hebrew); and HCJ 253/88 *Sajadiya v the Defense Minister*, ver 42(3), 801 (1988).

[37] HCJ 7015/02 *Ajuri v Commander of IDF Troops in the West Bank*, ver 54, 56(6), 352 (2002).

[38] HCJ 2056/04 *Beit Surik Village Council v Israeli Government*, ver 58(5), 807 (2004).

[39] HCJ 3451/02 *Almadani v The Defense Minister*, ver 56(3), 30 (2002).

[40] HCJ 769/02 *Public Committee against Torture in Israel v Israeli Government*, ver 72(1), 507 (2005), President Barak's opinion at [60]–[61].

However, in most cases, the HCJ also stated that a balance should be found between the rights of the Palestinians and Israel's security needs.[41] As a result, the HCJ almost always provided the Israeli policy in general with a legal seal of approval, while qualifying and restricting it.[42]

The use of international law suggests the importance of 'custom' as a constitutional source in Israel. Customarily, Israeli governments presented the Knesset with peace accords they had signed before finally committing the state to the agreement or treaty. These agreements were acknowledged as being of particular importance and were expected to greatly impact on the nation's life. Thus, the executive decided, on its own accord and while it was free of any such obligation, to obtain the approval of the legislature before making political commitments.

In the past, the HCJ suggested that the presidency should be the most appropriate and suitable national institution to approve and absorb international treaties, but practice over the years has shown that the government asks the Knesset to approve peace treaties and does so as a constitutional custom. In the *Kamiar* case,[43] the Court accepted the government's position that it is authorised to sign and ratify such treaties exclusively, without the Knesset's involvement. The Court established the government's authority to make pacts and sign treaties within its general authority to manage the foreign affairs of the state and upon the existence of a 'constitutional custom' whereby all the treaties that had been pending ratification were endorsed by the government without the Knesset's participation. The Court accepted the government's position, according to which the President's signature is required only under special circumstances and only when the government asks the Knesset to ratify such a treaty.[44]

In 1983, a government resolution stipulated that it must present treaties to the Knesset before ratifying them. In practice, however, the government asked the Knesset to approve only important covenants

---

[41] This issue will be discussed at length in a separate part on the war on terrorism within the framework of ch 8.

[42] A prominent exception to this rule was the absolute ban on employing the so-called 'neighbor procedure', which the HCJ ruled was in violation of international law. See HCJ 3799/02 *Adalah v IDF's Central Command Commander* ver 60(3), 67 (2005); and see Cohen (n 33) 193.

[43] HCJ 131/67 *Kamiar v The State of Israel*, ver 22(2), 89 (1968).

[44] Yafa Zilbershatz 'The Adoption of International Law into Israeli Law: The Real is Ideal' (1996) 25 *Israel Yearbook on Human Rights* 243.

on issues such as territorial concessions, security issues and human rights.[45]

This custom applies to international covenants and treaties that the State of Israel signed, namely, mainly peace accords and ceasefire agreements. The most important of these acts included the signing of the UN Charter (1948), the ceasefire agreements with Lebanon, Egypt, Jordan and Syria (1949), the Convention on the Prevention of and Punishment for the Crime of Genocide (1949), the Camp David Accords (1978), that is, the peace agreement with Egypt, which was presented to the Knesset as a political government statement and was followed by a discussion and a Knesset vote of confidence in the government, the Israel–Lebanon agreement (1983) and so on.

The scope of foreign law application in constitutional jurisdiction was greatly influenced by the fact that Israel is a legally mixed jurisdiction, having characteristics both from civil law and common law. Recent research[46] reveals that the HCJ makes extensive use of foreign law in its constitutional cases. It seems that Israel's constitutional history, as discussed above, can shed some light on the importance of comparative law, particularly when it pertains to human rights. Though Israel's institutionalised constitutional law is mostly organised within the textual framework of basic laws, this model is faulty when it comes to laws pertaining to human rights because they are textually lacking and because Israel does not have a formal bill of rights. Even after the constitutional revolution, the Court's interpretative means of including human rights that have not been explicitly anchored in basic laws under 'human dignity' have been constantly accompanied by extensive reference to foreign law.

CONCLUSION

In this chapter we have seen that the Israeli constitutional system derives from several different sources. Although incomplete, the basic laws are the main source of the constitution. Until the 1980s, there was a tight nexus between Israeli law and common law that shaped key features of the Israeli constitutional system, the most important of which was the

---

[45] Shimon Sheetrit, 'The Knesset's Role in Covenant Signing' (1995) 36 *Hapraklit* 349, 386–87 (Hebrew).
[46] Navot, *The Use of Foreign Precedents by Constitutional Judges* (n 1)

use of court rulings as a binding source of law. Stare decisis and the status of judges were also drawn from the common law system. Since the 1980s, American jurisprudence has made a significant impact on Israeli constitutional law. The use of US precedents has overtaken the use of UK law in recent years as one of the results of the constitutional revolution. This process of Americanisation has influenced both Israeli academic literature and the Supreme Court's rulings.

We have seen the crucial role played by the Supreme Court in formulating Israel's constitutional law, which will be discussed further in the next chapters. Following the constitutional revolution and the Knesset's subsequent constitutional silence, developments in human rights have relied on constitutional interpretation. The interpretative means by which rights that had not been explicitly listed are included in the human rights basic laws have been the most recent important development in Israel's constitutional law, a revolution carried out chiefly by the Supreme Court.

FURTHER READING

Barak, Aharon, *Purposive Interpretation in Law* (Princeton, Princeton University Press, 2005).

Barak, Aharon, *Proportionality: Constitutional Rights and their Limitations* (Cambridge, Cambridge University Press, 2012).

Barak-Erez, Daphne, 'The International Law of Human Rights and Constitutional Law: A Case Study of an Expanding Dialogue' (2004) 2 *International Journal of Constitutional Law* 611.

Benvenisti, Eyal, 'The Attitude of the Supreme Court of Israel Towards the Implementation of the International Law of Human Rights' in Francesco Francioni and Benedetto Conforti (eds), *The Role of Domestic Courts in the Enforcement of International Human Rights* (Kluwer, Martinus Nijhoff Publishers, 1997).

Friedman, Daniel, 'The Effect of Foreign Law on the Law of Israel' (1975) 10 *Israel Law Review* 192.

Friedman, Daniel, 'Independent Development of Israeli Law' (1975) 10 *Israel Law Review* 515.

Friedman, Daniel, 'Infusion of the Common Law into the Legal System of Israel' (1975) 10 *Israel Law Review* 324.

Harris, Ron, Kedar, Alexandre (Sandy), Lahav, Pnina and Likhovski, Assaf, *Israeli Legal History: Past and Present: The History of Law in a Multi-Cultural Society: Israel, 1917–1967* (Dartmouth, Ashgate, 2002).

Kretzmer David, 'Israel', in David Sloss (ed), *The Role of Domestic Courts in Treaty Enforcement: A Comparative Study* (Cambridge, Cambridge University Press, 2009)

Menahem, Mautner, *Law and the Culture of Israel* (Oxford, Oxford University Press, 2011).

Navot, Suzie, *The Constitutional Law of Israel* (Kluwer, 2007).

Weil, Rivka, 'Reconciling Parliamentary Sovereignty and Judicial Review: On the Theoretical and Historical Origins of the Israeli Legislative Override Power' (2012) 39 *Hastings Constitutional Law Quarterly* 457.

3

Constitutional Principles

—————

Introduction – 'Jewish and Democratic' – The Rule of Law – Separation of Powers – Independent Judiciary

INTRODUCTION

ANY DISCUSSION OF the Israeli constitution must deal with the tension which arises from the definition of Israel as both a Jewish and a democratic state, two principles that apparently contradict one another. Israel was defined as a 'Jewish and Democratic state' in the 1992 basic laws. This description of Israel is taken for granted by most of Israel's Jewish political leaders. It was presupposed by the UN Resolution of 29 November 1947 to the effect that Palestine should be divided into two states, both democratic, one Jewish and one Arab. It is part of the most basic political sentiments of most citizens of Israel, Jews and non-Jews alike.[1] Yet, the argument that Israel cannot simultaneously be both Jewish and democratic is presently expressed on all sides of the political spectrum.

Israel is divided by at least two major rifts that relate directly to this definition: the Jewish–Arab tensions (that is, the tension between the Jewish state and the rights of its non-Jewish population) and the tensions between religious and non-religious Jewish citizens. Both these rifts pose serious challenges to Israel's society today. The tensions between religious or Orthodox Jews and non-religious Jews are latent and occasionally erupt in demonstrations and clashes between them. At the same time, Jews and the Arab world are still involved in a persistent

---

[1] Ruth Gavison, 'Can Israel Be Both Jewish and Democratic'- in *Tensions and Prospects* (The Van Leer Jerusalem Institute, 1999) (Hebrew). For the English version, see Ruth Gavison, 'Can Israel Be Both Jewish and Democratic?', *Israel as a Jewish and Democratic State* (2011) 115. Available at: http://ssrn.com/abstract=1862904.

conflict, including numerous violent spells, with no end in sight. The conflict in Israel is fuelled by serious allegations of violence, dispossession, persecution and oppression by Israeli Arabs and Palestinians against Jews and the Jewish state. It should be recalled that Israel is situated in a region with a huge Arab majority and that, since 1967, it has controlled the territory between the Mediterranean Sea and the Jordan River (the West Bank), which originally was to be divided into a Jewish and an Arab state.[2]

These challenges require an examination of the concepts of democracy and the Jewish state. The Supreme Court has made an important contribution in trying to demonstrate that 'Jewish' and 'democratic' are compatible as constitutional characteristics, which will be explored below.

Another point to be discussed is the concept of the rule of law as one of the basic principles in Israel's constitutional law. Once regarded as deriving from the supremacy of Parliament, the rule of law concept is nowadays much more difficult to define.

'JEWISH AND DEMOCRATIC'

Hence, there could be no doubt – as the text of the declaration of the state's independence clearly indicates – that not only is the State of Israel a sovereign, independent, and freedom-seeking state, whose regime is characterized by the rule of the people, but it was also established as 'A Jewish state in the Land of Israel', and the act of its establishment primarily followed from 'the natural and historic right of the Jewish Nation to live as any other nation: self-reliant in its sovereign state', and that act was the realization of the age-old aspiration for Israel's redemption.[3]

The State of Israel was established as a Jewish state – a characteristic determined by the international community as part of the Partition Plan decreed by the UN General Assembly on 29 November 1947.[4] This characteristic was explicitly mentioned in the State of Israel's Declaration of Independence, which was drafted before the State of Israel was

---

[2] ibid 118.

[3] CA 1/65 *Yardor v Chairman of the Central Elections Committee of the Sixth Knesset*, ver 19(3), 365 (1965), Justice Agranat's opinion at 385–86.

[4] UN Resolution 181 (II). Future Government of Palestine, available at: unispal. un.org/unispal.nsf/0/7F0AF2BD897689B785256C330061D253.

established. The HCJ has acknowledged that the Jewish nature of the state is part of its 'constitutional data' or the basic principles of its legal system. Currently, the Jewish nature of the state is anchored in basic laws on human rights that established 'the values of the State of Israel as a Jewish and democratic state' and clarified that the Knesset may restrict basic rights through legislation that follows 'the values of the State of Israel' – namely, its values as a Jewish and democratic state.[5]

The failure to enact a constitution for Israel is primarily due to disagreements on the appropriate balance between the state's Jewish and democratic elements. Basic laws on human rights did not resolve these disputes and, in the absence of an agreement on Israel's predominant political philosophy, it is up to the courts to find the balance between these seemingly conflicting values, since the values of the State of Israel as a Jewish state might conflict with its democratic values.[6] There are several meanings to the term 'Jewish state', some of them more problematic in their relationship with democracy than others. The state may be deemed 'Jewish' because a majority of its population is Jewish, which is a very thin definition of a Jewish state. Jewish may mean that Israel is the state in which the Jewish people exercise their right to political self-determination, that is, a 'nation-state'. Jewish may also mean that Israel is a religiously Jewish state – a *Halakic* (Jewish law) state governed by religious rules, in which political decisions are made according to Jewish law. Only certain aspects of the Jewish state concept may be compatible with democracy.

Since Israel was established, many attempts have been made to balance out these ostensibly conflicting aspects, even though there is no full state–religion separation in Israel. The Knesset left many questions undecided because it was unable to reach political agreement, resulting in the courts being called upon to fill this void. Adjudication of issues that pertain to the tensions between these two sets of values has been particularly cautious, attempting to bridge the gap and find compromises between them,

---

[5] Basic Law: The Knesset also addresses Israel's values as a Jewish and democratic state. Section 7 states that a list of candidates may not run in Knesset elections 'if its objects or actions, expressly or by implication . . . negate the existence of the State of Israel as the state of the Jewish people' or 'the democratic character of the State'.

[6] Aharon Barak, *Judicial Proportionality: Infringements on Constitutional Rights and its Restrictions* (Jerusalem, Nevo, 2010) 316 (Hebrew); *Proportionality: Constitutional Rights and their Limitations* (Cambridge, Cambridge University Press, 2012).

often by assigning restrictive interpretations to avoid conflict as much as possible.

The State of Israel is Jewish in the sense that it serves as the political framework within which the Jewish nation's right to self-determination is realised. In addition, it is the 'state of the Jewish nation' – namely, the state in which the Jewish nation's right to national independence is realised. If Israel is, in fact, the 'state of the Jews', it indicates that Jews are the majority in the country and it does not, in itself, suggest that the regime in this country cannot be fully democratic. As Ruth Gavison described it, 'the relationship between the Jewishness of the state and democracy gets more complicated inasmuch as the Jewish majority is not only a description of a stable state of affairs at a given point in time, but rather a situation where the Jewishness of the state reflects the goal of ensuring, strengthening, and maintaining that Jewish majority through deliberate policies'.[7] Interestingly, when the Supreme Court was called upon to address the nature of the State of Israel and its conflicting values, it opted to adopt a narrow and minimalist approach to both concepts.

According to the HCJ, the State of Israel's fundamental characteristics shape the minimalistic definition of Israel as a Jewish state, primarily the right of every Jew to immigrate to the State of Israel, where Jews are the majority, the first official language is Hebrew, Jewish tradition is a key element of its religious and cultural heritage, and the major holidays and symbols reflect the historical revival of the Jewish nation. The Jewishness of Israel is, first of all, inherent in the recognition of the fact that Israel is the state in which the Jewish people exercise their right to national self-determination. A minimising definition, such as the one given by the Supreme Court, was meant to prevent, as much as possible, conflicts between Jewish and democratic values.[8] There are, however, issues in relation to which this clash is inevitable. Israel's definition as a Jewish state legitimises legal arrangements such as the Law of Return, restrictions on individual liberties in order to protect and promote the

---

[7] Gavison (n 1) 121.

[8] For example, when it delivered its judgment in a petition to disqualify a political party because it negated the existence of the State of Israel as a Jewish and democratic state, the Court adopted a 'narrow' interpretation of the term 'Jewish' and a 'slim' interpretation of the 'democratic' concept so as to avoid denying the right to be elected as much as possible. See AB 11208/02 *Central Elections Committee v Tibi*, ver 57(4), 1 (2003).

Jewish nature of public life in Israel,[9] granting 'semi-national' status to institutions that represent the Jewish nation.[10]

Being the nation-state of the Jewish people justifies the enactment of arrangements that express the nation's right to entertain a public life whose characteristics for the most part reflect Jewish culture and heritage. The incorporation of arrangements that shape Israel's public life according to Jewish tradition often means that originally religious norms are imposed on the public as a whole. These include, for example, Sabbath labour rules and public transportation restrictions, and the ban on the sale of pork. The sweeping application of *Halakic* rules in matrimonial issues is an extreme case of the prioritisation of Jewish values over human rights. The jurisdiction of the rabbinical courts is anchored in the Rabbinical Courts' Jurisdiction Law (Marriage and Divorce) (1953). According to this law, marriages and divorces of Jews who are citizens or residents of Israel are conducted exclusively in accordance with Jewish religious law. Rabbinical courts follow religious law,[11] which is why women may not serve as judges there. The rulings apply to all Jewish Israelis, whether they are Orthodox, Conservative, Reformist or secular. Pursuant to the court's interpretation of Jewish religious law, for example, a husband's consent is necessary to end a marriage. As has been the case for centuries, a Jewish divorce is not final in Israel until a divorce ritual is held: the husband delivers a handwritten divorce decree,

---

[9] A few examples of this are as follows: the Jurisdiction of Rabbinical Courts Law (Marriage and Divorce) 1953, which grants those courts unique judicial powers over all Jews' matrimonial issues; the amendment of Family Law (Alimony) 1959, according to which alimony decisions should follow the religious law; the Child Adoption Law 1960, whereby citizens may only adopt children of their own religious denomination; the Legal Capacity and Guardianship Law 1962, which restricts the conversion of minors exclusively to their parents' religion; the Law of Meat and Meat Products 1994, whereby only kosher meat stamped by the Chief Rabbinate Seal may be imported to Israel; and the (religiously self-evident) Ban on Growing Pigs Law 1962.

[10] Amnon Rubinstein and Barak Medina, *The Constitutional Law of the State of Israel* 6th edn (Jerusalem/Tel Aviv, Shoken, 2005) 320 (Hebrew).

[11] With the exception of property issues to which Israel's civil laws apply: 'The HCJ does not accept the approach by which civil courts must follow Jewish law when addressing asset-sharing issues. Rules pertaining to asset sharing that the HCJ had developed do not follow from the act of marriage and are not marital issues at all . . . When the general, civil law applies to issues that do not belong in the realm of marital status issues, religious courts must follow the general civil law as enacted by the legislator and as interpreted and developed by [civil] courts.' HCJ 1000/92 *Hava Bavli v The High Rabbinical Court*, ver 48(2), 221, 233 (1994) 246–47.

called a *get*, into the cupped hands of the woman, who must hold the paper aloft. A rabbi then tears a piece of the document. Only then the woman is free to re-marry.

The Rabbinical Courts' Jurisdiction Law (Marriage and Divorce) assigned to rabbinical courts three areas of jurisdiction: unique and exclusive jurisdiction on issues associated with marriage and divorce; parallel jurisdiction on 'matters pertaining to divorce suits', including alimony; and jurisdiction that depends on the litigating parties' consent and additional matters of marital status and inheritance.

One of the clearest reflections of the State of Israel as a Jewish state is the Law of Return, whereby all Jews may immigrate to Israel and become citizens of the state. Designed to guarantee a continuous Jewish majority in Israel, the law automatically naturalises Jews who immigrate to Israel and pronounce their desire to live there. The state acknowledges every Jew's right to Israeli citizenship without reservation or preceding formalities. The courts have acknowledged that every Jew has a 'fundamental right' to receive Israeli citizenship. This is coupled with a right to citizenship that the Law of Return accords to all Jews' spouses, children and grandchildren. This extension of the Law of Return not only pertains to personal issues – granting the option to immigrate to Israel to families in which just a few members are Jews – but has a national impact as well. It is assumed that even if those immigrating Jews are not religious, they could be expected to culturally associate with the Jewish sector and thus bolster the Jewish majority in Israel.[12] Referring to the alleged contradiction between granting the right of return to Jews only (which follows from the Jewish nature of the state) and the principle of equality of every citizen (which follows from its democratic nature), Justice Cheshin wrote:

> All of Israel's citizens, Jews and non-Jews, are 'shareholders' in this state . . . The statement that Israel is 'a state of all of its citizens' does not detract from the fact that it is the Jewish state or, if you will, the state of the Jewish Nation. We must know and remember – and how could we ever forget – that the Jewish Nation never had and does not have a state other than the State of Israel, the state of the Jews. Yet, within that state, all of the citizens have equal rights.[13]

---

[12] Rubinstein and Medina (n 10).
[13] LCA 2316/96 *Miron Isaacson v Party Registrar*, ver 50(2), 529 (1996), Justice Cheshin's opinion at [23].

The nature of the State of Israel as a Jewish state is further restricted by the acknowledgement of individual liberties. Jewish cultural heritage is closely associated with the Jewish religion, which maintains a complicated relationship with the state. The state does not impose religious edicts as a matter of principle. Religious laws are not part of the Israeli law that civilian courts must apply. The only exception is the status of rabbinical courts, which rule exclusively on issues of marital status.

In relation to other matters, such as Kosher food certification and burial, laws grant official powers to specific religious institutions. The fact that Israel is a Jewish state does not give the Israeli government the power to enforce religious laws: 'It is a basic principle in Israel that civilians and citizens enjoy freedom of religion and freedom from religion. Religious edicts and principles that draw on religion are not laws in Israel.'[14]

In the *Horev* case, for example, the HCJ was asked to rule on a request to close a main traffic artery that runs through a Jerusalem region inhabited mainly by ultra-Orthodox Jews during prayers on Sabbath and Jewish holidays. The minority judges felt that the street should not be closed to traffic because it was not a neighbourhood alley or even a minor street connecting other streets, but a 'main road that serves large communities and a very large number of vehicles, even on holidays. That street is public property and thus should serve the entire public. It cannot be seized, entirely or in part, from the public'.[15] The majority, however, ruled that because reasonable transportation alternatives existed and given that the sought traffic restriction was limited to the times of prayers, the decision to close it periodically was justified.

Another case, *Solodkin*, addressed the power of local governments to ban the sale of pork products within their boundaries. Here the court addressed the need to find a balance between religious sentiments offended by shops selling pork, potential harm to the freedom of conscience, and the freedom of occupation accorded by law to people who choose to deal in pork products. The HCJ ruled that an appropriate balance should be introduced: 'The local government needs to examine the nature of its territorial unit. It needs to examine the extent of social coherence and mutual tolerance within that unit. It needs to examine the

[14] HCJ 3872/93 *Mitral v The Prime Minister and the Religious Affairs Minister*, ver 47(5), 54 (1997), Justice Orr's opinion at 485 and 506.
[15] HCJ 5016/96 *Horev v Transportation Minister*, ver 51(4), 1 (1997), Justice Orr's opinion at 99.

various alternatives, particularly the proximal availability of shops where pork products can be purchased.[16] Both cases reflect cautious judicial intervention in decisions that required the consideration of the Jewish nature of the state.

Though defined as Jewish, the State of Israel is also a democracy, foremost in the formal sense that its parliament (the Knesset) is made up of representatives of all the state's citizens, regardless of their religion or ethnicity, and the state is representative of all its citizens, including non-Jews. The State of Israel is the national home of the Jewish people, but according to its own laws, it is also home to its Arab citizens. This arguably thin or 'formal' conception of democracy, dealing mainly with the rules and decision-making process, may minimise the tension between Jewish and democratic characteristic. The 'thinner' the definition of democracy, the lower the tension between the Jewish and democratic principles. Professor Gavison suggests that it is appropriate to speak of societies as being 'more democratic' or 'less democratic' than others. Democracy is an 'ideal type' of a political regime with rich variation over time and place.[17]

The basic elements of democracy have been mentioned by the Supreme Court:

> The democratic nature of the State of Israel has been embedded in it since establishment day. It clearly and openly emerges from the text of the Declaration of Independence, which expresses the fundamental concepts that have been with this state since that day. The democratic perception and its practical implementation are reflected in the government structure, in the practical and legal status of the state's citizens and residents and, among other things, in the principles of the rule of law and equality before the law.[18]

Gavison argues that the formal element of establishing the legitimacy of a regime on the consent of those ruled by it is extremely important and theoretically and practically significant. The requirement of consent as the source of political power indicates that democracy is committed, first and foremost, to humanism. This kind of state seriously considers the actual preferences and wishes of the public. It gives individuals the

---

[16] HCJ 953/01 *Solodkin v Bet Shemesh Municipality*, ver 58(5), 595 (2004), President Barak's opinion at [36]–[37].

[17] Gavison (n 1) ch 1.

[18] CA 1/88 *Neiman v Chairman of the Central Elections Committee*, ver 42(4), 177 (1988), President Shamgar's opinion at 188.

positive liberty and the legal power to participate in decisions that affect their lives and to choose their leaders. This principle and its moral significance are far from being self-evident or trivial. Therefore, Professor Gavison argues that a thin, formal interpretation of democracy should be adopted in order to allow for the compatibility of the Jewish and the democratic elements of the State of Israel.[19]

Arab citizens partake in Israel's political life and enjoy significant civil and political rights and representation, although attempts have been made by MKs to disqualify certain Arab political parties, as we shall see in the next chapter. Further, Arab citizens enjoy reasonable, if not always equal, levels of welfare and education. However, being a permanent minority in a Jewish state, they argue that the country does not truly accord its non-Jewish citizens with equal status and rights, meaning that Israel is not sufficiently democratic. In recent years, Israeli Arab leaders have advocated that Israel abolish the Jewish definition of the state and become 'the State of all its citizens', stressing its commitment to civic equality, a view that is unacceptable to the vast majority of Jewish citizens and provokes new tensions between Jews and non-Jews.[20]

Many Jews believe that the Arab citizens of Israel are a 'fifth column' and potential supporters of their enemy, which is why they are excluded from one of the main melting pots of the Israeli society: military service. Therefore, one of the main challenges of Israel and its political leaders in years to come is to strengthen the sense of equality and belonging of non-Jewish citizens in Israeli society. This may necessitate not only a new manner of allocating public funds – as we shall see later on – but also a new approach to the entire issue of that minority group.

The tension between the concepts of 'Jewish' and 'democratic' also relates to the 'intra-Jewish' debate between Jewish groups in Israeli society. The diversity among Jewish groups and the varying concepts of Judaism that they embrace is fascinating, extending from Orthodox and ultra-Orthodox Jews at one end of the scale to Jews who define themselves in a secular-ethnic way as Israelis at the other end. Tensions between different groups erupt every time an issue dealing with the

---

[19] Gavison (n 1),

[20] For example, new bills have being tabled recently advocating a new basic law regarding the Jewish nature of the State of Israel in response to Arab minority demands that the definition of the state be changed.

religious 'status quo'[21] arises on the public agenda. Writing on this tension, Professor Gavison argues that Orthodox Jews feel that the status quo arrangement is eroding: She states that there is less observance of *Shabbath* laws and practices, more avoidance by many of the rabbinical courts' monopoly over matters of marriage and divorce, and a general weakening of the consensus concerning the orthodox monopoly generally, in favor of religious pluralism and recognition of the non-orthodox versions of Judaism. Interestingly, secular Jews too feel that the status quo is shifting in the wrong direction. There is a greater presence of religion in public life and the political power of the religious and ultra-religious parties is growing.[22]

Cases like *Solodkin*, discussed earlier, demonstrate that the Supreme Court has been restrained, though not neutral, in relation to this matter. It seems that the Supreme Court is taking a position against religious coercion and in support of people's freedom from religion.

THE RULE OF LAW

The State of Israel is a constitutional democracy. Israel's constitutional democracy is built upon two pillars: The majority rule and basic principles such as the rule of law, separation of powers and the independence of the judiciary; chiefly: human rights.[23]

Israel's basic laws do not mention all of its fundamental principles. The two basic laws on human rights clearly intend to protect human dignity, liberty and freedom of occupation so as to anchor the state's values as a democratic state. Israel's democratic nature, however, can be discerned from many other sources such as the Declaration of Independence, state laws and rulings by the HCJ, which over the years have acknowledged fundamental values such as the rule of law, separation of powers, the judiciary's independence and a range of human rights. These fundamental rights do not appear in any particular book, but follow directly

---

[21] The term 'status quo' refers to political arrangements and understanding between the religious and the secular political parties as to different religious issues, mainly those concerned with everyday life both in religious neighbourhoods as well as in the public and secular environments.

[22] Gavison (n 1) foreword.

[23] The opening words in Aharon Barak's book, *Interpretation in Law: Constitutional Interpretation* (Jerusalem, Nevo, 1994) 37–38 (Hebrew).

from Israel's democratic nature and were in part accorded 'supra-constitutional' status.

The rule of law principle played a major role in Israel's constitutional development, and in the early years, it was understood together with the doctrine of parliamentary sovereignty, as in the UK. Formally defined by Dicey, it has several meanings. The first is that government and public bodies require lawful authority in order to act. This formal view of the rule of law was employed to restrict and limit government powers, particularly on human rights issues, before the basic laws of 1992. For example, the HCJ emphasised that one aspect of the rule of law is expressed in the principle of the administration's legality, according to which a public authority may act only within the framework of its lawfully assigned powers and authority. This principle had been expressed even in the earliest adjudication in Israel. Ruling in the 1949 *Bejerano* case, the HCJ established that in the absence of an explicit legal power to that effect, the Police Minister could not deny the freedom of occupation of those who filed others' car registration applications.[24] In the *Shayeb* case, the HCJ reversed an instruction issued by the then Defense Minister David Ben-Gurion according to which Dr Shayeb was not entitled to a teacher's permit because he had been a member of an underground movement and held – according to the Defense Minister – 'extreme and dangerous views'. 'The state is based on the rule of the law, not individual rules', Justice Cheshin wrote in his opinion, and 'even if a citizen holds misguided and wrong views, his life and blood are not forfeited'.[25]

A second approach to the rule of law requires equality before the law, meaning that all of the state's authorities – including the President and the security agencies – are subject to the law. The Supreme Court has often established that no authority is above the law. For example, Former President of Israel Moshe Katzav was tried, convicted and imprisoned as an ordinary citizen, as we shall see below. In cases dealing with the war on terror, President Barak stated that there is a difference between a democratic state that fights for its life and terrorists who attack that state. While terrorists fight against the law and violate it, the state fights in the name of, and for the protection of, the law: 'Here, we established

---

[24] HCJ 49/1 *Bejerano v The Police Minister*, ver 2(80), (1949).
[25] HCJ 144/50 *Shayeb v The Defense Minister*, ver 5, 399 (1950), Justice Cheshin's opinion at 406–07.

a law-abiding state that realises its national goal and the vision of past generations, while acknowledging and observing human rights in general and human dignity in particular.[26]

Another aspect of the rule of law principle refers to the moral dimension of the legal system. President Barak suggested a set of criteria in the absence of which the system is not lawful at all: 'The law should be . . . general, known, and published; clear and understandable; steady; never apply retroactively or conflict with another law; must not demand deeds that cannot be performed; and the government in charge needs to properly enforce the law.'[27] Many principles that follow from the essential meaning of the rule of law principle are not explicitly anchored in basic laws or even in ordinary legislation. This means that the courts will not invalidate a law on the basis that it conflicts with the rule of law. Nevertheless, certain decisions handed down in recent years reveal a trend that attempts to anchor requirements deriving from the rule of law principle in Basic Law: Human Dignity and Liberty. For example, the Supreme Court established that the penal principle – 'no act may be called felony, and no punishment for it may be imposed unless it had been defined as such in or according to an existing law' – is anchored in Basic Law: Human Dignity and Liberty by the power of the legal recognition of people's right to dignity and liberty.[28]

One of the most important requirements of the rule of law, which the Knesset occasionally violates, is the 'general application rule', which means that legal norms should express universal principles and should not address individuals in an attempt to impose these norms on them. The so-called 'personal' laws that address specific individuals conflict with the rule of law, although the Knesset has passed many such laws in recent years. These laws are popularly known by the name of the individuals to which they refer. For example, the 'Halutz Law' relates to a 'cooling period' for chiefs of staff before they may stand for elections; the 'Deri Law' instructs that convicted felons may not run in elections before the end of the seventh year after they have been released from

---

[26] HCJ 3451/02 *Almadani v The Defense Minister,* ver 56(3), 30 (2002).

[27] Aharon Barak, *Interpretation in Law – Vol 1: General Interpretation* (Jerusalem, Nevo, 1994) 292 (Hebrew).

[28] ACP 4603/97 *Meshulam v The State of Israel,* ver 51(3), 160 (1998); Aharon Barak, 'The Constitutionalization of the Judiciary in the Wake of the Basic Laws and its Implications on Criminal Trial (Essence and Litigation)' (1996) *Mehkarei Mishpat* 5, 13 (Hebrew).

prison; and the 'Amir Law', for different reasons, prevents pardoning or shortening the prison term of a 'lifer' who had been convicted for murdering a prime minister for political-ideological reasons. Although they have general application after they are passed, these laws specifically respond to a particular person's situation and have not, in fact, been applied beyond that situation.

SEPARATION OF POWERS

The separation of governing powers into three independent authorities – legislative, judicial and executive – is a clear characteristic of democracies and is a cornerstone of modern democratic regimes. It is meant to avoid the concentration of power in the hands of any single body.

The separation of powers has two major characteristics. The first of these is that the distribution of powers makes a distinction between exercising powers 'politically', which characterises the legislature, and impartial powers that generally characterise the judiciary and, to some extent, also the executive branch. The second characteristic is the concept of mutual supervision and the establishment of 'checks and balances' between them. Judicial review of other authorities is a clear example of this system of checks and balances, as is the Knesset's supervision of the government's work. The separation of powers does not mean that there are barriers resulting in a complete lack of contact between these authorities, but principally refers to the practical and theoretical pre-defined reciprocal supervision that reinforces independence from, and balance between, the powers.[29] Thus, ruling in the *Bank Hamizrahi* case, the HCJ judges stated that when the court judicially reviews a law, 'it does not impair the principle of separation of powers, but actually realises it'.[30]

In Israel, the relationship between the legislature and the judiciary is complex. The HCJ is the authorised interpreter of legislation and often partakes in the legislative process, as was clearly seen in *Bank Hamizrahi*. This interpretative liberty gives rise to tension between these two powers, but such tension exists in many democratic regimes.

---

[29] HCJ 73/85 *KAKH Faction v The Knesset Chairman*, ver 39(3), 141 (1985) 158.

[30] CA 6821/93 *United Bank Hamizrahi v Migdal Cooperative Village*, ver 49(4), 221 (1995), President Barak's opinion at 421.

Even when the Knesset exercises its authority to deal with 'judicial' (or semi-judicial) decisions – as it does, for example, when it rules on the status of MKs – the HCJ still has the authority to review Knesset acts. As we shall see in the discussion on judicial activism below, the Israeli judiciary has the power to judicially review parliamentary proceedings, which is quite unusual, particularly in common law countries. In turn, the Knesset may respond to court rulings by amending legislation. For example, when the HCJ judges remarked that they do not have the power to ban anti-democratic parties from standing for election, the Knesset amended the law and added a section that permitted such a ban. The Court has frequently asserted that 'the judiciary is not harmed when the legislator amends a law after the court had spoken, leaving the former displeased with the latter's interpretation'.[31]

The separation of powers exists to restrain the executive branch, as principally expressed in the 'principle of administration's legality', according to which the Executive is authorised to act according to powers assigned to it by law. This fundamental principle of democratic regimes mainly refers to the application of powers that might impair basic human rights. Presently, this principle is explicitly anchored in limitation clauses of the basic laws on human rights, meaning that human rights must not be harmed except by virtue of a law or by regulation enacted by virtue of a law.

One of the most important constitutional aspects of the administration's legality principle, as developed by Israeli adjudication, is the Knesset's assigned duty to set the principal arrangements by which the administrative authority may act. For example, according to HCJ rulings, the Knesset may not settle for generally establishing a certain government authority, but must outline the main arrangements that it must follow in legislation. This issue has been dubbed by the HCJ the 'primary arrangements'.[32]

This rule was not meant to negate the Executive's power to establish regulations – that is, to set general standards for exercising its assigned authorities – because secondary legislation is a practical necessity. Reference here is predominantly made to the scope of considerations that the Knesset delegates to the executive power. The 'primary arrange-

---

[31] Alfred Vitkon, *Law and Judgment* (Jerusalem/Tel Aviv, Shoken, 1988) 136 (Hebrew).

[32] HCJ 11163/03 *The Supreme Monitoring Committee [of the Arab Citizens] v Israel's Prime Minister* (published by Nevo on 27 February 2006).

ments' rule is based on the general aspiration that essential decisions concerning state policies and society's needs are made by the nation's elected representatives. The legislative authority is the body elected to make laws, which therefore enjoys social legitimacy when it does. Decisions that are essential to the citizens' lives should be made by the body that the people elected for that very purpose. Thus, society's views must be formalised by the legislative body. The Knesset, which represents that public's views, is the body empowered to determine the primary arrangements that government bodies must follow,[33] which is why the Supreme Court may invalidate secondary legislation merely by stating that it is up to the Knesset to deal with the issue through primary legislation.

One of the most interesting examples of how the rule of the 'primary arrangements' turned into a duty assigned to the legislative branch can be found in the *yeshiva students' recruitment* affair.[34] Mandatory military service is required by law in Israel. The 1986 Defense Service Law (Combined Version) imposes a duty on every Israeli citizen to serve in the military. Males serve at least three years while women usually serve some 20 months.[35] Yet, as an administrative practice dating back to the first days of the State of Israel, the Minister of Defense enjoys discretionary powers to exempt individuals from that duty, which particularly applies to male ultra-Orthodox Jews who have reached the age of service but are full-time students at higher religious institutions, known as *yeshiva*. David Ben-Gurion, the first Prime Minister of Israel, reached a compromise with the ultra-Orthodox Jewish parties, exempting *yeshiva* students from service.[36] As a result, the ultra-religious sector is, as a practical matter, exempt from any military duty. This exemption has been the source of continuous conflict between secular and Orthodox Jews for more than 60 years.

---

[33] HCJ 3267/97 *Rubinstein v The Defense Minister*, ver 52(5), 481 (2000), President Barak's opinion at 508.

[34] For a discussion of the various aspects of this affair, see Suzie Navot, 'Exemption from Military Service Granted to Orthodox Students in Israel – A Case Study on Justiciability, Equality, and Judicial Review' (2000) 6 *European Public Law* 12.

[35] A married woman at the age of recruitment may choose to volunteer for the military, although she is not obliged to serve.

[36] However, the word 'exemption' is not used and formally the enlistment of *yeshiva* students is 'postponed' as long as they keep studying in a *yeshiva*.

This arrangement is important not only because it breaches the basic principle of equality, but also, and mostly, due to the security situation in Israel. The main reason why this exemption policy prevailed for so long is Israel's political structure in which pro-exemption religious parties play a crucial role in every government, being able to tip the coalition scales at will. In many, if not in all, cases, the survival of the governing coalition depends on the support of the religious parties, which felt that the exemption policy was a legitimate political demand during coalition negotiations.

Over the years, many citizens have petitioned the Supreme Court against this policy and, in most cases, have asked it to reconsider and review the discretion granted to the Minister of Defense. In the early years, the majority of these cases were held to be lacking in 'standing' or were considered to be unjusticiable because of the 'political questions' with which they were associated. Then, as a result of radical changes in the HCJ, particularly in relation to judicial review and judicial activism, this traditional approach of judicial restraint in political questions was almost entirely abandoned.

When the HCJ was asked to address this issue in the 1988 *Ressler* case, after the above restrictions were lifted, it established that the Defense Minister has the right to exempt *yeshiva* students from service by the power of his general legal prerogative to exempt individuals from service 'for other reasons', as the law states. It held that 'once the legislator established that "other reasons" may justify the deferral of the security service duty, it at the same time allowed the Defense Minister to establish what those "other reasons" are' and that these may include 'religious reasons.'[37]

Later, when dealing with a new petition on this matter, in the *Rubinstein* case, the HCJ's statement was modified. President Barak stated that 'quantity makes quality' and that the quantity of exemptions dictates a need to change the quality of the Court's attitude. The Court referred to the distinction between 'primary' and 'secondary' arrangements, stating: 'The Israeli Parliament, the Knesset, must formulate a policy concerning those exemptions. It is the Knesset's duty and responsibility, and thus the delegation of powers to the Defense Minister in this case is unconstitutional. The minister is not authorised to establish principles

---

[37] HCJ 910/86 *Ressler v The Defense Minister*, ver 42(2), 441 (1988), Justice Barak's opinion at 502.

and rules for exemption from military duty because these rules should be specified by "primary regulations" that define the general policy and its guidelines, which should be introduced as a state law."[38]

The Court therefore instructed the Knesset to pass a law governing this matter, which it did. And so, after decades of avoiding the issue for political reasons, it ordered the Knesset to address it, and so the exemption of *yeshiva* students was prescribed by law. The constitutionality of this law will be discussed in chapter eight on human rights. In a dramatic 2012 ruling, the HCJ declared this law unconstitutional as it disproportionally impairs the equality principle.[39]

INDEPENDENT JUDICIARY

A discussion of the separation of powers would not be complete without considering the arrangements that ensure the independence of the judiciary. In Israel, the judiciary is an independent body that is not part of the political system:

> Judges are not elected by and do not answer to the people the way that members of the legislature are and do. To be appointed, judges are not required to present a social platform that they intend to realise in the courtroom, and their term in office is not terminated when they fail to meet the people's expectations . . . Exercising judicial discretion, judges should not be viewed as 'representing' or 'accountable to' the people. Judges must stay 'above politics' and be constantly aware of that position.[40]

The independence of the judiciary is expressed in the statement that: 'A person vested with judicial powers shall not, in judicial matters, be subject to any authority but that of the Law.'[41] The judges' independence is primarily guaranteed by the way they are appointed and promoted, the process by which candidate judges are selected and the fact that their rulings are both immune from any criminal or civil liability and autonomous from any external pressures.

---

[38] *Rubinstein v The Defense Minister* (n 33).

[39] HCJ 6298/07 *Ressler v The Knesset* (rendered on 21 February 2012).

[40] Aharon Barak, *Interpretation in Law – Vol II* (Jerusalem/Tel Aviv, Nevo, 2003) 676–77 (Hebrew). See also Shimon Sheetrit, 'Developments in Constitutional Law: Selected Topics' (1990) 24 *Israel Law Review* 368.

[41] Section 2 of Basic Law: The Judiciary.

Nonetheless, the judiciary is not administratively independent. The Israeli courts are a unit of the Ministry of Justice in practice. According to the *Courts Law*, the Justice Minister determines the courts' administrative arrangements and, with the HCJ President's consent, even appoints the courts' director. Arguably, this dependence on the Ministry of Justice has not crucially impacted on the independence of the judiciary, but Supreme Court presidents have nonetheless argued that the ties with the Justice Minister should be severed.

Judges are selected by a Judges' Appointment Committee, appointed by the President of the State, and serve until they reach the age of 70. The Appointment Committee represents the concept of 'the combination of powers' – a notion of 'checks and balances' – rather than the separation of powers. The Committee comprises nine members, five of whom are not in the political system (namely, three HCJ judges, including the President and the Vice President, and two representatives of the Israeli Bar Association) and four politicians (two MKs selected by the Knesset, and two Cabinet members, including the Minister of Justice, who serves as the Committee Chairman). Thus, the Committee represents all three branches of government. A candidate for presidential appointment as judge must be selected by the majority of the Committee members (that is, at least five) and a Supreme Court candidate must secure the votes of at least seven Committee members.

Over the years, reservations concerning the composition of this Committee have been voiced, but a special national committee that was appointed to examine the issue resolved to retain the current composition. Several attempts that were recently made to change this composition have also failed. Critics have mainly argued that Israel's judges, particularly the members of the HCJ bench, are not 'representative' enough as far as the various population sectors are concerned. Some even suggested that a special constitutional court should be established to address 'constitutional issues', representing the various sectors of the Israeli society. This suggestion was rejected as dangerous. Some believe that it might politicise the judiciary because, if endorsed, judges would not be appointed on the merits of their skills, but as clear representatives of popular movements.[42] The main problem with this suggestion is the fact that Israel does not have a complete constitution and it is rather

---

[42] Rubinstein and Medina (n 10); Aharon Barak, 'The Supreme Court as a Constitutional Court' (2003) 6 *Mishpat uMimshal* 315 (Hebrew); Yoav Dotan 'Does Israel Need a Constitutional Court?' (2000) 5 *Mishpat uMimshal* 117 (Hebrew).

difficult to envisage a constitutional court before a fully fledged constitution is introduced or the existing one is completed.

In fact, the Israeli judges' election system has been said to be 'better' than the systems of other Western countries.[43] Past experience has shown that, thanks to its unique composition, the Committee makes decisions that are generally free of political considerations and appoints judges who are both of high professional standing and free from political bias. It is the candidates' professional competence and not their political agenda that is evaluated. Presently, Israel's judges are not appointed as sector representatives, although while evaluating a candidate's personal data, the Committee considers the 'reflection principle', which means that it intends for the bulk of Israeli judges to reflect (or represent) Israeli society as much as possible. In recent years, political pressures have been exerted in the Committee, primarily by the political members, especially during discussions of appointments for the Supreme Court. Former Minister of Justice Daniel Friedman, a renowned law professor, launched a fierce campaign against the nominations of the judges to the Supreme Court, arguing that they all come from the same 'clique' and the same background.[44] During his term as Minister of Justice, the Committee appointed two private lawyers as Supreme Court judges – a first in Israel's judicial history. The tensions, discussions and pressures involved in nominations to the Supreme Court in Israel derive mainly from the role that the Court plays in Israel's public life. As we shall see in the following chapters, claims that judicial activism undermines the government's authority and ability to implement policies were among the main reasons why politicians demanded that their influence on the appointment of judges should increase.

The idea that has been central in this chapter is that of balance. The first aspect of this balance relates to the balance between the notions that define the state of Israel: 'Jewish' and 'democratic'. It was the Knesset that combined these two principles in the basic laws of 1992 as part of a political compromise. It was up to the Supreme Court to interpret these

---

[43] The report by the Committee for the Judges' Selection Arrangements (2001) 24–25 reads: 'Based on a comparative study, opinions that the committee heard, relevant considerations, and accumulated experience, the committee feels that the Israeli method for electing judges . . . is better than all the methods as applied in other countries.'

[44] See Daniel Friedman, *The Purse and the Sword: The Trials of the Israeli Legal Revolution* (Tel Aviv, Yedioth Ahronoth, 2013) (Hebrew), which deals with the rise of judicial activism in Israel.

principles in such a way as would diminish the tension embodied in them. Careful balance made both principles compatible with each other and allowed the Supreme Court to declare that Israel can be both Jewish and democratic at the same time.

Second, balance was also the key concept arising from the rule of law and separation of powers. In Israel's constitutional framework, the division of power is based on a system of checks and balances rather than a strict separation of powers. This notion of balance between the different branches of governments could also be observed within the discussion regarding the independence of the judiciary. The Israeli Appointment Committee for the election of judges created a satisfactory checks and balances model, despite some fierce discussions held every now and then over appointments to the Supreme Court. Still, the question remains as to whether this method, which has been in force since the establishment of the State of Israel, will be retained in the future, due to the growing demand from politicians to increase their influence on the appointment of judges.

Although the Supreme Court has been trying to diminish the tensions between the principles of 'Jewish and democratic', some Jewish groups argue that the interpretation by the Supreme Court is insufficiently 'Jewish'. A recent bill was tabled for a new basic law entitled 'the Jewish State Law', proposing the predominance of the country's Jewish identity over its democratic identity, particularly with regard to future judicial rulings. As we shall see in the following chapters, it seems that the strong divisions in Israeli society pose a great challenge to the constitutional process and the completion of the constitution.

FURTHER READING

Agmon-Gonnen, Michal, 'Judicial Independence: The Threat from Within' (2005) 38 *Israel Law Review* 120.

Ben Porat, Guy, *Between State and Synagogue: The Secularizations of Contemporary Israel* (Cambridge, Cambridge University Press, 2013).

Barak-Erez, Daphne, *Outlawed Pigs: Law, Religion, and Culture in Israel* (Madison, University of Wisconsin Press, 2007).

Barak-Erez, Daphne, 'Citizenship and Immigration Law in the Vise of Security, Nationality, and Human Rights' (2008) 6 *International Journal of Constitutional Law* 184.

Dowty, Alan, *Israel/Palestine*, 3rd edn (Cambridge, Polity Press, 2012).

Gavison, Ruth, 'Jewish and Democratic? A Rejoinder to the Ethnic Democracy Debate' (1999) 4(1) *Israel Studies* 44.

Gavison, Ruth, *Can Israel Be Both Jewish and Democratic? Or: Israel between Jewishness and Democracy* (Jerusalem, The Van Leer Institute and Hakibbutz Hamehuhad, 2011).

Kasher, Asa, 'Justice and Affirmative Action: Naturalization and the Law of Return' (1985) 15 *Israel Yearbook of Human Rights* 101.

Klein, Claude, 'Right of Return in Israeli Law' (1997) 13 *Tel Aviv University Studies in Law* 53.

Maoz, Asher, *Israel as a Jewish and Democratic State* (Liverpool, Deborah Charles Publications, 2011).

Rubinstein, Amnon, 'Can Israel Be Both Democratic and Jewish?' (24 May 2009). Available at: http://ssrn.com/abstract=1409291.

Smooha, Sammy, 'The Model of Ethnic Democracy: Israel as a Jewish and Democratic State' (2002) 8(4) *Nations & Nationalism* 475.

Shapira, Anita, Stern, Yedidia and Yakobson, Alexander, *Nationalism and Binationalism: The Perils of Perfect Structures – Contemporary Challenges to the Nation State: Global and Israeli Perspectives* (Volume 1) (Brighton, Sussex Academic Press, 2013).

Shetreet, Shimon, 'Judicial Independence and Accountability in Israel' (1984) 33 *International and Comparative Law Quarterly* 979.

Yakobson, Alexander, 'Jewish Peoplehood and the Jewish State, How Unique? A Comparative Survey' (2008) 13(2) *Israel Studies* 1.

Yakobson, Alexander and Rubinstein, Amnon, *Israel and the Family of Nations* (New York, Routledge, 2009).

4

Parliament: The Knesset

Introduction

Part I: Elections and the Role of Political Parties – The Electoral System – The Party System –Disqualification of Political Parties

Part II: Composition and Privileges – Composition – The Political Mandate of MKs – Parliamentary Immunity

Part III: The Legislative Process – Bills – Judicial Review of Parliamentary Proceedings

Part IV: The Knesset as Watchdog – Questions and Committee Debates – Parliamentary Commissions – The Annual Budget – Conclusion

INTRODUCTION

THE KNESSET IS the State of Israel's house of representatives.[1] It is a single-chamber parliament that is both a legislative body and a constituent authority that may enact and amend basic laws. Israel's parliamentary system was influenced by UK tradition and the government is based on the Knesset's confidence in it. In addition, the Knesset supervises the executive and the state budget. In practice, the Israeli Parliament is quite weak. The government rules the legislative process, minimising the possibility of passing laws that it does not support. The tools at the disposal of the Knesset for scrutinising the government are not terribly effective. A real opposition to the government within Parliament rarely exists due to the many parties that comprise the

---

[1] Section 1 of the Transitional Law (1949) stated that: 'The house of legislators in the State of Israel shall be named The Knesset.' Section 1 of Basic Law: The Knesset reads: 'The Knesset is the state's house of representatives.'

opposition, which ideologically have almost nothing in common between them. Many of these flaws in the Knesset's functioning are a result of the unique electoral system.

This chapter will consider the Knesset and its role in Israel's constitutional framework. Here, we examine the Knesset proceedings, working methods and MKs' (Knesset members) immunity, but first we focus on Israel's election method.

The entire State of Israel is a single constituency that sends 120 representatives to the Knesset. Israel permits only officially registered parties to run in elections. Voters cast a single ballot with which they elect parties, not MKs, and the parties select their Knesset candidates. This is known as a 'list system'. This simple rule has a substantial impact on Israel's political public life, as MKs do not represent geographical areas. The concept of a constituency is problematic, as are the principles of responsibility and representation, as we shall see. While Israeli parties are elected democratically, their inner election processes do not have to be democratic – a fact that is critical for understanding Israel's political life. Furthermore, like constitutional arrangements in Germany and Spain, for example, Israel allows for the disqualification of undemocratic, pro-racist or terror-supporting parties, as well as parties whose platforms deny the State of Israel's right to exist. The presence of the Supreme Court is also visible in this chapter. Unlike many common law countries, where proceedings in Parliament are not questioned in the courts, Israel has a long tradition of judicial control of parliamentary proceedings. The Supreme Court has played an important role in protecting the rights of the political minorities within the Knesset, and many MKs turn to the Supreme Court not only when their rights have been infringed but also as part of their political agenda, seeking a judicial remedy when they disagree with the outcome of a political process.

PART I: ELECTIONS AND THE ROLE OF POLITICAL PARTIES

THE ELECTORAL SYSTEM

The Israeli parliamentary system was inspired by the UK system. Although it originated from the British Mandate, the Westminster system was not adopted in full. While Britain is divided into constituencies so that regional representatives are elected personally, Israel is a single electoral zone and Israelis vote for parties rather than individuals. Since the early days, there has been extensive debate about the need to change Israel's electoral system, mainly by introducing regional elections, at least for half of the Knesset. This debate peaked in the 1980s when a national unity government was formed after the two large political blocs (traditionally characterised as right (*Likud*) and left (Labour)) were practically tied in their representation in the legislature. Labour was the largest party elected and *Likud* came in second, but neither could form a stable coalition on its own. This situation stemmed from the fact that, while Israel's citizens elect the house of representatives, it is the MKs who nominate the Prime Minister, since, after consulting the party leaders, the President of the State of Israel assigns the formation of the government to the most suitable candidate, who, generally, is the leader of the largest Knesset faction. This is a common parliamentary practice, although the President of the State of Israel may assign the formation of government to the candidate who has the best chance of forming a government, even if he or she is not the leader of the largest faction in the Knesset.[2] This method makes forming a coalition-based government imperative because no Israeli party has ever won 61 Knesset seats alone or has been able to prevent the formation of a coalition without it. Institutionally, such a process encourages the abuse of political power for personal gain or other benefits. Clearly, it promotes what is known as 'crossing the floor', that is, MKs quitting their original parties after other political groups offer them positions or benefits. The Knesset's history is rife with cases of MKs resigning from the faction on whose ticket they were elected, as we shall see below.

Israel is a fine example of a state whose citizens have strongly divided views over a host of issues, but which has nevertheless remained a democracy with a reasonable degree of stability in governance. However, governments seldom complete their four-year terms and elections are generally held every three years or so. This has been the case over the past two decades and it impacts on the quality and execution of the processes of democratic government. The public and political reactions to unstable coalition governments, and the fact that relatively small minority

---

[2] A remarkable case in point was the elections of 2009: although *Kadima* emerged as the largest party, the *Likud* eventually formed the cabinet and headed the coalition, leaving *Kadima* in the opposition.

and sectarian factions gain tremendous influence because they can tip the scales of power, have led to many Israelis seeking electoral reform.

Israel's governance difficulties are deeply rooted in the election method outlined in section 4 of Basic Law: The Knesset: 'The Knesset shall be elected by general, national, direct, equal, secret, and proportional elections, in accordance with the Knesset Elections Law; this section shall not be altered save by a majority of the members of the Knesset.' This section presents six terms that, read together, reflect the State of Israel's election method. The elections are: (1) general – all eligible voters may exercise their right to vote; (2) national – the entire state is a single constituency; (3) direct – voters elect their representatives directly, without the mediators that are employed, for example, by American electors; (4) equal – a dual stipulation: everyone has an equal right to vote once and the right to be elected; (5) secret – when casting their ballots, voters are alone behind a curtain in practice, placing their chosen slip in a sealed envelope that does identify them; and (6) proportional – Knesset seats are distributed relative to the nationwide votes that each party received, provided it won enough votes to cross the election threshold of two per cent.[3]

Section 4 of Basic Law: The Knesset also states that the election method cannot be changed save by a majority (61) of MKs. This means that Knesset elections are national and proportional, which is an extreme case of proportional representation based on a single multi-member district and a low minimal election threshold.[4]

The problematic Israeli election method and the public's displeasure with it was well described by MK Uriel Lynn, who served as Chairman of the Knesset Law, Constitution and Justice Committee when the 1992 amendment of Basic Law: The Government was introduced, instituting the 'direct election' of an Israeli Prime Minister:

---

[3] Proportional representation is an election method whereby the elected body is composed according to the ratio of votes received by the various groups running in those elections. This method assigns seats in the elected body proportionally to the votes that each group received. Most democracies employ mixed proportional methods, so that part of the parliament is elected by relative and national elections, while another part is elected in regional (proportional or plurality) elections, representing the various groups in each region. Israel, Slovakia and the Netherlands are the only three veteran democracies that employ a 'pure' proportional national election method.

[4] Gideon Doron, *Presidential Regime for Israel* (Jerusalem, Carmel, 2006) 46 (Hebrew); Gideon Rahat, The Election Method 1948–1959: From Default to Entrenchment' (2001) 11 *Discussions of Israel's Revival* 369, 372 (Hebrew).

Ever since Israel was founded, people have been bitter about and disappointed with the government election method. Its faults are well known: At the end of the Election Day, no one knows who was elected Prime Minister. It takes longer to establish a cabinet. Mandatory coalition negotiations force the majority to make far-reaching concessions for minority groups. The government is not stable even after it is formed and cabinet members waste too much time struggling to keep the cabinet stable instead of performing their duties. Dependence on minority parties impacts on cabinet resolutions. There are too many flaws and they undermine the public's trust in our democracy. This bill took 39 months to prepare, but it perfectly matches Israel's needs, resolving the main problems of Israel's government: lack of stability, inefficiency, and lack of resolution power.[5]

The arrangement tested by Israel at the time, which will be discussed in chapter five, was to have a directly elected Prime Minister rather than one placed in office by the power of the Knesset's confidence. The main goal for the initiators of this law was to prevent the prevailing situation in which the Prime Minister is at the mercy of small factions or even a few MKs who might prevent a coalition from forming or destabilise it once it is formed.[6] Yet, as we shall see below, this experimental election method failed to achieve its goals and soon the parliamentary method was reinstated with slight modifications.

In terms of the election process, the valid votes of all eligible voters who exercised their right to vote are counted. Next, the lists of candidates (or parties) among which these votes are to be distributed are determined based on the election threshold principle, so that only parties that win at least two per cent of the total valid votes are eligible to partake in the distribution of Knesset seats. The threshold was established in an attempt to minimise the number of parties represented in the Knesset and to make sure that each faction comprises at least three MKs. Once the eligible lists are determined, only the votes they received are counted. Votes for parties and lists that failed to cross the threshold are dismissed. The final stage deals with the distribution of surplus votes, that is, votes that failed to attain the quota needed to elect a single MK.

[5] Uriel Lynn, 'An Infrastructure for a Written Constitution in Israel' (1993) *Hamishpat* A 81 at 86 (Hebrew).

[6] Avraham Diskin and Hana Diskin, *The Direct Election of the Prime Minister: An Initial Inspection of Basic Act: The Government* (Jerusalem, Jerusalem Institute for Israel Studies, 1991) (Hebrew).

The Knesset's term is four years, a period that may be extended only under justifiable irregular circumstances and only after 80 MKs have endorsed a law to that effect. The Knesset may also shorten its term. The House may choose to dissolve before completing its full term by passing a law for that purpose by a majority of members. Elections must also be held if a budget law is not introduced three months into a fiscal year or if, after a new Knesset is elected, no MK is able to form a Cabinet that would win the Knesset's confidence. Additionally, a Prime Minister may dissolve the Knesset (with the approval of the President of the State of Israel) if a majority of the Knesset opposes the government and prevents it from performing effectively.

The election system seems to be constantly on the public agenda and is part of many party platforms. Either before elections or after them, NGOs[7] which deal with governmental reforms regularly present proposals and raise debates – in the Knesset and in the media – aimed at promoting electoral and governmental changes. For example, in 2013, after the elections, a bill was tabled aimed at raising the election threshold to four per cent, a proposal that was supported by these NGOs.

THE PARTY SYSTEM

Political parties play a key role in Israel's public and political life. The parties serve as means for realising the freedom of association and mediate between the government and the population segments they represent. In addition, the representative democracy structure helps various political and interest groups reach compromises that cannot be attained in a direct democracy. Parties are central in Israel in the sense that only they may present lists of candidates for Knesset elections. They are at the centre of all political power groups and thus, to a great extent, they determine the candidates and the ideological shape of the government, since political agreements between parties often include governance commitments, and the parties that form the coalition dictate government policies.[8]

---

[7] For example, the Israeli Democracy Institute, the Citizens' Empowerment Center in Israel and 'Israel's Hope'.

[8] Amnon Rubinstein and Barak Medina, *The Constitutional Law of the State of Israel*, 6th edn (Jerusalem/Tel Aviv, Shoken, 2005) 758 (Hebrew).

Still, despite their central role in Israel's public life, the legal status of political parties is disputed. A party is ordinarily described as 'complex legal body' that is both 'a personal-law association and a public-law constitutional unit'.[9] While Israel has laws that regulate their activities (the Parties Law of 1992 and the Party Financing Law of 1973), parties are, in practice, free to manage their internal affairs as they see fit.

According to the Parties Law, a party is 'a group of people who joined together to legally promote political or social goals and to have elected individuals represent them at the Knesset'. A party is officially founded once it is registered in the Parties Log (managed by the Party Registrar). Parties are further legally required to include institutions such as a central body that is in charge of managing its affairs, and an auditing body.

Before the Parties Law was endorsed, attempts were made to have it include requirements for democratic structures within parties. These attempts failed and eventually the Parties Law was the result of a political compromise that made its endorsement possible. As Avnon described it: 'The normative message is vague: parties should be conducted in an orderly fashion, but not necessarily democratically.'[10]

Thus, both the Parties Law and the courts acknowledge the parties' freedom to manage their own affairs as they see fit. The courts clearly refrain from intervening in resolutions of party institutions that have followed their own procedural rules. Since the law did not stipulate internal democracy, courts abstain from forcing parties to actually conduct their affairs democratically. For example, the Knesset representatives of several religious and ultra-Orthodox parties are chosen by spiritual leaders, and women may not hold Knesset seats for those parties.

At the same time, bigger parties such as the *Likud* and Labour hold primary elections in which the party's candidates for Prime Minister and the Knesset are elected democratically by registered party members. The introduction of these 'primaries' heralded significant and practical political changes. The fact that MKs who represent these parties, including some who represent specific sectors, are elected in primaries made many of them conduct themselves as if they were elected in personal, national or regional elections.[11] The Parties Law prescribed the conduct of those

[9] HCJ 1635/90 *Zarzhevsky v The Prime Minister*, ver 45(1), 749 (1990), 836.
[10] Dan Avnon, 'The Parties Law' (1992) 1(1) *Mishpat uMimshal* A 181–82 (Hebrew).
[11] See R Hazan, 'Those Who Laid You Waste Depart From You: The Impact of Primaries on Parties' in D Koren (ed), *The End of Parties: Israel Democracy Distressed* (Hakibbutz Hamehuhad, 1998) 78 (Hebrew).

primary elections, which were mainly designed to guarantee due process in terms of parties' organisation, financing, candidates' campaigns and so on. Primary elections, which have now been held for more than 20 years, have become a regular part of the mainstream Israeli political process. Still, such primary elections are expensive, which makes them particularly vulnerable to corruption. The law limits the total amount that may be contributed to an individual's campaign in the primaries and the State Comptroller investigates the financial aspects of the primaries and fines MKs who do not observe the regulations. Many criminal proceedings have arisen from these primaries. The growing criticism from politicians, academia and the media, as well as calls for a re-evaluation of the process, seem to have been effective, with new parties now being reluctant to adopt primary elections.

According to the Party Financing Law (1973), parties represented in the Knesset are entitled to have their ongoing as well as their campaigning activities financed by the state. The state's duty to pay the parties through the Finance Ministry is absolute in the sense that it is not subject to budgetary constraints. The law further outlines certain restrictions on donations that parties may collect. One key reference to the constitutional status of parties in Israel is section 7A of Basic Law: The Knesset, which, establishes that lists of candidates that deny the democratic nature of the State of Israel may not partake in the elections. We shall focus on this issue below.

DISQUALIFICATION OF POLITICAL PARTIES

The fundamental right of each citizen to partake in the elections process is a basic tenet of a democratic regime. Basic Law: The Knesset imposes several restrictions on the right to vote. Every Israeli national of or over the age of 18 may vote unless a court has deprived him or her of that right by law. In practice, however, there is no law by which the right to vote may be denied. This right can only be denied if citizenship itself is nullified, and the Interior Minister may deprive Israeli citizens of their citizenship when their acts constitute a breach of loyalty to the state. Therefore, prisoners may vote in Israel.

In addition to the age and citizenship requirements, the law outlines a few more conditions for realising the right to vote – mostly administrative conditions such as being registered in voter logs or the population census. Thus, for example, Israelis may not exercise their right to vote while abroad. The Knesset has often discussed bills attempting to allow votes to take place in Israeli embassies and consulates abroad, but none has been endorsed. As a result, only civil servants and persons who work abroad for a specific list of organisations, such as the Jewish Agency for Israel, may participate in elections abroad.

Unlike several other countries, Israel does not impose sanctions against individuals who do not exercise their franchise. A blank slip is a disqualified vote and is not counted at all.

Some restrictions exist concerning the right to be elected. For example, the Elections Law prescribes 'cooling-off periods' for various position holders that are mainly intended to prevent them from using their public positions to promote political goals and to prevent the politicisation of the civil service. Thus, it was established that civil servants and senior army officers must wait 100 days before announcing their candidacy, and that army officers holding ranks of Major General and higher, as well as holders of parallel ranks with other security services, require a six-month cooling-off period. This clause has been amended, however, so that the Chief of Staff and the heads of the *Shin Bet* (the General Security Service) and the *Mosad* must wait three years. Section 6 of Basic Law: The Knesset states that 'a person who had been handed down a final prison term of more than 3 months may be elected (or rather, enter his candidacy) only after the end of a 7-year period that starts on the day of his release from prison – except if the chairman of the CEC decides that the felony that person had been convicted of does not constitute moral turpitude'.

The most significant restriction of the right to stand for election is found in section 7A of Basic Law: The Knesset, which states: 'A list of candidates shall not participate in elections to the Knesset if its objectives or actions, expressly or by implication, include one of the following: (1) Negation of the State of Israel's existence as a Jewish and democratic state; (2) Incitement to racism; (3) Support for an armed struggle by an enemy state or terror group against the State of Israel.' This section expresses a view held by other democracies as well, justifying restrictions imposed on the right to be elected with the concept of 'self-defending' or 'militant democracy'.[12]

---

[12] 'Militant democracy' is a paradigmatic concept in the study of democratic responses to political extremism. Its origins are usually traced back to Karl Loewenstein's

Israel has a fascinating history of disqualifying political parties, which clearly and uniquely demonstrates the prevailing tension between the Jewish and the democratic aspects of the state. Upon establishment, Israel imposed no ideology-based restrictions on civilians or candidate lists.[13] Despite its establishment soon after the Second World War, no law was introduced in Israel that restricted the right to vote or to stand for elections (apart from some technical restrictions) so that any Jew who immigrated and was registered as a citizen, and all the Arabs who were listed in the 1948 population census, had a right to vote.[14] Since 1948, all Israeli citizens, both Jewish and non-Jewish, have enjoyed these political rights.

A historical review of Israeli constitutional law's stand on party disqualifications reveals three distinct periods. First, between the state's establishment and the 1980s, there was a period during which there was no law that allowed for the disqualification of a party on the basis of its political platform. The second period was between 1985 and 1992, when for the first time Israel introduced a law by which parties could be disqualified for their platform or political views. The third period started in 1992 when the Parties Law was endorsed and peaked in 2002 when election laws were amended to allow party disqualifications for new reasons, mainly aimed at banning parties that supported or encouraged terror. This last amendment of 2002, which has been argued to be an *ad casum* initiative, is one of a series of amendments endorsed around the same period with similar goals and of a similar nature, namely, to include the case of 'support for the armed struggle of a terror organization' against the state as a general restriction on the right to vote or stand for elections. These three periods were triggered by events in the political arena, causing the Knesset to react by introducing new grounds for party disqualification, which will be discussed below.

appeal for strong responses to the rise of fascism in 1930s Europe. See Gregory Fox and Georg Nolte, 'Intolerant Democracies' in Gregory Fox and Brad Roth (eds), *Democratic Governance and International Law* (Cambridge, Cambridge University Press, 2000) 389; Markus Thiel, *The Militant Democracy Principle in Modern Democracies* (Aldershot, Ashgate, 2009).

[13]   In its Declaration of Independence, Israel stated that it will grant all of its citizens full civilian rights.

[14]   In practice, however, no independent Arab movement managed to send representatives to the Knesset before the late 1980s. Political associations in the Arab sector were mostly sponsored by 'Jewish' parties such as the Communist Party. Zionist and leftist parties accepted Arabs as members and over time allocated them realistic slots on their candidate lists.

The first period, in which all political parties were allowed to participate in the elections, reached a turning point in 1965. A party called *The Socialists' List* filed for Knesset candidacy with the Central Elections Committee (CEC). The list included several members of the *Al-Ard* (Arabic: The Land) movement, which had been defined by the Defense Minister as subversive and acting against the state's existence.[15] The CEC is the body legally empowered to approve or reject a list of candidates if it fails to meet the formal legal terms.[16] The CEC refused to approve the *Al-Ard* list of candidates, arguing it was an illegal association whose members denied the State of Israel's integrity and very existence. It seemed that this decision was ultra vires, as the CEC did not have the power to make such declarations, and an appeal was filed with the HCJ. The Court's majority opinion endorsed the disqualification and rejected the appeal.

The HCJ decision on this matter, known as the *Yardor* case,[17] is viewed as one of the most important judicial decisions ever rendered in Israel. It was considered most unusual and, in many respects, became a symbol of the 'militant-democracy' doctrine. That was the first time in Israel's history that the Supreme Court clearly deviated from the principle of legality, which is the foundation of the rule of law, and justified its decision to disqualify a list of Knesset candidates by citing 'natural law' and 'supra-constitutional' principles.

The three judges on the bench, however, were not in full agreement. Expressing the dissenting view, Justice Chaim Cohn[18] stated that the list should be allowed to stand for election because of the application of the legality and rule of law principles. The two majority judges decided

[15] The *Al-Ard* movement was not allowed to operate as an association. Its appeal against this decision was rejected by the HCJ, which stated: 'It is the elementary right of states to safeguard their liberties and very existence against foreign enemies and their domestic supporters.' See HCJ 253/64 *Giris v Haifa District Governor*, ver 18(4), 673 (1964), 679, 681.

[16] The Central Elections Committee is a political body comprising Knesset faction representatives. It is chaired by an HCJ judge who is expected to explain legal issues pertaining to elections, but has a single vote. The procedure by which a political body may disqualify political parties has been criticised and disputed. Legally, its decisions may be challenged before the Supreme Court, which guarantees that the final decision on a disqualification move is in the hands of a judicial instance.

[17] EA (Elections Appeal) 1/65 *Yardor v The CEC*, ver 19(3), 365 (1965).

[18] Cohn was one of the most prominent judges in Israel's judicial history. One of his best-known books deals with the trial of Jesus: Chaim Cohn, *Processo e Morte di Gesù – un Punto di Vista Ebraico*, translated to Italian by Professor Gustavo Zagrebelsky (Torino, Giulio Einaude editore, 1997).

to approve the CEC decision to disqualify *Al-Ard*. President Agranat concurred with Cohn that the law does not speak of a disqualification power, but explained that when interpreting the state's laws, a 'constitutional datum', whereby the State of Israel is viable and eternal, should also be considered. Justice Zussman explicitly referred to the principles of natural law, including the right of any state to defend itself.

This decision judicially disqualified a party because of its platform, when no law actually permitted such disqualification. The Knesset, however, did not make the seemingly natural move of amending the legal situation by legally enacting the disqualification power.[19] Thus, the legal situation remained as it was before, probably because the MKs assumed that *Al-Ard* was an extreme case that would never recur. Nearly 20 years passed before the issue resurfaced on the Israeli public agenda.

The second period commenced in the 1980s, when Rabbi Meir Kahana established the *Kakh* movement, which advocated the Jewish nature of the state to the point of exclusivity. At the same time, the all-Arab *Progressive Movement for Peace* (PMP) was formed to represent the entire Arab population of Israel and called for the establishment of a Palestinian state. The CEC disqualified both lists: *Kakh* because its racist goals negated the democratic nature of the state and the PMP because some of its key figures allegedly identified with the state's enemies. Again, the decisions were made without an explicit legal authority to do so. When the CEC decisions were challenged, a five-judge HCJ panel unanimously ruled in favour of the appellants and, handing down the *Neiman* verdict,[20] allowed the two parties to run in the elections.

The majority of the bench in this case opined that the *Yardor* verdict of 1965 was correct due to its particular, irregular circumstances, but that it could not be extended so as to disqualify parties that do not negate the state's very existence.

---

[19] Writing about the *Yardor* case, Dr Menahem Hofnung said that the HCJ ruling created 'a strange situation. First, the scope of the reasons for disqualification remained unclear because they were not defined by law. Second, the decision created an asymmetry because it (apparently) applies only to new lists and parties. It is hard to see it applied to parties that took part in elections before, even if anyone should argue that their ideology denies the State of Israel's right to exist'. Menahem Hofnung, *Israel – Democracy, Law and National Security* (Aldershot, Ashgate, 1996) 214–15.

[20] See EA 84/2, 3 *Neiman and Others v CEC*, ver 39(2), 225 (1984). For a detailed discussion of the verdict and the judges' arguments, see Claude Klein, 'The Defence of the State and the Democratic Regime in the Supreme Court' (1985) 20 *Israel Law Review* 397.

The court's decision forced the Knesset to address the issue of party disqualification by legislation. After *Kakh* was allowed to run in the elections, its leader, Rabbi Kahana, became an MK and between 1984 and 1988 attempted to promote his racist platform, filed racist bills and spoke out harshly against the Israeli Arabs. The Knesset made several attempts to restrict Kahana's activities and he repeatedly filed petitions against these moves with the HCJ.[21]

A year after the *Neiman* verdict was handed down, the Knesset introduced section 7A of Basic Law: The Knesset, the provision that denied a party's right to participate in the Knesset elections if it denies Israel's existence as a Jewish state and/or its democratic nature, or if it provokes racism. The Knesset further amended the Knesset Elections Law, stating that the CEC shall have the authority to refuse lists for reasons cited in section 7A. As noted, the CEC comprises party representatives who are, naturally, motivated by political and ideological considerations. Parties whose lists have been rejected have the right to file appeals against CEC decisions with the HCJ. The new law – section 7A of Basic Law: The Knesset – clearly covers a very broad spectrum of cases. Nevertheless, although the clause that permits the disqualification of parties due to their 'implicit goals' (not only their explicitly stated ones) is particularly broad and although the phrase that refers to parties that negate the democratic nature of the state is rather vague, the HCJ interpretation of this law has subsequently been very narrow.

The HCJ was called upon to interpret this clause in 1988 when the CEC disqualified the *Kakh* list after Kahana had already served a four-year Knesset term. The *Kakh* list appealed (in the second *Neiman* case) and the HCJ unanimously rejected their appeal and approved *Kakh*'s disqualification.[22] The Court's position was that the instructions in section 7A should be interpreted strictly and applied only in the most extreme cases, because it is a law restricting a constitutional right. This narrow interpretation should be expressed by a series of 'tests' or 'requirements' that have to be met entirely before the power to disqualify

---

[21] Among other things, Kahana was denied the right to table motions of no confidence and racist bills, and his pledge of allegiance was revoked. His HCJ appeals in relation to these matters started an interesting discussion concerning the judicial control of parliamentary proceedings in Israel.

[22] EA 88/1 *Neiman v The CEC*, ver 42(4), 177 (1988). This was the first time in Israel that a political list was disqualified by the CEC's exercise of its explicit legal power to do so.

a list may be exercised. These tests include, among other things, proof that the list under discussion actually takes steps to realise its goals, that its wrongful moves and goals are central and dominant, not marginal and unimportant, and that evidence of these activities is clear, conclusive and unequivocal. When all of these tests were applied to the *Kakh* movement, the Court unanimously concluded that it was a racist list and disqualified it. In 1992, two other movements that identified with extreme-right ideologies were also disqualified.

The Parties Law of 1992 empowered the Party Registrar to refuse to register a party if its goals or actions explicitly or implicitly deny the State of Israel's right to exist as a Jewish and democratic state, incite racism or might serve as a front for illegal activities. This law marks the third period and introduced a 'two checkpoint' system into Israel's constitutional law, theoretically allowing the system to disqualify a party at two distinct points in time: when it files for registration (under the Parties Law) and when it runs in Knesset elections (by the power of the CEC according to section 7A of Basic Law: The Knesset). Thus, a new party may be registered legally before it becomes truly active. Then, closer to election day, it may be disqualified from running for the Knesset if it turns out that its actions violate the law. Still, over the two decades since the Parties Law was introduced, no party was denied registration for these reasons.

The third period peaked in 2002. In 2000, a year before the 9/11 attacks on the US and the global struggle against terrorism, a violent uprising erupted in the occupied territories and spread into Israel proper. Riots in Israeli Arab villages climaxed when, attempting to quell the riots, the police shot and killed several Israeli Arabs, further extending the rift between the two national groups. The Palestinian uprising (known as *intifada*) included a series of gruesome terror attacks staged by mainly Palestinian suicide bombers against Israeli citizens. The violent struggle resonated in the Knesset as well. Arab MKs made a series of disputed statements that implicitly supported the terror attacks. These remarks were met with grave responses from many MKs who promoted a rapid and comprehensive legislative move that was meant to address the situation.

The most prominent and interesting legislative change made in the wake of the *intifada* was the amendment of section 7A of Basic Law: The Knesset. Introduced in July 2000, it added a new cause for the disqualification of a political movement in Israel: 'Support for armed struggle by a hostile state or terrorist organization against the State of

Israel.[23] The law further allowed the disqualification of a candidate personally, regardless of his party's stand. This innovation allowed for the separation between the party as a legal entity and its individual members. As a precaution, the law provided that the disqualification of a candidate must be approved by the Supreme Court.

This new amendment was extensively discussed by a panel of 11 Supreme Court judges when addressing the *Tibi* case in early 2003. This case started with the CEC decision to disqualify the Arab-based *Balad* Party (headed by Dr Azmi Bishara) and the candidacy of Dr Ahmad Tibi of the *Ra'am* movement, while allowing the candidacy of a former *Kakh* movement leader who wished to run on the ticket of another party.

A majority of seven Supreme Court judges decided to allow all the parties and candidates mentioned to participate in the elections. The majority opinion was delivered by President Aharon Barak. The verdict examined Israel's militant-democracy tools, but ruled that the right to vote and to stand for elections prevails, stating that, although the Basic Law: The Knesset allows the disqualification of parties, the Supreme Court would not easily approve such disqualifications.

The Court stated that a list of candidates may be disqualified under the pretext of 'denying the Jewish nature' of Israel only if it invalidates 'the core characteristics' that comprise the minimalistic definition of the State of Israel as a Jewish state. The core characteristics that define the Jewish state and whose denial, according to Justice Barak, might serve as cause for the disqualification of a party include the following premises: 'Hebrew is the main official language of the state; the majority of its holidays and symbols reflect the national revival of the Jewish Nation; and the Jewish heritage is a key component of the state's religious and cultural heritage.'[24] Accordingly, the Court acknowledged the legitimacy of *Balad*'s aspirations to establish 'a state of all of its citizens . . . where the Arab minority could realise its collective rights in a manner similar to the way the Jewish majority realizes its collective rights'.[25]

Referring to the second cause – the disqualification of a party that negates the state's democratic nature – the Court stated that the term 'democratic state' should be given a narrow interpretation so as to prevent

---

[23] Also added to the Parties Law.
[24] President Barak's opinion in the *Tibi* case, EA 11280/02 *Central Elections Committee for the Sixteenth Knesset v Tibi*, ver 57(4), 1 (2003) 22.
[25] ibid 36–37.

too many restrictions from being imposed on the right to stand for elections. It was of the view that a democracy needs to defend only 'the most basic democratic principles: acknowledging national sovereignty as expressed in free and equal elections, and recognizing the nucleus of human rights, including dignity and equality, the separation of powers, the rule of law, and an independent judiciary'.[26] Thus, a list of candidates who advocate violence as a means of changing the state's regime cannot take part in the same democratic process that it wishes to destroy by force.

The Court concluded that the aspiration to change national arrangements by way of supporting an armed struggle against the state deviates from the democratic framework and a democracy may defend itself against it.

Referring specifically to the cases at hand (the claim that MKs Bishara and Tibi supported the armed struggle of the Lebanese Hezbollah organisation and the terrorist activities of Palestinian organisations against Israel), the Court stated that the step of disqualifying candidates because they support an anti-Israeli armed struggle may be taken only if this kind of support is a dominant and central trait of the party's, list's or individual's platform, and if that support had been expressed repeatedly and continuously, not just sporadically. Thus, the majority of the Supreme Court judges ruled that MK Bishara could enjoy the benefit of the doubt as to the meaning of remarks attributed to him, which may be viewed as supporting the opposition to the occupation in non-violent ways, and unanimously ruled that Tibi's remarks had not been proven to express support for any type of terrorist activity.

The State of Israel went from a situation where no substantive legal restrictions existed to one in which parties that deny the state's existence, or that are racist, anti-democratic or pro-terrorist, may be legally disqualified. Nevertheless, over the years and despite the extensive introduction of such laws, HCJ interpretations have limited the application of those laws and firmly defended the right to stand for elections. The disqualification of a political party in Israel was and still is a very rare phenomenon.[27]

According to the Israeli Supreme Court, the damage liable to ensue from silencing political views and excluding parties from the political

---

[26] ibid 23.
[27] See Suzie Navot, 'Fighting Terrorism in the Political Arena: The Banning of Political Parties' (2008) 14 *Party Politics* 745.

game may well exceed the benefit gained from such action. In the words of the Supreme Court: 'It is preferable that non-democratic pressures find expression within the legitimate frameworks of democracy and not outside it.'[28]

PART II: COMPOSITION AND PRIVILEGES

COMPOSITION

The Knesset sits in Jerusalem. It comprises 120 MKs, who are headed by the Knesset speaker (known by the Hebrew term *Yoshev-Rhosh*, which means chairman), and its main forum of operation is the Knesset Plenum. The Knesset may hold discussions and vote on issues regardless of the number of MKs present in the plenum hall since Israel has no legal quorum for legislative or other votes. Plenum resolutions are made by the majority of present voters, unless the law orders otherwise, which means that laws may be actually passed by a very small number of MKs.

Traditionally, the Knesset elects one MK as speaker and several others as deputy speakers according to the party composition of the Knesset. Together, they form the Knesset Presidency. Since the Knesset speaker must be impartial, he may not simultaneously serve as a member of any Knesset committee. The Knesset speaker serves as director of plenum discussions and holds extensive powers in managing Knesset affairs, presides over discussions, determines the order of votes on tabled motions and the Knesset's weekly agenda, and is authorised to give the floor to MKs, call them to order and even remove them from the plenum hall. The speaker serves as acting President of the State of Israel when that position is vacant and performs the President's duties when the latter is temporarily incapacitated or abroad.

Another prominent Knesset position is the head of the opposition. The Israeli opposition does not follow the British tradition of maintaining a 'shadow government', but the head of the opposition plays a key role in House deliberations. A law creating this position was enacted in 2000, prescribing the opposition head's status, roles, salary and reciprocal

---

[28] Justice Levi in the *Tibi* case (n 24).

relations in relation to the Prime Minister (the coalition head). The opposition head is a member of the largest opposition faction and it is the Prime Minister's duty to update him or her on state affairs at least once a month. When the bill on the opposition head was tabled, the accompanying explanatory notes stated that the new law was meant 'to assign special status to the opposition head – namely, the head of the largest Knesset faction [that is not in the ruling coalition], provided it comprises at least 15 MKs. This bill symbolically and practically expresses the importance of the opposition in Israel and encourages it to arrange its activities around the largest Knesset faction. It further intends to shape Israeli parliamentarism and bolster the Israeli democracy. It is also important because it would help the opposition perform its duties more effectively.' Israel has a multi-partisan system and the current opposition includes left-wing, Jewish religious Orthodox parties and Arab parties, which makes it rather difficult for the opposition head to properly represent all their interests and for the opposition parties to serve as a viable alternative government.

The tenure of all MKs ends when the Knesset term ends or when they resign. According to section 42A(a) of Basic Law: The Knesset: 'If a Knesset member has been convicted of a felony in a final verdict, and the court – by its own initiative or at the request of the Attorney-General – has determined that the offense bears moral turpitude, his Knesset membership shall end on the day the court issued its final verdict.' This termination of duty is automatic.

When a Knesset seat becomes vacant, the seat is taken by the next person on the same faction's list of candidates. The same rule applies to the seat of a suspended MK for the duration of the suspension. If the faction list does not have a candidate, the seat remains vacant, which is the only scenario in which the Knesset may comprise less than 120 members.

THE POLITICAL MANDATE OF MKS

The legal status of MKs is a rather complicated issue, mainly because it is not clear whether their loyalty lies with the Knesset, the party that placed them there, their electorate or the entire public. The basic legal approach in Israel is that the MK is a 'public trustee' and thus must 'inherently act in the best interests' of 'the nation' or 'the people',[29] and

[29] Suzie Navot, 'Members of the Knesset as "Public Trustees"' (2000) 31(2) *Mishpatim* 466, 519 (Hebrew).

avoid taking action that might fundamentally and seriously harm the government's foundations and human rights.

In the *Velner* case,[30] the Israeli Supreme Court reviewed the question of the duty of loyalty of MKs while discussing the validity of political agreements. Justice Barak established that MKs must be loyal to the entire public: 'MKs are not "representatives" of a party; they are state organs. When they are sworn in, each one of them pledges to bear allegiance to the State of Israel and faithfully perform their mission in the Knesset. They do not pledge allegiance to their party or swear to faithfully perform its mission in the Knesset. Every MK is a representative of the entire nation and must act as a public trustee.'[31] Thus, MKs must primarily promote the interests of the general public. In that spirit, the House Committee stated in the Knesset's ethical code that MKs 'are public trustees and it is their duty to represent their electors in a manner that serves human dignity, the advancement of Man, and the good of the state'.

Nevertheless, theoretically pure and 'free' representation does not exist in parliamentary regimes as a whole, and in Israel in particular, because political parties mediate between MKs and the public. In the Israeli parliamentary system, significant weight is assigned to the party and, by definition, to the Knesset faction that represents it. The Israeli representational model is a three-way system comprising the public, the party and the MK. The 'public–party' and the 'public–MK' relationships match the 'free representation' model whereby the public gives the party and the MK a 'free' mandate that, at least theoretically, compels the latter two to do all that is required to promote the good of the entire public. Nevertheless, MKs are not elected personally, but as part of a candidate list presented by the party with which they are affiliated or of which they are members. As a result, they are 'trustees and emissaries of their party and their electorate'.[32]

In view of the above, it seems that MKs are subject to a complex duty of loyalty: they must be loyal to the public as a whole and must exercise

---

[30] HCJ 5364/94 *Velner v Labour Party Chairman*, ver 49(1), 758 (1995).

[31] ibid 807.

[32] HCJ 4031/94 *Bezedek Organization v Israel's Prime Minister*, ver 48(5), 1 (1994) 23: 'According to our [election] system, a Knesset member is elected within the framework of a list that runs in the elections. The voting citizen gives his vote to the list, not to the single MK. Our election rules do not express a tendency to grant the elected MK a political-parliamentary status outside his faction.'

their powers according to their best judgement, conscientiously, professionally and without bias. When they are sworn in, they pledge allegiance to the State of Israel and vow to faithfully perform their Knesset duties. At the same time, however, because they were elected as part of a partisan framework, they are subject to 'factional discipline' and must follow and act in accordance with their faction resolutions. A series of legislative instructions and the Knesset Rules of Procedure further authorise factions to restrict the independence and freedom of action of MKs.

An interesting example of this kind of party control over MKs is the section in Basic Law: The Knesset that prevents MKs from quitting their factions, which was originally designed to prevent them from crossing the floor. This clause was enacted because the Knesset has a history of MKs quitting the factions on whose tickets they had been elected, while retaining and even trading their seats and votes. In 1990, this phenomenon reached troubling proportions, both quantitatively and substantially, in terms of the promised benefits and the impact the various 'crossings' had on the composition of the government. Subsequently, the Knesset amended Basic Law: The Knesset in order to severely limit the freedom of MKs to leave their parties once elected. The amendment allows MKs to quit their factions and ignore faction discipline in votes, but punishes them if they do so. Section 6A of Basic Law: The Knesset now states:

> (a) A member of Knesset who leaves [quits] his faction and does not resign from office at the same time may not, in the election of the subsequent Knesset, be included in the list of candidates of a party that was represented by a faction in the outgoing Knesset; this regulation shall not apply to a faction split under circumstances determined by Law.
>
> (b) For the purposes of this section: 'resignation from a faction' includes a vote in the Knesset plenum on a no-confidence motion not in accordance with the position of his original faction. Such voting shall not be construed as resignation if the Knesset member has not received compensation in exchange for his vote; 'compensation' – directly or indirectly, by a promise or future commitment, including the assurance of a place on the list of Knesset candidates, or the appointment of the Knesset member himself or another person to whatever position. (Introduced on 12 February 1991)

Interestingly, the basic law makes a distinction between 'quitting' a faction (which is banned) and 'splitting' from a faction (which is allowed). MKs 'quit' when they so announce or when they vote against their faction's position in a vote of no confidence in the government. Yet, MKs who leave their faction by 'splitting' from it are not viewed as if they had 'quit' it. The law determines that to 'split' from a party, the splinter faction they form must include at least three MKs who together form at least one-third of the original faction members. The distinction between splitting from and quitting a party was introduced on the basis of the theory that when a group of MKs decides to split as a group, their motivation is not personal but ideological, which is acceptable.

An MK who quits his faction is subject to a series of sanctions. For example, MKs who do not resign from the Knesset soon after quitting their party may not be included in a list of candidates for the subsequent Knesset of a party that already has a Knesset faction, they may not assume Cabinet positions during the same Knesset term and they are not entitled to state funds, while allocations to the faction they quit remain the same as prior to their resignation. At the same time, a faction has no legal option to 'expel' an MK, nor can it deny an 'undesired' MK's right to file bills and table motions.

PARLIAMENTARY IMMUNITY

MKs are subject to the law, just like every other citizen, but – as is customary with many parliaments worldwide – they are immune from liability in criminal or civil lawsuits. 'Professional immunity' or 'substantive immunity' are terms that describe the kind of protection enjoyed by MKs from criminal or civil responsibility for wrongs performed as part of their duty. MKs may not be tried for expressing their views, voting or performing other acts which form part of their Knesset duties, and this immunity is 'absolute', as it may not be lifted by the Knesset and remains in effect after they end their term – a situation also known as inviolability.

MKs' parliamentary immunity is established by Basic Law: The Knesset, according to which the 'particulars' of their immunity shall be 'described by law'. This is an important rule, although it lacks a few basic details.[33] The 'particulars' to which the basic law refers are outlined in

---

[33] Incidentally, relevant details feature in constitutional arrangements worldwide addressing the nature of parliamentary immunity under the constitution. Such basic arrangements should be introduced in Israel as part of Basic Law: The Knesset. While immunity to various extents (primarily when it comes to political opinions or votes) guarantees stability in this respect, the Israeli version that allows its 'particulars' to be

the Knesset Members (Immunity, Rights and Duties) Law (1951). Referring to the expression of opinion in the course of performing a parliamentary duty, section 1(1a) of this law reads: 'MKs shall bear no criminal or civil responsibility and shall be immune to any legal action in response to their vote, expression of opinion orally or in writing, or any other act they perform in or outside the Knesset – whether voting, opining or acting for the fulfilment of their functions.'

The immunity law was not intended to allow MKs to deliberately violate the law, and the interpretation of this law has assumed that staying within the boundaries of the law is within the definition of MKs' duties. At the same time, if MKs do engage in unlawful acts and there is a 'link' between their acts and their parliamentary position, their unlawful acts may be seen as having been performed in the fulfilment of their functions. This immunity is meant to guarantee that MKs are free to act and perform their duties without fearing that they might be sued for them, and that they remain independent and free from other government branches.

In the *Gorolowsky* case,[34] which will be discussed below, President Barak determined that substantive immunity is meant to secure the independence of the House and 'the representational-democratic nature of the Israeli regime', so as to safeguard the MKs' independence. According to him, it is meant to allow the MKs to use their judgement, to act on the 'representation principle', 'realise the democratic process' and 'bolster the democratic regime'. The HCJ President remarked similarly in the *Bishara* case[35] that substantive immunity is meant to defend basic political liberties.

Nonetheless, unduly broad immunity harms and conflicts with fundamental constitutional principles. Israeli case law has so far named three main democratic goals that parliamentary immunity contradicts: the need to safeguard the democratic nature of the state, the rule of law and the principle of equality. While ordinary citizens must pay for their wrongdoing, MKs do not and thus the principle of equality before the law is violated. This inequality has been addressed by Israeli and foreign

'described by law' leads to frequent amendments, some of which are 'personal' in nature, which is both undesirable and comparatively unacceptable.

[34] HCJ 11298/03 *The Movement for Government Quality v The Knesset House Committee*, ver 59(5), 865 (2005).

[35] HCJ 11225/03 *Azmi Bishara v Attorney General* (published in Nevo on 1 February 2006).

courts and, subsequently, the scope of procedural immunity was restricted in several European countries in recent years. For example, the Italian and French constitutions were amended in the 1990s so that the law no longer requires the House's consent before procedural immunity is lifted. The two Parliaments are only asked to approve such moves when, for example, the authorities wish to further restrict MPs by placing them in custody or detention.

The question of balance between the various purposes of immunity was discussed when the HCJ interpreted the phrase 'in the fulfilment of his function' from the Knesset Members (Immunity, Rights and Duties) Law. The Supreme Court established that parliamentary immunity is meant to protect activities that fall within the 'realm of natural risk' which performing parliamentary duties entails, 'where the wrongful act is performed within the line or for the sake of the MKs' duty'.[36] This approach considers the possibility that action performed within the 'realm of natural risk' might slip from being legal to illegal or be inappropriate. Accordingly, immunity protects MKs only when their 'illegal activities fall within the realm of natural risk that the MKs' legal activities might create by nature'.[37]

The scope of substantive immunity was extensively discussed in the *Pinhasi* case, in which MK Pinhasi allegedly presented the State Comptroller with false reports. Reviewing the case, the HCJ judges concluded that this act did not fall within the realm of immunity for acts done in the fulfilment of the MK's function. They determined that immunity applies only to activities that are closely affiliated with MKs' parliamentary work, but does not protect MKs when they deliberately commit a criminal offence or attempt to deliver political messages through illegal or unjust acts. The verdict stated that 'MKs who believe in equality between rich and poor should not enjoy immunity if they steal from the rich to give to the poor. Similarly, an MK who is also a physician and believes that women should be free to choose whether or not to have an abortion should not enjoy immunity if he performs an illegal abortion'.[38]

In 2002, the Knesset introduced a series of amendments to the Immunity Law after some MKs allegedly supported anti-Israeli terror organisations. Like the amendments made concerning the disqualification

---

[36] HCJ 1843/93 MK *Pinhasi v The Knesset*, ver 49(1), 661 (1995) 677.
[37] ibid 695–96.
[38] *Pinhasi v The Knesset* (n 36).

and registration of parties, the Immunity Law was amended to state that MKs shall not enjoy immunity from criminal charges if they 'negate the existence of the State of Israel as the state of the Jewish nation . . . or if they support the armed struggle of an enemy state or terror groups against the State of Israel'.

There is a clear link between this amendment of the Immunity Law and the reasons mentioned above that led the Knesset to ban political candidates. The amendment was first discussed by the HCJ in the *Bishara* case after it had been argued that MK Bishara expressed support for the armed struggle of a terror group. Handing down its verdict in 2006, the HCJ ruled that MK Bishara should not be tried for speeches he made several years earlier, in which he praised Hezbollah for its struggle against the IDF in southern Lebanon, and voiced his support for 'resistance to the occupation'. In a majority ruling, the HCJ decided that the MK's remarks were protected by his parliamentary immunity. This was the first time that an MK was charged for expressing political views, hence the great importance of this verdict in relation to the scope of the substantive immunity of MKs in particular and to the protection of freedom of expression as a whole.

In a majority opinion, Justices Barak and Rivlin stated that MK Bishara's remarks did not actually express support for the armed struggle of terror groups, but rather were made 'as part of his parliamentary duties', because the speech was defined as being 'political' in nature. President Barak described the purposes of immunity as measures designed to allow Israel's elected representatives to speak their minds freely, stressing the representation principle: 'First of all, such protection is particularly essential for minority groups; second, immunity is vital as it is meant to guarantee the existence of a free market of views and ideas . . . and thirdly, in view of the above, immunity is essential for guaranteeing the democratic nature of the government.'[39]

The HCJ stated that the right to stand for elections entails and practically presupposes a scope of parliamentary activity which in most cases may be considered as part of the fulfilment of parliamentary duty: 'It would not be easy to throw out the window that which had been allowed in through the main entrance.'[40]

---

[39]   *Azmi Bishara v Attorney General* (n 35) President Barak's opinion at [8].
[40]   ibid, Justice Rivlin's opinion at [6]–[7].

Thus, the Court established that Bishara's remarks were political and that the nature of his remarks and the circumstances in which they were made were closely associated with the MK's political credo, and were therefore legitimate. The verdict in this case clearly stated that 'political remark' and 'political speech' are the key issues that the parliamentary freedom of speech protects, and that the 'realm of natural risk' test has so far strictly guarded MKs' liberties, particularly their freedom of speech. Thus, libel suits against MKs are routinely rejected,[41] which often creates the sense that ordinary citizens would have no recourse if they attempted to defend their reputation in court after having been slandered by an MK. The test has not explicitly examined the necessary balance between the MKs' freedom of speech (which is protected by immunity) and the right of others to defend their dignity and reputations.

Interestingly, in all the cases that the Israeli courts have so far addressed, the freedom of speech of MKs has clashed with public interests such as public safety or the need to defend democratic values. Cases (mainly in the lower courts) in which immunity clashed with an individual's right to defend his dignity and reputation were all decided in favour of parliamentary immunity.

In addition to substantive immunity, MKs enjoy 'procedural' immunity, which protects them from being searched and detained by the authorities, and from facing criminal charges. Procedural immunity is temporal – it applies only during the MK's term in office and even then, it is not absolute because, unlike substantive immunity, the Knesset has the power to lift it. Procedural immunity is meant 'to guarantee the regular operation of the Knesset as a legislative authority so as to prevent MKs from being harassed for wrongful reasons by the executive, which might attempt to go this way and unlawfully impact on the freedom of action of the people's representatives and deny them the right to speak freely'.[42]

Immunity from searches is included in section 2 of the Immunity Law: 'MKs shall be immune against searches of their premises, persons, or belongings . . . and [protected] from searches in, perusal, or seizure of their private documents.' MKs are also immune from arrests and may not be detained unless they are apprehended *in flagrante delicto*, while

---

[41] Suzie Navot, 'Freedom of Speech of MKs: A License to Libel?' (2010) *Mishpatim* 67 (Hebrew).

[42] HCJ *Abu-Hazira v Attorney General*, ver 35(4), 567 (1981).

perpetrating a crime that includes the use of force, disturbance of public order or treason. Yet, according to the provisions of the Immunity Law, MKs are not immune from testifying in court or from investigations by authorities that have the power to launch investigations. Before 2005, Israeli MKs were immune from criminal prosecution even for acts and speeches outside the scope of their duties, effectively meaning for every criminal act committed. Their procedural immunity could have been lifted by the Knesset even then, and once it was lifted totally, MKs could be tried just like any other citizen. In 2005, the scope of parliamentary immunity was limited in the wake of a case that was later dubbed the 'Double Votes' or the *Gorolowsky* case, which is of particular interest and sheds light not only on the rules of immunity, but also on the courts' judicial review of Knesset proceedings. The case demonstrates the unique 'dialogue' on constitutional issues that often takes place between the Israeli Supreme Court and the Knesset.

Gorolowsky was an MK who voted twice (as himself and as another) during a series of votes on a law that accompanied the *Budget Law*.[43] His act did not have any impact on the voting result or the law. This particular vote was cancelled and repeated. Gorolowsky pleaded guilty, faced the Knesset's disciplinary action and was suspended from the Knesset for four months. Gorolowsky's reputation was badly damaged. He quit the Knesset after the elections and never returned to the public ring.

If the case had ended with the expulsion of the MK from the House and public life as a whole, Israel could have been spared an entangled and extensive legal affair, a crisis between the legislature and the judiciary, and a series of hasty legislative amendments. After the Knesset disciplinarily sanctioned Gorolowsky, the Attorney General (Israel's chief prosecutor) decided to file criminal charges against him for 'forgery with intent to receive benefits under grave circumstances, deception, and breach of trust'. Next, the Attorney General asked the Knesset to lift MK Gorolowsky's procedural immunity so that he could face trial. Following this request, the House Committee examined the case in various frameworks.

The House Committee decided not to lift MK Gorolowsky's procedural immunity. According to the Knesset Members (Immunity, Rights

---

[43] Voting on laws of this kind – including budget and economic arrangements laws – often last hours and even days. The Supreme Court has often criticised this practice.

and Duties) Law, the Committee's decision is final in the sense that the issue was not to be further discussed at the Knesset plenum. A petition was filed with the HCJ against the Committee's resolution and a seven-judge bench endorsed the petition unanimously. Thus, the HCJ stepped right into the very heart of Knesset proceedings and reversed the House Committee's decision, strongly intervening in the legislature's affairs.

Writing for the majority, President Barak wrote that the Knesset is not authorised to review criminal charges, may not determine whether or not the MK in question was speaking the truth, may not address the issue of sufficient evidence at all and must not create a special 'prosecution policy' for MKs. Therefore, Barak stated, the House Committee may only 'examine the reasons of the Attorney General and make sure they include no flaws such as bias and wrongful discrimination, deviation from the general prosecution policy, or biased by political influence'. The entire panel concurred with Barak's opinion and thus concluded that the Committee may only consider whether the Attorney General was acting with bona fides and was not motivated by political considerations. Therefore, because the Committee had addressed other considerations, such as the fact that Gorolowsky had already been 'punished' by the Knesset in an internal disciplinary procedure, the HCJ quashed its decision.

The verdict took the House Committee by surprise and the media cited protests by Committee members. In its wake, the Attorney General officially requested that the Committee hold another vote on Gorolowsky's parliamentary immunity, but subsequent remarks in the media by Committee members left little doubt as to what was to take place in the second Committee discussion.[44] The House Committee convened for a second time to vote on the fate of Gorolowsky's immunity in June 2005 and once more decided against lifting it, which essentially expressed contempt for the HCJ decision. It seemed that the two authorities were defying one another. The public, however, reacted harshly to the Knesset's decision and openly sided with the Court. Consequently, the House had to respond to much criticism, which even arose from within the Knesset. It

---

[44] On 17 March 2005, the *Haaretz Daily* reported: '*Likud* MK Michael Eitan will vote against lifting MK Gorolowsky's immunity as an act of protest against the HCJ's intervention in the Knesset's resolution. *Likud* MK Yuli Edelstein said he would vote against lifting the immunity, and *Likud* MK Daniel Benlulu remarked: "With all due respect to the HCJ, Gorolowsky had already been punished once, which is why I will not vote for lifting his immunity".'

responded with a quick amendment of the Knesset Members (Immunity, Rights and Duties) Law in a particularly rushed procedure.

The amendment introduced a reform of procedures, the outcome of which was that the Knesset in fact waived the rights of MKs to procedural immunity. This meant that the Attorney General can file charges against MKs with the court directly and does not have to ask for the Knesset's permission. The amendment created a situation in which procedural immunity is the exception: after the Attorney General presents the Knesset speaker with a copy of a charge sheet concerning an MK, the charged MK has 30 days in which he may submit a written request to the speaker that the House Committee grant him procedural immunity.

This story provides an example of the dialogue sometimes held between the Supreme Court and the Knesset, and of how 'hard cases make bad law'. In practice, since 2005, this amendment has been a success, in the sense that all the MKs who were charged for acts not covered by the substantive immunity, namely, for acts that were outside the scope of their functions, have chosen not to request procedural immunity.

PART III: THE LEGISLATIVE PROCESS

Neither the Knesset's working procedures nor Israel's legislative processes have yet been anchored in a basic law. A chapter dealing with the legislative process – arguably one of the most important features of a constitution – is still lacking in Israel. Several bills have been tabled over the years, paying particular attention to the enactment of basic laws, but none has yet ripened to a basic law. Rules pertaining to the legislative processes are listed only in the Knesset Rules of Procedure.

Section 19 of Basic Law: The Knesset reads: 'The Knesset shall determine its procedures. Insofar as such procedures have not been prescribed by law, the Knesset shall prescribe it by rules; so long as the procedure has not been prescribed as aforesaid, the Knesset shall follow its accepted custom and practice.' The term 'rules' in this section refers to the Knesset Rules of Procedure. However, as these Rules were endorsed by a Knesset plenum vote, their legal status is not clear and the Supreme Court has not yet ruled on this issue. The working assumption is that the Rules of Procedure are normatively inferior to state laws. In principle, the Court considers itself authorised to judicially review the Rules of Procedure, but has determined that it would do so only in extreme circumstances or when an endorsed House regulation is substantively flawed and damages fundamental principles of Israel's constitutional regime.[45] In practice, however, the Court has never nullified a Knesset rule or instruction.

The Knesset's chief operating platform is the plenum – that is, all of the MKs. Since Israel's legislative procedures do not require a quorum, the Knesset may hold deliberations and issue resolutions with any given number of MKs present at the plenum hall.

In most cases, Knesset votes are held openly, with secret votes being held only in exceptional circumstances, such as for the election of the President of the State of Israel or the State Comptroller. Knesset debates are also public, currently even being broadcast on the Knesset TV channel that airs plenum discussions in full.

The Knesset's work is performed in various committees, which hold the main discussions on the wording of bills and audit the government's performance. Several Knesset committees are permanent (for example, the Foreign Affairs and Defense Committee, the House Committee, the Economics Committee, the Ethics Committee and the Finance Committees), while others are established ad hoc for a given period. The Knesset may also establish parliamentary commissions of inquiry, which will be discussed below.

Knesset committees are composed according to the faction representation principle. The committee members elect their chairperson, who is then assigned numerous powers for managing the working procedures of that committee. Chairpersons may summon committee meetings and their presence is the only condition required for a committee to hold legal working sessions. Thus, committees may reach 'unanimous' resolutions that are passed with the presence of only the chairperson. The chair's powers include the right to order disciplinary measures against committee members that are rather similar to the sanctions that the Knesset speaker may impose in the plenum. Unlike plenum deliberations, which are open to the public, committee discussions are only public when the committee decides they may be. Yet, over the past several years, committees have regularly opened their discussions to the public, and some of their deliberations have even been broadcast live on the Knesset TV channel.

---

[45] HCJ 669/85 *Kahana v The Knesset Speaker*, ver 40(4), 393 (1985) 399.

By virtue of Basic Law: The Government, Knesset committees have the authority to demand information from the Cabinet, and the government is under an obligation to help the Knesset perform its duties. Knesset committees have the power to summon Cabinet members and civil servants to testify before them. In relation to particular issues, committees may also summon representatives of organisations and establishments that are interested parties and may ask academics to appear before them as expert witnesses on specific issues.

BILLS

The legislative process, described in the Knesset Rules of Procedure, comprises several stages. Bills may be initiated by the government (government bills) or by MKs (private bills), and in some cases by Knesset committees. For example, the Harari Resolution established that the Knesset Constitution, Law, and Justice Committee was to initiate the enactment of basic laws, but in most cases, this Committee has not been responsible for initiating the legislation.

All MKs who do not additionally serve as Cabinet members may submit private bills. No minimal quota of MKs is required to file a bill, so even a single MK may initiate the legislative process. As a result, a large number of private bills are filed (some 12,000 in the past decade alone and 4,600 in the last Knesset term), far exceeding the customary number of bills in other democracies. MKs have often been accused of filing bills in an attempt to reach the media and to 'grab headlines'. Thus, more often than not, bills are submitted immediately after, and in reaction to, events that are broadly covered by the media. The majority of these bills never mature into real laws, which is why they are popularly known as 'legislative statements'. In an attempt to restrict this phenomenon, an amendment to Basic Law: The State Economy states that if a bill requires budgetary funding of more than NIS 5 million and the government does not support it, it must be endorsed by at least 50 MKs.

Government and Knesset committee bills are submitted for a first Knesset plenum reading. Private bills, however, must scale two preliminary stages before they are presented for a first reading: first, they must be approved by the Knesset Presidency (the speaker and his deputies); and then the Knesset needs to endorse them in a preliminary reading.

They are then transferred to the relevant committees that prepare them for the first reading.

The Knesset Presidency approval stage is interesting in light of Israel's history with racist bills. According to the Knesset Rules of Procedure, the Presidency is authorised to verify that a submitted bill is not 'racist by nature, or denies the existence of the State of Israel as the state of the Jewish nation'. Based on that instruction, the Knesset Presidency disqualified several bills filed by MK Kahana (who served between 1984 and 1988), as well as other bills it classified as racist – for example, a bill asserting that only a Jew can be elected Israel's prime minister. This instruction actually complements section 7A of Basic Law: The Knesset, which denies the participation in elections of racist parties or lists that deny the fundamental values of the State of Israel. Yet, the legality of Knesset's procedural instruction that allows such disqualification is not entirely clear because it restricts the basic rights of MKs. In any event, the right to disqualify bills is reserved only for particularly extreme cases.

Although MKs may present private bills almost at will, the government controls the legislative agenda and it is very difficult for a private bill to become a law without the approval of the government. The government has a Ministerial Committee for Legislation whose main objective is the formulation of the government's position on proposed legislation and private bills. MKs may present their private bills for approval by the Ministerial Committee for Legislation, and the Committee may decide to support it, to oppose it or to support it subject to changes.

Each bill is read three times. The first reading merely constitutes a general discussion at the end of which the bill is either transferred to a relevant committee or dismissed. If transferred to committee, it is discussed there in the presence of the Attorney General and the committee's legal advisors, and interested parties are summoned to offer opinions. The discussion ends when the committee produces the final draft of the bill and submits it to the House for a second reading. A Knesset committee may not reject a bill that passed the first Knesset reading. In the second reading, the MKs discuss each section individually. Debates on the wording of the various clauses may be held at this stage between the members of the committee or with other MKs who were authorised to table their reservations. After votes are held on all the bill chapters and the second reading is complete, the Knesset holds a third reading. When the bill is then approved, the legislative process comes to an end. The new law is then endorsed and published in *Rashumot*, at which stage it takes effect.

JUDICIAL REVIEW OF PARLIAMENTARY PROCEEDINGS

Judicial review of parliamentary proceedings is an issue that strikes at the core of the separation of powers. While certain countries follow the *interna corporis* doctrine – whereby parliamentary proceedings are not subject to judicial review – the Israeli situation is particularly interesting and comparatively irregular. Few Western democracies allow judicial supervision of parliamentary proceedings. Following the British tradition, whereby 'proceedings in Parliament shall not be questioned', the Knesset's sovereignty principle was, until the 1980s, viewed as applying to the House not only as the legislature, but also to all other parliamentary activities. Section 7 of the Courts Law formally gave the HCJ the right to issue warrants against individuals who 'held a public position by law'[46] and thus – formally at least – all Knesset resolutions are viewed as if they were made by 'a body that holds a public position by law'. Although this section formally grants the judiciary the right to intervene in parliamentary proceedings, the Supreme Court traditionally avoided any and all such intervention. This approach, however, changed in the 1980s.

In 1981, the HCJ addressed a petition against the Knesset speaker who decided to change the date of a vote of no confidence, allegedly violating the Knesset Rules of Procedure. In what was known as the *Sarid* case,[47] Justice Barak offered a brief opinion in which he reviewed the pros and cons of court intervention in parliamentary proceedings. He established that there should be 'balance' between two principles: the fact that the House working procedures are its own concern and the principle of the rule of law. He set out a test that allows for judicial intervention in the inner affairs of the House that measures 'the extent of harm to the parliamentary work life and the extent of [the] impact it has on the foundations of the structure of our constitutional regime'.[48]

Applying this new test to the *Sarid* case, the Court established that the deviation from the Rules of Procedure in this case was minor, and so

---

[46] This arrangement is currently found in s 15(D) of Basic Law: The Judiciary.

[47] HCJ 652/81 *Sarid v The Knesset Speaker*, ver 36(2) 197 (1981).

[48] ibid 204.

rejected the petition. In this respect, the *Sarid* verdict is yet another example of an interesting peculiarity of Israel's constitutional law, particularly over the past 20 years, in which the Court issues verdicts that establish new tests or change the rules of the game, but does not apply them in the specific case in which it so ruled.[49]

The test formed in the *Sarid* case is based on the division of parliamentary proceedings into three categories – legislative, semi-judicial and administrative – stipulating a different form of intervention for each category. Thus, the Court established that it would 'narrowly' intervene in legislative activities and would 'regularly' supervise the Knesset's semi-judicial activities (such as suspension of MKs or Ethics Committee resolutions), while the judicial review of administrative Knesset activities should match the extent of harm it causes to parliamentary life as a whole.

The *Sarid* verdict was handed down before the 'constitutional revolution', when judicial review did not allow for the invalidation of legislation. Therefore, in a later case that took place after the enactment of these basic laws, the HCJ reiterated its traditional distinction between types of Knesset activities, while asserting that different categorisations may apply: 'After all, a final [legislative, semi-judicial, or administrative] decision is not the same as an interim decision . . . and a Knesset act that harms a right protected by a basic law is not the same as an act that impairs on the Knesset Rules of Procedure or its administrative regulations.'[50]

Nevertheless, though Knesset proceedings may be judicially reviewed, it should be noted that this rarely occurs due to the HCJ's self-restraint in this respect. A clear exception of this was the previously discussed *Gorolowsky* case.

In recent years, the HCJ began intervening on a new front – the judicial review of laws which came before it due to flaws in the legislative process. The issue was raised in the context of the introduction in Israel of a series of votes on what are known in Israel as Arrangements Laws (and sometimes internationally known as Omnibus Laws)[51] that are introduced along with the Annual Budget Law. These laws are typically

---

[49] The most important of which, of course, is the *Bank Hamizrahi* verdict.

[50] Justice Barak in HCJ 90700/00 *Livnat v Chairperson of Knesset Constitution, Law, and Justice Committee*, ver 55(4), 800 (2000).

[51] For information on the custom in Spain, see, for example, Saturna Moreno Gonzalez, *Constitucion y Leyes de 'Acompañamiento' Presupuestario* (Navarra, Aranzadi, 2000).

rushed through the Knesset, the coalition discipline that applies to the Budget Law applies to them too, and they address a bulk of issues and en-bloc legal amendments in various fields. Most of these laws are initiated by the Finance Ministry, with Knesset committees rarely being involved in the process. Over time, the Arrangements Laws have turned into a platform for legislation and amendments, and are viewed as a general means of making structural changes in the market and society, addressing issues that the government might have had a hard time changing through regular legislative procedures.

The first petition against legislative procedures that resemble the Arrangements Laws was filed in 2003, seeking a unique remedy – that the law be nullified not because it unlawfully impaired rights anchored in basic laws, but also because its enactment process was flawed. This petition, known as the *Poultry Growers Organisation* case, was the first time that the HCJ extensively discussed the possibility of judicially reviewing a law due to its allegedly flawed enactment process. Justice Beinisch wrote in her opinion: 'It is not enough to prove that a fundamental principle of the legislation proceeding has been harmed to make the court intervene in that proceeding. One needs to show that the said principle had been greatly and significantly harmed . . . Only in extreme and rare cases . . . which we may hope are not to be expected in our parliamentary reality, may the court declare a law null and void due to a flawed legislation proceeding.'[52]

Although this petition was rejected and the law was not quashed,[53] the Court's verdict sharply chastised the Arrangements Law proceedings. Justice Beinisch stated that this type of law is problematic in terms of due democratic process. It is characterised by a hasty legislative procedure that makes it practically impossible for MKs to seriously debate the law, impairing the decision makers' ability to reach educated conclusions and to form opinions. Not only is the bill insufficiently discussed, it also detracts from the Knesset's ability to effectively supervise the legislative process itself.

Justice Beinisch's ruling introduced new concepts regarding the fundamental principles of the legislative process that had not previously

---

[52] HCJ 4885/03 *The Poultry Growers Association v Israel's Government*, ver 59(2), 14 (2005) [25].

[53] This is yet another example of a court's decision that acknowledges a reason to intervene, but rejects the initial petition that called for it.

been systematically and thoroughly discussed. Beinisch named four such principles which, when seriously harmed, might constitute 'a flaw that impairs on the root of the process' and might render the law null and void: (1) the majority ruling principle, whereby a bill becomes a law only if it is supported by a Knesset majority; (2) the formal equality principle, whereby each MK has a single vote; (3) the publicity principle, whereby the legislative process should be open to the public; and (4) the participation principle, whereby all MKs have the right to participate in the legislative process. The HCJ recommended that the Knesset reconsider the future use of the problematic mechanism of the Arrangements Law. The verdict significantly influenced the scope of the Arrangements Law, as the Knesset has subsequently changed the legislative process. The Court did not impose on the Knesset a 'duty' to follow a due legislative process, although this issue was discussed in the verdict. For example, the Court did not order the Knesset to establish its resolutions on the basis of a proper factual foundation.

While the four basic principles of the Israeli legislative process were outlined in the *Poultry Growers Association* case, Western parliamentary democracies acknowledge additional institutionalised principles such as the representation principle, the free-mandate principle and more. When these principles are acknowledged, additional parliamentary rights and duties may derive from them.

Although the intervention of the Supreme Court in the Knesset's internal affairs has been limited, the test for judicial intervention is vague. Therefore, MKs sometimes appeal to the Supreme Court as part of their political agenda when they disagree with the outcome of a political process. Research on this issue[54] shows that politicians bring cases to the Court primarily to increase their media exposure. Politicians tend to seek litigation even when their chances of success are not high, and they do so because they usually receive immediate media coverage, an important factor when they need to be selected as party candidates for election. This phenomenon of 'legislators' litigation' may be one of the main reasons for the expansion of judicial review of parliamentary decisions. Nonetheless, the power for judicial review has been exercised with self-restraint, meaning that not every minor violation of constitutional principles has triggered judicial intervention.

---

[54] Yoav Dotan and Menachem Hofnung, 'Legal Defeats – Political Wins: Why Do Elected Representatives Go to Court?' (2005) 38 *Comparative Political Studies* 75.

PART IV: THE KNESSET AS WATCHDOG

The Knesset is not only the legislative body but is also the institution that monitors and supervises the executive – namely, the government. To effectively perform this role, the Knesset employs a variety of measures, although the effectiveness of each of those measures is disputed. Still, as we shall see, the Knesset powers to scrutinise the executive are quite limited.

The main tool at the Knesset's disposal is a vote of no confidence in the government. Since 2001, however, this tool has undergone a 'constructive' rearrangement such that presently, such a vote must be endorsed by at least 61 MKs, and all the MKs who vote in favour of the no-confidence motion must also agree on the identity of the MK to whom the task of forming a new government should be subsequently assigned. Since the introduction of this new arrangement, no Israeli government has lost a vote of no confidence. Votes of no confidence will be discussed in the next chapter.

QUESTIONS AND COMMITTEE DEBATES

The Knesset is authorised to demand and receive information from the government. Such information is regularly imparted when government representatives respond to MKs' queries and when Cabinet members appear before Knesset committees. Government activities are regularly supervised by these committees, which are authorised to demand that government representatives present them with facts and figures, and may also summon civil servants to testify. Basic Law: The Government acknowledges the government's duty to provide Knesset committees with the information they require and orders it to assist these committees in the performance of their duties. As part of their duties, Knesset committees may summon and even order Cabinet members and civil servants to appear before them, but they have not been authorised to impose sanctions against individuals who do not appear when summoned.

Furthermore, according to the Knesset Rules of Procedure, every MK has the right to table a query on factual matters that is addressed specifically to the Cabinet member in charge of the relevant issue. Such queries are first presented to the Knesset Speaker, who has the right to decide whether they are in order. The queried Cabinet member must respond to all such queries within a specified period of time, but since this instruction appears only in the Knesset Rules of Procedure, it is not always strictly observed.

It would seem that the most effective tool that Knesset committees can use is secondary legislation. When enacting primary laws in Israel, Cabinet members (ministers), who are authorised to introduce regulations for the execution of primary laws, must have these regulations approved by a relevant Knesset committee. For example, section 21A(a) of Basic Law: The Knesset states that: 'Regulations that are set by a minister and that determine criminal punishment if they are violated shall not take effect unless they are approved, before being issued, by the Knesset committee responsible for the subject.' Similarly, according to Basic Law: The State Economy, taxes, compulsory loans or other payments that are not prescribed by law require prior approval by the Knesset or by a Knesset committee.

The legislative process serves as yet another tool that the Knesset may use to supervise the government. In theory, the Knesset makes laws and resolutions about issues on the public agenda, which the government then executes. In practice, supervising government activities through legislation is a very limited instrument because the MKs are subject to their faction and coalition discipline. Since the Cabinet is generally supported by a Knesset majority, votes against government bills are fairly rare. In Israel, therefore, the government in practice dominates the legislative procedure.

PARLIAMENTARY COMMISSIONS

The Knesset is authorised to establish parliamentary commissions of inquiry. Section 22 of Basic Law: The Knesset established that: 'The Knesset may appoint inquiry commissions – either by empowering one of the permanent committees in that behalf or by electing a commission from among its members – to investigate matters designated by the Knesset; the powers and functions of a commission of inquiry shall be prescribed by the Knesset.' This mechanism can help the Knesset overcome incidents in which committees fail to obtain all the information they require concerning a certain event. The Knesset is authorised to determine the powers of such commissions, which usually comprise MKs, but rarely uses this tool. It may be argued that this reluctance is justified by the fear that a Knesset commission of inquiry might be biased because MKs represent particular political positions. Furthermore, reports that such commissions have issued thus far have failed to acquire the prestige and public status attributed to national commissions of inquiry, as will be explained later.

THE ANNUAL BUDGET

In theory, the Knesset can further supervise government activities through the state budget vote. The state budget is introduced as a state law that the Knesset must endorse as a form of approval of the government's budgetary activities and serves as a vote of confidence in the government. According to Basic Law: The Knesset, when a budget bill is voted down, the Knesset must disband and early elections are called. As may be recalled, in the *Bar-On* case of 2011, the HCJ was asked to rule on a petition against an ad hoc, provisional instruction that amended Basic Law: The State Economy so that the state budget is determined biennially. Ruling on the issue, the HCJ stated that the annual approval of the Budget Law is a cornerstone of democratic regimes and is the main tool at the disposal of the legislature to supervise the government's budgetary activities and priorities. Thus, it found that the provisional instruction impeded the Knesset's supervisory powers and was actually intended to weaken the Knesset and strengthen the government.

The Court further argued that the introduction of a biennial budget law conflicts with a long trend of tightening the Knesset supervision of the executive through, among other things, establishing specific dates by which the government must present the budget bill to the Knesset. The petitioners in this case argued that the amendment impairs the Knesset's ability to disband and thus overthrow the government if the budget law is rejected. They argued that this powerful instrument, with which the parliament can attempt to replace one Cabinet with another, is given to the Knesset only once a year. The provisional amendment restricts it, allowing that tool to be applied only every other year, which further disrupts the balance of power and alters the relationship between the government and the Knesset.

As mentioned earlier, the HCJ accepted the petitioners' arguments, but rejected the petition itself because it felt that the harm caused by this specific amendment was not so grave as to necessitate the Court's intervention in the law-making process. It should be remembered that in this case, the HCJ was asked to nullify an amendment to a basic law – a product of the constituent authority – when the legal power to judicially review even ordinary laws has not yet been anchored in a basic law or a solid constitution.

CONCLUSION

The Knesset is the Israeli legislator, both of regular laws and of constitutional basic laws. However, the government's dominance of the legislative process, the weakness of an opposition comprised of different parties with no real common ideology and the restricted control over the executive impose serious limitations on the efficacy with which the Knesset carries out its role. The Knesset's main role should be to improve government legislation by providing scrutiny. Achieving this is almost impossible in Israel today. The last Knesset's ruling coalition included two-thirds of the MKs, leaving the last third with a seriously weakened capacity of oversight. At the same time, the Knesset lost its legislative inhibitions and flooded the floor with private legislation. These flaws in the Knesset's functioning are the reasons for new bills proposed recently, which seek to limit the size of the Cabinet, and therefore allow more MKs to perform their public duties in the Knesset rather than in government.

More positively, the Knesset has greatly improved its control over the state budget following the HCJ decision on the Arrangements Law. The Knesset is still the arena in which the important political questions are debated and is the only institution entrusted with the important task of completing the constitution.

FURTHER READING

Akirav, Osnat, 'The Use of Parliamentary Questions in the Israeli Parliament, 1992–96' (2011) 17(2) *Israel Affairs* 259.

Arian, Asher, *Politics in Israel: The Second Republic* (Washington DC, CQ Press, 2005).

Barak-Erez, Daphne, 'The Primaries System and Its Constitutional Effect: Where is the Revolution?' (2002) 3 *Theoretical Inquiries in Law* 197.

Bendor, Ariel, 'Parties in Israel: Between Law and Politics' (2000) 1 *San Diego International Law Journal* 101.

Cohen-Almagor, Rafael, 'Disqualification of Lists in 1988 and 1992: A Comparative Analysis' in Michel Troper and Mikael M Karlsson (eds), *Law, Justice and the State* (Stuttgart, Franz Steiner Verlag, 1995).

Hazan, Reuven, 'Executive–Legislative Relations in an Era of Accelerated Reform: Reshaping Government in Israel' (1997) 22(3) *Legislative Studies Quarterly* 329.

Hazan, Reuven, *Reforming Parliamentary Committees Israel in Comparative Perspective* (Columbus, Ohio State University Press, 2001).

Hazan, Reuven and Rahat, Gideon, *Israeli Party Politics: New Approaches, New Perspectives*, A Special Issue of *Party Politics* Vol 14 (6), November 2008.

Hofnung, Menahem, *Israel – Democracy, Law and National Security* (Aldershot, Ashgate, 1996).

Hofnung, Menahem and Dor, Gal, 'Litigation as Political Participation' (2006) 11 *Israel Studies* 2.

Klein, Claude, 'The Defence of the State and the Democratic Regime in the Supreme Court' (1985) 20 *Israel Law Review* 397.

Krezmer, David, 'Judicial Review of Knesset Decisions' (1988) 8 *Tel Aviv University Studies in Law* 95.

Mersel, Yigal, 'The Dissolution of Political Parties: The Problem of Internal Democracy' (2006) 4 *International Journal of Constitutional Law* 84.

Navot, Suzie, 'Fighting Terrorism in the Political Arena – The Banning of Political Parties' (2008) 14 *Party Politics* 745.

Navot, Suzie, 'Judicial Review of the Legislative Process' (2006) 39(2) *Israel Law Review* 182.

Rahat, Gideon, 'Israel: The Politics of an Extreme Electoral System' in Michael Gallagher and Paul Mitchell (eds), *The Politics of Electoral Systems* (Oxford, Oxford University Press, 2005).

Shamgar, Meir, 'Judicial Review of Knesset Decisions by the High Court of Justice' (1994) 28 *Israel Law Review* 43.

5

The Government and the Executive

Introduction

Part I: The President of the State – Presidential Powers – *Katzav*: The Trial of an Acting President

Part II: The Government – Formation and Working – Elections and Government Formation – The Rise and Fall of the Prime-Ministerial Regime – Caretaker Government – Responsibility and Accountability – The Role of the Military – The Civil Service – Local Government – Conclusion

INTRODUCTION

THIS CHAPTER FOCUSES on the government in Israel. Although a separate branch and not part of the executive, its origins lie with the State's President, who is head of the State of Israel. Unlike in presidential regimes such as the US, the Israeli President's duties are merely representational and symbolic, having little real authority. Yet, although the Israeli President's duties are almost all ceremonial, some of his functions require consideration, as defined in Basic Law: The President of the State. Israel has even seen the indictment and prosecution of a serving President. This unique case will be discussed later in this chapter.

In relation to the executive branch, a public and political debate has been waged concerning the best model for the executive power in Israel. The parliamentary regime was introduced in Israel when the state was founded. In 1992, the election method and regime were changed. The new method, which came into effect in the 1996 elections for the 14th Knesset, was dubbed 'semi-presidential'. In this system, the Prime Minister was elected directly, but the Knesset reserved its power to terminate the Prime Minister's tenure through a vote of no confidence in the government, while the Prime Minister had the power to dissolve the Knesset.[1] This new system did not, however, enhance the government's freedom of operation as expected. As a result, the Knesset once again decided to change the system in 2001. Coming into effect for the 2003 elections for the 16th Knesset, the new system actually reverted to the original regime in which the government governs by the power of the Knesset's confidence. We will discuss the formation and work of the government, as well as the special features of a caretaker government, whose powers have been limited by the HCJ. In addition, we will explore the principles of responsibility and accountability, and the role of the military in the constitutional context. Finally, we will discuss the civil service in Israel, which serves any government in power, much like in the UK, and local governments.

PART I: THE PRESIDENT OF THE STATE

PRESIDENTIAL POWERS

The State's President is elected by a secret Knesset vote for a single, seven-year term and the role is mainly symbolic – both in public life and in the constitutional sphere. His formal involvement mainly concerns the validation of resolutions by other bodies. For example, the President endorses laws that the Knesset has introduced, signs conventions with other countries that the Knesset has ratified and reviews letters of credence presented by foreign diplomatic representatives. He also appoints judges, but does not select them.

The President has three types of discretionary function: involvement in composing a government; ratifying the Knesset dissolution and early elections as requested by the Prime Minister; and the power to pardon prisoners.

According to Basic Law: The Government, after Knesset elections are held, in order to form a government, the President consults party

---

[1] Avraham Brichta, *Political Reform in Israel: The Quest for a Stable and Effective Government* (Brighton, Sussex Academic Press, 2001); Reuven Y Hazan, 'Presidential Parliamentarism: Direct Popular Election of the Prime Minister – Israel's New Electoral and Political System' (1996) 15 *Electoral Studies* 21.

representatives and assigns the duty to form a government to an MK who agrees to assume this duty. The basic law imposes no restrictions on the President's discretion, although he must act reasonably. The President's goal is to install a government that retains the Knesset's confidence as soon as possible, which means that he needs to consider which candidate is most likely to be able to form a government most rapidly.

Basic Law: The Government also grants the President a role in a Prime Minister's decision to dissolve the Knesset, which is similar to the power granted to the President regarding the formation of a government, though his powers on this issue are narrower. Here too, the President has some discretion. He needs to examine whether a Knesset majority opposes the government to the point of obstructing its performance.

Third, the President has the power to pardon convicted felons. Section 11(6)(b) of Basic Law: The President of the State reads: 'The President of the State shall have power to pardon offenders and to lighten penalties by the reduction or commutation thereof.' This follows the power included in the 1922 King's Order-in-Council, which granted the British High Commissioner the power to pardon offenders. This power was transferred to the Provisional Government, which in turn assigned it to the President. As a result, the government has no pardoning authority. Decisions that it makes to release (mainly terrorist) prisoners as part of political agreements require the President's consent.

The basic law assigns the President certain privileges that are representative of his unique public standing. For example, the President is immune from criminal investigation while on duty and remains immune concerning issues that pertain to his term even after it ends, like the immunity assigned to MKs. This immunity prevents judicial deliberations of petitions filed directly against the President, although the President's resolutions may be subject to judicial review. Thus, a President's pardoning decision may be challenged, but such petitions are generally filed against an administrative body. For instance, such a petition might be filed against the governor of the prison authorising the release of a felon whom the President pardoned. The scope of judicial review, however, is rather restricted given the President's status and the nature of his resolutions. As Justice Cheshin pointed out: 'The President's considerations for pardoning a felon fall within the realm of mercy and compassion, and it is obvious that we may not and it would be inappropriate to apply the rules of administrative justice to these considerations . . . By nature, mercy and compassion may not be judged by ordinary judicial standards, which means that special legal rules are required when addressing pardons.'[2]

Considering the scope of the President's operative and symbolic powers, it may be concluded that the law was intended to establish an institution that would serve as a 'symbol of the state'. It creates a President who acts as a representative and apolitical figure who stands above the nation – a role model for the entire population.[3] The Supreme Court has recently addressed the President's position, saying:

> The State's President stands apart from every other authority in Israel. His deeds express the spirit of the nation, its core values, the fundamental issues its parts share, and its founding narrative. The President symbolizes the state and its moral and democratic values. He stands high above power struggles in the state, representing politically undisputed values of social morality. He stands for stateliness and the lines that unify and connect the various currents of Israeli society. His personality is supposed to reflect all that is good, fine, unique, and value-based that characterizes the Israeli public.[4]

KATZAV: THE TRIAL OF AN ACTING PRESIDENT

In July 2006, Attorney General Meni Mazuz ordered the police to commence a criminal investigation into President Moshe Katzav, who was suspected of committing sexual offences against and sexual harassment of several female employees of the presidential residence and ministries where he had served before being appointed President. Upon conclusion of the investigation, Mazuz decided to file charges of rape and other sexual offences against President Katzav, subject to the outcome of a pre-trial hearing. Subsequently, the President notified the Knesset

---

[2] See HCJ 706/94 *Ronen v Minister of Culture and Education*, ver 53(5), 389 (1994) 414, a case in which the court nullified a President's decision to pardon a felon who, as it turned out, falsified his medical condition.

[3] For comparison's sake, see a description of the US President's position: 'The President is not merely the principal executive officer of the federal government, like the prime minister in a parliamentary system of government, he is the head of the state, and it is natural to think of the head of the state as constituting a powerful example for the population.' Richard A Posner, *An Affair of State: The Investigation, Impeachment, and Trial of President Clinton* (Cambridge, MA, Harvard University Press, 1999) 153.

[4] HCJ 1002/06 *Nir Zohar v The Justice Minister* (verdict handed down on 23 December 2008).

Speaker that he was 'temporary incapacitated', which prevented him from fulfilling his duties, but he retained his status as President of the State of Israel. At the same time, the Knesset was unable to depose him by way of the statutorily-based impeachment procedure, failing to attain the 75 per cent majority of the Knesset House Committee required before an impeachment proposal can be transferred to the plenum for confirmation by a similar majority.

In May 2007, the Attorney General conducted two pre-trial hearings before making a final decision on the indictment. These hearings produced a particularly lenient plea-bargain deal between the prosecution and the President. This deal omitted the rape charges and resulted in a guilty plea on the less serious offences. Immediately after the deal was signed, petitions challenging the reasonableness of its terms were filed with the HCJ. Petitions seeking the annulment of the plea bargain were heard, but the majority of the expanded five-judge panel, headed by President Dorit Beinisch (who was in the minority), rejected them. Nevertheless, the media and leading legal pundits openly opposed the deal. Moreover, hostile public opinion was manifested with the staging of several stormy demonstrations. In essence, the feeling was that the state was being too lenient on a President who was apparently a serial sexual offender.

The saga did not end there, however. The stage was set for a trial court to approve the plea bargain – a proceeding that required the President to enter a guilty plea on the reduced charges. Instead, the President notified the Magistrate Court of his decision to withdraw from the plea bargain and cancelled the deal. It should be mentioned that the President is immune from prosecution only during his term, and Katzav resigned from office in July 2007, two weeks before his term had expired.

Subsequently, the Attorney General's office proceeded to re-examine the indictment and ordered the police to conduct supplementary investigations. In March 2009, the Attorney General notified the government of his decision to indict Katzav for rape and additional sexual offences relating to three different complainants. The trial was conducted *in camera* over the course of one year and, in December 2010, the judges of the Tel Aviv District Court unanimously found Katzav guilty as charged on all counts. The President was then handed a seven-year prison sentence and his subsequent appeal to the Supreme Court was dismissed.

For the State of Israel, the Katzav affair represented a momentous event. Clearly, the criminal conviction of an acting President is a source of great embarrassment, but the actual unfolding of the case further gave rise to an array of constitutional questions concerning the status of the Israeli President, the proceedings of the President's election and ways of supervising his activities while in office.[5] At the same time, Israeli democracy demonstrated that equality before the law is not just a fundamental principle de jure, but that the state's legal system applies the same criteria and moral standards to the head of state as to its lowliest citizen.

PART II: THE GOVERNMENT

FORMATION AND WORKING

In Israel, the government is the executive branch and is mainly comprised of MKs from factions that form the coalition. The Prime Minister who heads the government is usually the leader of the largest political party. The government has extensive powers that are not only executive but also legislative in nature. Since the government is generally established on the basis of a Knesset majority, it can easily introduce bills that serve its interests.

While the office of Prime Minister is not defined by the basic law, it is responsible for the most important decisions on domestic and foreign affairs. The government (or Cabinet, interchangeably) comprises a Prime Minister, ministers and deputy ministers. In Israel, the Prime Minister is generally viewed as 'first among equals' and has a single equal vote in Cabinet resolutions. The Prime Minister forms the Cabinet and appoints ministers at will. His extensive powers in this respect allow him to appoint anyone – even non-Knesset members – as Cabinet members and to dismiss ministers. The ministers' positions are political in nature, in the sense that they are not appointed on the basis of their professional skills or expertise.

---

[5] For more on the *Katzav* case, see Suzie Navot, 'The Former President Guilty of Sexual Crimes: Some Constitutional Thoughts Following the Katzav Affair' (2012) 16 *European Public Law* 1–15.

After election results are published and after consulting representatives of Knesset factions, the President of the State of Israel assigns the task of forming a coalition-based Cabinet to one MK, who must accept this task. The task of forming a government is not automatically assigned to the leader of the largest Knesset faction if, for example, other parties have managed to create a 'preventive bloc' against him.[6] The President needs to assign this task to the MK who he believes has the best chance of forming a Cabinet, based on his consultations with party representatives. After the chosen MK has managed to form a Cabinet, he or she must present it – its composition, portfolio distribution and main policy guidelines – to the Knesset and win a vote of confidence.

Basic Law: The Government lists several additional situations in which the President must order the initiation of a new Cabinet composition process, namely, when a Prime Minister resigns, passes away or is unable to serve in office for more than 100 consecutive days (for example, where he is suffering from a sudden illness). In such cases, a Cabinet member, who is an MK from the Prime Minister's faction, is appointed by the Cabinet to serve as acting Prime Minister until a new Cabinet is formed. The President must launch the formation of a new Cabinet in two additional situations: if the Prime Minister is found guilty of an offence that bears moral turpitude and if the Prime Minister ceases to serve as an MK for any reason.

Naturally, the procedure for forming a new government is also launched when the Knesset overthrows a presiding government in a vote of no confidence. When the direct election reform was eliminated in Israel, the Knesset established the 'constructive non-confidence' – a restriction on votes of no confidence, according to which the Knesset may vote down a Cabinet only when a Knesset majority supports an alternative one. This means that the majority of MKs must agree on the MK who would form the next Cabinet before tabling a motion of no confidence. This requires a separate vote of confidence, and the basic law states that if the MK who was so nominated by the Knesset fails to establish a Cabinet within a given period of time, the Knesset would be

---

[6] This, for example, was the case after the 2009 elections: while the largest party was *Kadima* under Tzipi Livni (with 28 Knesset seats), the task of forming a Cabinet was assigned to Benjamin Netanyahu, Chairman of the *Likud* (with 27 seats). See Mario Sznajder, 'The 2009 Elections in Israel' (2010) *IEMed*. Available at: www. iemed.org/anuari/2010/aarticles/Sznajder_elections_en.pdf.

deemed to be dissolved before completing its four-year term and general elections must be held within the next 90 days.

In addition, should the Prime Minister realise that a Knesset majority opposes his Cabinet, he may dissolve the Knesset even if that majority cannot form an alternative government. Thus, should the government fail to realise its legislative initiatives or national policies, the Prime Minister may, with the President's consent, issue a decree that dissolves the Knesset.

The basic law originally stated that the Cabinet shall comprise no fewer than eight and no more than 18 members, including the Prime Minister. Yet, in 1999, when the old election method was still in effect, and given the large number of Knesset factions, the basic law was rapidly amended and this restriction was eliminated. A petition was filed against this amendment,[7] and though the Supreme Court established that the endorsement or amendment of basic laws for ad hoc situations is undesirable, it rejected the petition and chose not to intervene. It stated: 'It is most doubtful that motivations for the enactment of basic laws – even if arguably unworthy – could in and of themselves constitute a legal flaw that justifies judicial review.'[8] Presently, there are no restrictions on the number of Cabinet members. The Cabinet formed in 2009, for example, comprised 39 ministers and deputy ministers, which meant that approximately one-third of the MKs were also members of the Cabinet. The Cabinet formed in 2012 comprised 20 ministers.

Nevertheless, the Court's intervention in the Cabinet composition issue is a rather interesting subject. For example, it was the Israeli judiciary – not the legislature – that banned individuals charged with crimes from serving as Cabinet members. The question of whether a person suspected of illegal activity may serve on a Cabinet rarely emerges in other countries and is usually a political issue. This issue first surfaced in Israel in the 1990s when the prosecution filed bribery charges against the Interior Minister. According to Basic Law: The Government, the Prime Minister 'may' depose a Cabinet member. In theory, this is a Prime Minister's prerogative and he may employ it when he sees fit, but when the Attorney General decided that Interior Minister Arie Deri (Chairman of the ultra-Orthodox *Shas* movement) should face criminal

---

[7] HCJ 5160/99 *The Movement for Government Quality in Israel v The Knesset's Constitution, Law, and Justice Committee*, ver 53(4), 92 (1999).
[8] ibid 96.

charges in court, Prime Minister Yitzhak Rabin chose not to exercise this prerogative and did not dismiss him.

A petition was filed, asking the HCJ to order the Prime Minister to dismiss the suspected minister and, in one of its more 'activist' verdicts, the Court accepted the petition. HCJ President Meir Shamgar established that, in certain circumstances, the Prime Minister must exercise his power and depose a Cabinet member. The Court stated that it was the Prime Minister's 'duty' to dismiss Minister Deri, as such a duty arises when 'the event in question . . . reflects on the Cabinet's status, public appearance, ability to rule and serve as a role model, power to instil appropriate norms of conduct, and mostly when it affects the public's trust in our regime and governance system'.[9] This approach presupposes that the government needs to act properly and be trustworthy. This precedential HCJ ruling pertains not only to the Prime Minister's prerogative to depose a Cabinet member, but also applies when a Cabinet is formed or a new member joins it.[10] The ruling in the *Deri* case still stands, and ever since it was made, whenever the Attorney General has decided to file an indictment against a minister, the minister has resigned from the Cabinet. Nonetheless, the HCJ refused to expand the ruling so that it would also apply to a minister's misconduct for which he has not faced charges. In other words, a Cabinet minister does not have to be removed from his position when a criminal investigation is conducted in relation to him, but only if and when the Attorney General decides to file charges.

Cabinet members may resign, and when they do, their resignation takes effect 48 hours after they give notice, which is the same timeframe that applies when a minister is dismissed by the Prime Minister. When a minister stops serving with the Cabinet or when he becomes temporary incapacitated, the Prime Minister takes his place or the Cabinet assigns his portfolio to another Cabinet member. Such a temporary position must not be held for more than three months.

Section 31(6) of Basic Law: The Government states: 'The Government will set work and debate procedures and decision-making processes in the

---

[9] HCJ 3094/93 *The Movement for Government Quality in Israel v Israel's Government*, ver 47(5), 422 (1993). A similar ruling was handed down in the case of a deputy minister who was charged with criminal offences (HCJ 4267/93, 4287, 4634 *Amitay, Citizens for Proper Administration and Morality v Israel's Prime Minister*, ver 47(5), 441 (1993)). Both verdicts were handed down on 8 September 1993.

[10] Amnon Rubinstein and Barak Medina, *The Constitutional Law of the State of Israel* (Jerusalem/Tel Aviv, Shoken, 2005) (Hebrew).

Cabinet, whether permanent or for a specific matter.' This provision allows the government to determine its own working methods. As a result, the Cabinet has established the rules of procedure for determining, among other things, the agenda of its sessions; the formation of ministerial committees and the transfer of issues to and from such committees; the handling of government bills, emergency situations and regulations; the organisation of trips abroad by the Prime Minister and other ministers; the appointment of an acting Prime Minister; and the regulation of confidentiality, report filing and publication. However, it is worth noting that judicial review does not apply to these resolution-making procedures, but only to the resolutions themselves. The Cabinet sometimes performs its duties through permanent or ad hoc ministerial committees. The Attorney General provides legal guidance for the government's work.

In recent years, the executive has been gaining power while the legislature has become weaker and often seems willing to condone the transfer of powers to the executive branch.[11] This appears to be a global phenomenon that does not depend on the type of constitutional system, be it republican or parliamentary. Of course, the main role of the government is to govern. Section 32 of the Basic Law: The Government provides that: 'The Government is authorized to perform, in the name of the State and subject to any law, all actions that are not legally incumbent on another authority.' This grants the government residual powers and is meant to serve as a constitutional umbrella clause for the government's daily activities that are not covered by explicit legislation. Indeed, these residual powers are widely used, for example, when dealing with the foreign affairs, arranging immigration issues, formulating criteria for recommending the release of prisoners, distributing budgets as allocated by law, signing contracts on the state's behalf and many other issues. In particular, the government relied on section 32 when it decided to allow the residents of East Jerusalem to participate in elections to the Palestinian Legislative Council by sending ballot forms from post offices.

Over the years, however, the HCJ has established restrictions and reservations that also apply to these residual powers. As President Aharon Barak put it: 'Residual powers apply within the boundaries of the Government's powers as the executive. They should be viewed as an instrument for the realization of the statement made in Basic Law: The

---

[11] Jenny S Martinez, 'Inherent Executive Power: A Comparative Perspective' (2005–06) 115 *Yale Law Journal* 2480.

Government, according to which the Government is the state's executive. These powers must not be used to determine that the Government is an organ whose powers apply to areas that lie beyond the authority of the executive.'[12] The main restriction on the government's residual powers relates to 'primary arrangements'. For example, in the *Supreme Monitoring Committee* case,[13] the HCJ was asked to decide whether the government is authorised to determine geographical 'areas of national priority'. This relates to the areas in which various economic benefits are distributed, on the basis of its residual powers. The Court quashed the Cabinet resolution in question, referring to the primary arrangements rule, according to which it is for the legislature to establish arrangements that pertain to fundamental issues in the society's life and that significantly impact the public as a whole.[14] It ruled that the legislators' duty to establish primary arrangements is based on the separation of powers principle and the authority to introduce laws is given to the legislature. It follows from the Knesset's supremacy that major decisions that pertain to the nature of the regime in principle be made by the Knesset, not by other powers. This is the Knesset's unique authority, and that authority is its duty and may not be assigned to another.[15] Furthermore, the rule of law and the democracy principles support the view that decisions on key issues must be made by the body that the public elected and whose legislative acts therefore bear legitimacy.[16]

In another verdict, addressing the limits of privatisation and quashing a law which endorsed privately operated prisons,[17] several HCJ judges were willing to acknowledge the 'hard core' of government powers that it may not deny. Although these powers remain undetermined, it would

---

[12] HCJ 8600/04 *Shimoni v The Prime Minister*, President Barak's verdict at [4] (published by Nevo on 16 January 2005).

[13] HCJ 11163/03 *The Supreme Monitoring Committee of the Arab Citizens v Israel's Prime Minister* (published by NEVO on 27 February 2006).

[14] ibid, Justice Cheshin's verdict at [32].

[15] Aharon Barak, 'The Parliament and the Supreme Court: A Look at the Future' (2000) 55 *Hapraklit* 5, 7 (Hebrew); Baruch Bracha, 'Towards Parliamentary Supervision of Secondary Legislation' (1993) 7 *Iyuney Mishpat* 390 (Hebrew).

[16] HCJ 3267/97 *Rubinstein v The Defense Minister*, ver 52(5), 481 (2000), Justice Barak's verdict at [18]–[31].

[17] HCJ 2605/05 *Academic Centre of Law and Business v Minister of Finance* (rendered 19 November 2009). See http://elyon1.court.gov.il/files_eng/05/050/026/n39/05026050.n39.htm for the English version.

seem that section 1 of Basic Law: The Government, which states that 'the Government is the executive authority' of the State of Israel, is not merely declaratory. It has been explained that: 'We tend to interpret section 1 so that the "hard core" of Government powers is anchored at the constitutional level; reference is to those duties that the executive must perform and may not transfer or delegate to private parties.'[18]

ELECTIONS AND GOVERNMENT FORMATION

Despite the fact that the government is elected for a period of four years, concomitant with the Knesset term, the prevailing public sentiment is that in recent years, Israel has gone to the polls too many times and government powers have changed hands too often. There are those who argue that these phenomena indicate a degree of chronic instability in Israel's political system that exceeds the norm in Western democracies. Certain aspects of the Israeli electoral system also contribute to this lack of stability. For this reason, there have been strong political and public debates over structural changes to Israel's parliamentary model. Debates on the preferable election method and executive model for Israel have been held since it was first established. In essence, it is a debate between political positions that accept the principles of democracy, but disagree on the appropriate shape that they should take.[19]

Israel 'inherited' the national-proportional election method from pre-state national institutions formed when the British Mandate was in effect. Economic and security hardships in the early years of the state, and the desire to hold democratic elections as soon as possible, influenced the leaders of the fledgling state to retain the existing electoral method, and initial institutions were modelled on the consociational democracy structure.[20] The proportional representation method created a situation in which numerous ideological groups were politically represented in the Knesset and thus could directly impact the exercise of governing powers by the executive branch, the legitimacy of

---

[18] ibid.
[19] Nir Kedar, 'The Struggle for Changing Israel's Election Method During the State's First Decade: A Tale of Democracy, Civil Culture, and Law' (2011) 33 *Iyuney Mishpat* 555, 557 (Hebrew).
[20] Arend Lijphart, 'Consociational Democracy' (1969) 21(2) *World Politics* 207.

governmental institutions and the extent of citizens' involvement in democratic life.[21] The combination of a parliamentary regime in which the government needs the Knesset's confidence to operate, the national-proportional election method in its pure Israeli version with a low threshold percentage and the absence of a written constitution that defines the rules of the democratic process have all led to the formation of a multi-partisan, divided and rickety political structure. The method of election profoundly impacts Israel's political culture and impairs the effectiveness of its system of governance.

The debate over the most desirable election method to adopt and the appropriate model of the executive resurfaced in full force in the 1980s. This decade witnessed the end of the era of single-party rule on the Israeli political scene. The new era was characterised by parity between the two major political blocs – Labour (left) and the *Likud* (right) with their affiliates of both blocs – which exemplified and made visible the flaws of the regime and the election method. The elections of 1984 and 1988 produced two equally-sized right and left blocs that were equally unable to form a stable coalition. Each of the blocs could form a 'preventive bloc' that stopped the other from winning a Knesset majority vote of confidence. Thus, the two large parties had only one option – to form a national unity government. This approach worked for a while, but the need to change the regime surfaced again after the breakdown of the unity government in March 1990. Believing he could form a Labour-led coalition, then Labour party Chairman Shimon Peres initiated a vote of no confidence in his own government. The motion, however, was endorsed by only 61 MKs and Labour was eventually unable to form a new coalition. Over the years, this tactic came to be known as 'the stinking trick'. This is because it took the flaws of the existing regime to a new extreme – it amounted to a form of political extortion at the public's expense based on cold opportunism and shameless 'floor crossing'. It also made the public lose faith in the political system. Popular protest movements formed, staged mass demonstrations and gained great support for their demands for political reform. Various reforms have since been suggested, but the main change that eventually

---

[21] Daphne Barak-Erez, 'Towards Democratic Rules in Israel' (2011) 33 *Iyuney Mishpat* 33, 527, 533 (Hebrew); Reuven Y Hazan and Gideon Rahat, 'Representation, Electoral Reform, and Democracy: Theoretical and Empirical Lessons from the 1996 Elections in Israel' (2000) 33 *Comparative Political Studies* 1310.

resulted was the replacement of Basic Law: The Government with a new basic law, known as the Direct Election Law.[22]

THE RISE AND FALL OF THE PRIME-MINISTERIAL REGIME

Before and after the 1992 amendment came into effect, Israel was and remained a parliamentary democracy, as reflected in the fact that the government can be established and can govern only with the confidence of the Knesset.

The new basic law (known as The Direct Election Law) established that the Prime Minister would be directly elected at the same time as the Knesset elections. The reformed law further stated that the Prime Minister must be elected by more than half the voters, and if none of the candidates achieve this majority, a second round of elections will be held with the two leading candidates from the first round.

The Direct Election Law further stated that the Knesset could depose a Prime Minister by a majority vote. Yet, should the Prime Minister realise that a Knesset majority opposes the Cabinet, the Prime Minister could dissolve the Knesset with the President's consent. The direct election reform was meant to create a de facto 'balance of terror' between the legislative and executive branches, since each could overthrow the other, but would have to disband at the same time. The new direct election method created an institutionally unique situation among democratic regimes that had never before been tried in other countries.[23] It is unique because it combined the characteristics of both a parliamentary and a presidential democracy. According to this new reform, the head of the executive would be answerable to the legislature, but, unlike in the purely parliamentary method, the parliament is not the Prime Minister's source of authority as his power comes directly from the people's vote.

This method gave rise to the use of two separate votes in elections: one for a Prime Minister and one for a party. The new direct elections reform was employed in Israel in an attempt to stabilise the government and to bolster the Prime Minister's status while attempting to prevent

---

[22] Basic Law: The Government (Amendment 7-1992).

[23] Though it was considered in Italy; see Mark Donovan, 'Semi-Presidentialism in Italy: From Taboo to Taboo', a draft paper that Donovan presented at the *Joint Panel of Specialist Groups: French Politics & Policy, Italian Policy* (on file with author).

party splits and restrict the power of scale-tipping parties. In practice, however, the reform produced the opposite result.[24] In their election campaigns, the two large parties focused mainly on promoting their prime ministerial candidates while the smaller sectarian parties addressed their specific constituencies. The direct election method allowed voters to split their votes. While voting for the prime ministerial candidate with the best chances of reaching an influential position, voters felt free to express their positions on a variety of issues and their support for specific concepts listed in the sectarian parties' platforms. As a result, the large parties further lost power, while sectarian parties – those that represented ethnic, religious or national groups – gained influence.

Subsequently, the large parties became even more dependent on the smaller ones, which were then able to exercise political leverage in exchange for their coalition membership. At the same time, the Prime Minister did not have enough political power to make tough decisions and execute policies. After two election campaigns were held using this method, and having realised that the direct election reform had failed, the Knesset endorsed the new Basic Law: The Government in 2001, removing the direct election method. The elections of 2003 marked the end of this unusual institutional concept. The parliamentary regime was restored and the direct election method was abolished. Basic Law: The Government of 2001 re-established the principle that the government governs by virtue of retaining the confidence of the Knesset.

At the same time, the legislature retained some of the arrangements that pertained to the relationship between the executive and the legislature, intending to bolster the standing of the Prime Minister and the government vis-a-vis the Knesset. For example, the constructive vote of no confidence was retained and further restrictions were imposed on moves to dissolve the Knesset, while the Prime Minister reserved his power to dissolve the Knesset by a Cabinet resolution. Nevertheless, this reversion to the previous system did not end the debates over the appropriate regime for Israel and the issue is still high on the Israeli political and public agenda.

---

[24] Ofer Kenig, Gideon Rahat and Reuven Y Hazan, 'The Political Consequences of the Introduction and the Repeal of the Direct Elections for the Prime Minister' in Asher Arian & Michal Shamir (eds) 'The Elections in Israel – 2003' (Israeli Democracy Institute, 2004); Naomi Himeyn-Raisch, 'The Return of the Direct Election?, *The Israel Democracy Institute*, available at: http://www.idi.org.il/sites/english/Pages/homepage. aspx (Hebrew).

CARETAKER GOVERNMENT

When a government is in power but does not have the Knesset's confidence – that is, when a decision to dissolve it has been made – it is known as a caretaker government. Typically this occurs after the Prime Minister resigns or is deposed. Section 30(b) of Basic Law: The Government states: 'When a new Knesset has been elected or the Government has resigned . . . the outgoing Government shall continue to carry out its functions until the new Government is in place.' This section outlines the 'governance continuity' principle whereby there may be no governance vacuum between two governments. The outgoing or caretaker government remains as the temporary executive of the state until the incoming government is formed and sworn in.

In principle, the powers of a caretaker government are not restricted in any way. Israel's Supreme Court was called upon to address the scope of powers and lawful activities of a caretaker government when, in 2000, the Cabinet decided to continue diplomatic negotiations with the PA, attempting to reach a peace accord before the elections, after the Prime Minister had resigned.[25] This decision was challenged by several petitioners, who asked the HCJ to order the Cabinet to cease its action, arguing that a caretaker government is not authorised to conduct negotiations that could lead to territorial concessions.

The Court rejected the petitions and stated that 'Israel's constitutional law does not acknowledge a unique doctrine whereby, after a Prime Minister resigns . . . the Government powers are restricted to the performance of ongoing [maintenance] operations exclusively'.[26] At the same time, the rule is that the 'reasonable scope' of the powers assigned to a caretaker government is narrower than those assigned to an ordinary government. When exercising its powers, a caretaker government must consider the fact that it no longer has the Knesset's confidence and therefore should avoid acting on central and disputed matters that might irreversibly change the existing situation, unless such actions are called for by an urgent and essential public interest. It has been explained that: 'The Prime Minister who resigned and the members of his Cabinet . . . must exercise

---

[25] HCJ 5167/00 *Weiss v The Prime Minister*, ver 55(2), 455 (2001); see also Claude Klein, 'The Powers of the Caretaker Government: Are They Really Unlimited?' (1977) 12 *Israel Law Review* 271.
[26] *Weiss*, ibid 468.

the level of restraint expected of an outgoing government. At the same time, they need to ensure stability and continuity. The restraint duty does not apply where there is a public need for government action.[27]

The majority of the HCJ bench has chosen to exercise judicial restraint and has recognised a wide range of reasonable caretaker government resolutions as legitimate, but has nonetheless established a rule whereby, in certain cases, the reasonable scope of the caretaker government's activities is narrower than the reasonable scope of activities by a Prime Minister and a Cabinet who serve in the ordinary fashion.

The power of the caretaker government to nominate civil servants has also been discussed. It was feared that nominations made by a caretaker government might be flawed due to conflicts of interest or improper considerations, and it could amount to an attempt to arrange certain important matters before the outgoing Cabinet's term ends. Discussing the *Weiss* case, President Barak addressed nominations made by a caretaker government: 'As a rule, it would be inappropriate for members of an outgoing Cabinet, the Prime Minister included, to fill high-ranking positions with their nominations, which should be left for the Prime Minister-elect and his Cabinet, except when under the circumstances of the specific case, it is essential that the position be manned without waiting for the Prime Minister elect to start working.'[28] One of the parameters that judges employ when ruling on the reasonableness of a government nomination is the degree to which it is reversible. If the decision is irreversible and might have long-term implications, the Court has tended to impose the duty of restraint on the Cabinet. In this spirit, the Court ruled in 2000 that the nomination of Israel's chief rabbis should be postponed until after the Knesset elections had been held and a new Cabinet formed.

The government and its ministers are political entities who assume their position after they win the public's confidence in a Knesset election. The Cabinet members, including those who are not MKs, are subject to the restrictions that follow from the MKs Immunity Law, including the ban on having additional occupations. Rules for preventing conflicts of interest by Cabinet members exist, but the Cabinet does not have a special ethical code as such. A public committee did draft such a code for the

---

[27] *Weiss,* ibid, President Barak's verdict at [9]. See also Instruction 1.1501 by the Attorney General regarding nominations during an election period.

[28] ibid, President Barak's verdict at [10].

Cabinet and ministers, but no Cabinet has endorsed it thus far. Nevertheless, the Attorney General, who serves as the Cabinet's authorised interpreter of the law and draws the legal boundaries of government activities, issued restrictions that apply to ministers' activities. These are particularly relevant when making decisions that might be affected by a conflict of interests or that reflect personal interests. According to section 3 of the Rules for the Prevention of Conflicts of Interests, which apply to ministers and deputy ministers, as drafted in 2003, 'when performing their duty, Cabinet members shall act without bias, maintain an honest approach to everyone, and shall not entertain personal interests, not even for appearances sake, in their decisions and activities. Thus, a minister who has a personal interest in a certain issue is required to avoid addressing it'.[29]

RESPONSIBILITY AND ACCOUNTABILITY

The principle of collective responsibility is a fundamental rule of government activity. Basic Law: The Government provides that: 'The Government is collectively accountable to the Knesset.' This collective accountability or responsibility is not viewed as a liability (that is, a legal responsibility), but as a public responsibility whose scope depends on the prevailing political culture, which is why it may not be legally enforced.

Collective responsibility is binding in principle, obliging Cabinet members not to dispute a Cabinet resolution and to support the government's position when addressing the Knesset plenum or committees. Nevertheless, since Israel is a parliamentary regime and the Cabinet includes members of different parties with different political views, ministers do not refrain from criticising the government. The collective responsibility principle means that once the Cabinet has decided to follow a certain course of action, all Cabinet members share that decision and are bound by it. Ministers who disagree with a certain Cabinet policy do not commonly resign in Israel, although there have been cases of ministers who have resigned over controversial political issues. As noted above, the Prime Minister may dismiss a Cabinet member and he is broadly empowered by law to do so.

---

[29] A Ministerial Conflict of Interests: A Matter of a Personal Relative – from the Attorney General's Instructions to the Cabinet (Instruction 21.470, dated 1 August 1980).

One of the most interesting examples of the Prime Minister exercising the authority to dismiss ministers who oppose government policies took place when the Israeli government decided to evacuate Jews who had settled in the Gaza Strip. In August 2005, the Cabinet decided to execute what was known as the 'disengagement plan'. The plan was devised by then Prime Minister Ariel Sharon, head of the *Likud* party, in early 2004. Believing that the *Likud* represented their interests in such matters, the political right was shocked and felt betrayed by this move. This was the first time that the State of Israel evacuated Jewish settlements built on territories that Israel occupied in 1967. While Israel did cede the Sinai as part of a peace accord with Egypt, it never forcefully evacuated settlements in Judea and Samaria (the West Bank) or the Gaza Strip. The disengagement plan deviated sharply from the *Likud* party platform that had won it the elections and the seat of the Prime Minister. Sharon needed his Cabinet to approve the plan before presenting it to the Knesset. As soon as he learned that two right-wing ministers were planning to vote against it in the Cabinet session, he decided to dismiss them from their posts, which was his prerogative according to section 22(b) of Basic Law: The Government.[30] An appeal was filed with the HCJ, arguing that the Prime Minister's action was illegal.[31]

The Court rejected the petitions unanimously. Nonetheless, although it approved the Prime Minister's right to act, the judgment criticised his actions and introduced restrictions on the scope of his discretion. President Barak stated: 'A Prime Minister has the authority to depose a Cabinet member only if he is convinced that the move would improve the Prime Minister's ability to perform properly.' He added: 'The Cabinet and the ministers are not beneath the Prime Minister. The state's executive is the entire Cabinet, not the Prime Minister alone, and once a minister has been nominated, he must not be deposed over trivialities.'[32] Furthermore, the court allowed the Prime Minister to take into account 'political' considerations, such as the need to sustain the coalition and guarantee the Knesset's confidence in the government, when deciding to dismiss a minister. Thus, the Prime Minister has a wide framework of discretion, and as long as the decisions he makes remain within these

---

[30] 'The Prime Minister may, by way of written notification, remove a Minister from his post.'

[31] HCJ 5261/04 *Fuchs v The Prime Minister* (published by Nevo on 26 October 2004).

[32] ibid, President Barak's verdict at [15].

boundaries, the Court would not intervene. At the same time, President Barak maintained that a minister should not be dismissed without solid factual infrastructure or relevant reasoning. Ruling on the case before him, however, he established that Sharon's decision was lawful and his considerations were relevant, meaning that political considerations are within the appropriate boundaries of discretion of the Prime Minister.

Justice Cheshin, however, took a different view. According to him, the Prime Minister's powers are 'so extensive . . . that it seems like a black hole that swallows almost every consideration'. He considered that it would be almost impossible to find a case in which the HCJ could intervene in relation to the firing of a Cabinet member.

At the parliamentary level, ministers and deputy ministers may not hold a Knesset position or table private bills. This arrangement reflects the view that Cabinet members are, at least publicly, held responsible for all of the government's activities and thus may not occupy posts that involve the supervision of government activities. Moreover, although they are MKs, they may not act contrary to any government policy in the Knesset.[33] The collective responsibility principle further assumes that the Cabinet makes resolutions after the ministers have discussed the relevant issues. In practice, however, Israeli Cabinets have a long-held tradition in which central decisions are made by small groups of ministers (dubbed 'the kitchenette' or 'the security Cabinet'), but these resolutions too are viewed as if they were endorsed by the entire Cabinet and are subject to the collective responsibility principle.

While all ministers are collectively responsible for Cabinet resolutions, each minister bears ministerial responsibility for the office (ministry) in relation to which he is in charge. Section 4 of Basic Law: The Government states: 'Each minister is responsible to the Prime Minister for the field of responsibility with which that minister has been charged.' This describes the ministers' key public responsibility, which is not a 'legal' responsibility, which means that it is for the public rather than for the courts to judge them.

Ministers are held responsible on two levels: they bear personal ministerial responsibility for deeds or misdeeds committed personally; and comprehensive ministerial responsibility for everything that happens within the ministry in relation to which the minister is in charge, even if the minister's personal conduct was flawless. The distinction between

---

[33] Rubinstein and Medina (n 10).

the two is the same as the distinction between accountability and responsibility. Many countries have adopted a custom whereby a minister who bears ministerial responsibility for grave misdeeds must resign. However, although resignation is the most extreme act of accepting this responsibility, no country that adopted the principle (mainly Britain and countries that were inspired by it) has included a formal legal sanction for failing to assume ministerial responsibility.

Over the years, very few Israeli ministers have resigned due to their ministries' failures or misdeeds. The scope of ministerial responsibility – both personal and comprehensive – has been mainly addressed by national commissions of inquiry that have examined this issue. Thus, when various commissions of inquiry recommended that certain Cabinet members resign due to their ministerial responsibility, the Cabinet adopted these recommendations. It is important here to note that such resignations only followed from the recommendations of inquiry commissions. Alternatively, ministers must resign (and if they do not, it is the Prime Minister's duty to dismiss them) when they face criminal charges, but this is a separate matter to ministerial responsibility.

In Israel, national commissions of inquiry have helped to shape the norm of ministerial responsibility and its consequences, as will be discussed later in chapter six. When referring to the ministers' personal responsibility, the custom is that the decisions and recommendations of commissions of inquiry regarding ministerial responsibility compel the government. Consequently, ministers have been forced to resign after commissions of inquiry have filed their reports.

Yet, in one of several reports that were issued in 2012, in the wake of a hugely mismanaged forest fire that resulted in 44 fatalities, the State Comptroller wrote that it has become customary for Israelis to 'find refuge in the bosom of' their ministerial responsibility. He stated that officials tend to hide behind a curtain of downsized, abstract and undetermined responsibility, the sole practical purpose of which is to help ministers shake off their personal responsibility for deeds or misdeeds in areas covered by their portfolios.[34] In his report, the State Comptroller coined a new term – 'special responsibility' – which lies between ministerial and personal responsibility and refers to a situation in which the minister has not done enough to prevent the failure from occurring.

[34] *The State Comptroller's Report on the Mount Carmel Fire* (issued 20 June 2012).

Though the Comptroller's report made rather harsh assertions, no minister resigned and the Prime Minister deposed no Cabinet members in
its wake.[35]

Ministers may exercise governance powers that are legally assigned to
other bodies by assuming those powers. Section 34 of Basic Law: The
Government states that: 'A minister charged with the implementation
of the law may assume any power, with the exception of powers of a
judicial nature, granted by law to civil servants.' Such powers may be
assumed when, for example, the minister and the civil servant in charge
have a difference of opinion on the desired approach or modus operandi in relation to a publicly disputed issue, and when the minister
believes he should personally take charge of the situation. For example,
in 1996, the Transportation Minister decided to enter into an area in
which the ministry's transportation supervisor had control and, intervening in a state-religion issue, ordered that Bar-Ilan Street in Jerusalem
be closed to traffic during holiday prayers.[36] The street, a major traffic
artery in Jerusalem, runs next to an ultra-Orthodox neighbourhood and
has often turned into a focal point of clashes between the ultra-
Orthodox followers and secular residents.

As for the accountability principle, it should be noted that Israeli
law has changed dramatically following the enactment in 1998 of the
Freedom of Information Law. This law was meant to revolutionise the
prevailing situation when it stated that every citizen has the right to
receive information from the government, a statement that both established a right in a law and would lead to the establishment of deadlines
and the appointment of freedom of information officers with the various authorities. The key innovation introduced by the Freedom of
Information Law was the confirmation that citizens have extensive rights
to receive publicly relevant information from public authorities, regardless of the reason why they request that information. The problem is that
the authorities have neither reasons to like nor incentives to follow this

---

[35] That situation prompted a recent petition to the HCJ demanding that the
responsible ministers be deposed.
[36] A petition with the HCJ was filed against this decision. Ruling in HCJ 5016/96
Horev v The Transportation Minister, ver 51(4), 1 (1996), Justice Barak wrote that 'in
Israel's public discourse, Bar-Ilan Street is not merely a road, but a social concept
reflecting a deep political dispute between secular and ultra-Orthodox citizens. That
dispute is not about the freedom of traffic on that street on Jewish holidays, but
mainly a serious dispute about the state-religion relations in Israel.' The HCJ eventually nullified the minister's decision.

law. In many respects, the authorities' interests directly conflict with the interests that the law serves. The authorities are not necessarily interested in being supervised in this manner, and though citizens have the right to receive such information, the law lists many reasons on which the authorities may rely in order not to divulge it. For example, the law states that a public authority is not obliged to provide information if 'its discovery might disrupt the proper functions of that authority or its ability to perform its duties' and may withhold 'information concerning in-house discussions and the minutes of inner consultations between the employees, members, or advisors of public authorities'. In addition, the law bans the distribution of information if it pertains to the privacy of individuals or if it might harm the state's security. On top of these restrictions, certain bodies have been explicitly placed beyond the scope of this law. This aspect of the law is the prerogative of ministers, who may issue secondary legislation in relation to this matter. Thus, for example, the law does not apply to certain security services and specific Israel police units.

Experience accumulated thus far indicates that Israeli government ministries have not yet internalised the transparency principle. The law is only partially implemented, and government offices have not done enough to advise the public of its ability to request and receive information from them. On its part, the public has not yet shown sufficient interest in the law and the possibilities it offers. At the same time, when courts are asked to decide on the disclosure of public information, they still tend to greatly respect and prioritise the authorities' considerations and freedom of action.[37]

It should be noted that the Israeli government has recently taken another step toward transparency when it joined the international Open Government Partnership initiative. Following this move, the government issued a statement on a precedential resolution it made on 4 January 2012, which stated that: 'Information that the government possesses is a public resource, and thus it will take steps to maximize public access to it and options to process and even improve it, and will make personal government services and information accessible so as to increase public control of the government performance.'[38]

---

[37] Yoram Rubin and Roi Peled, 'Seven Years of the Freedom of Information Law' (2005) 20 *Hamishpat* 89, 94 (Hebrew).

[38] A statement by the Cabinet Secretary at the close of a government session dated 4 January 2012. See also 'Open Government Partnership – Israel's Action Plan for 2012', available at:. http://www.idi.org.il/media/293904/action_plan.pdf

THE ROLE OF THE MILITARY

Israel is a civil society, but it is also a society in which the army plays a crucial role in everyday life. Since the establishment of the State of Israel, and particularly in view of the ongoing state of emergency, the IDF has been a key player in Israeli society. All Israeli citizens aged 18, both men and women, must serve in the army (although there is a broad exemption for religious *yeshiva* students, religious women and Arab citizens), meaning that the army serves as an important melting pot for Israel's multicultural society. The IDF's centrality in Israeli life dictated the need to clearly define its powers and, in particular, its subordination to the government and the law.

Like all other security branches, the army is subject to government supervision. The government is responsible for national security, and the subordination of the various security departments to governmental authority is a core principle of the Israeli democratic regime. This principle is explicitly stated in Basic Law: The Army: 'The army is subject to the authority of the government.' This law also states that the chief of the general staff (known as the Chief of Staff), who serves as the supreme commander in the army, is 'subject to the authority of the government and subordinate to the minister of defence'. This means that in the event of a conflict between orders given by the government and orders or guidelines given by the Defense Minister, the army must follow the government. The HCJ has ruled that government decisions bind the chief of staff even if they conflict with the Defense Minister's position.[39]

The scope of the government's power to give orders to the Chief of Staff and the army as a whole is unclear. Obviously, the Defense Minister is authorised to prescribe guidelines for the army concerning its general policies and fundamental goals or strategy. The question is whether this authority also extends to the means of achieving those goals or tactics. In practice, these questions actually do not arise in Israel because ministers of defense are quite frequently retired military men and even former chiefs of staff. Thus, in reality, the Defense Minister is actually a 'supra-chief of staff'.[40]

---

[39] HCJ 390/79 *Duikat v The Government of Israel*, 34 (1) PD 1 (1979), 10.
[40] Yehuda Ben-Meir, *Civil-Military Relations in Israel* (New York, Columbia University Press, 1995).

The Defense Minister also bears ministerial responsibility for the army's actions. This responsibility is expressed mainly in the determination of strategic goals and policies, but is rather limited when it comes to making operative decisions in battle. The distinction between the responsibility of the military authorities and civil powers has been examined by several commissions of enquiry, the most important of which were the Agranat Commission, which was established to examine the responsibility of the government in the aftermath of the army's failures in the 1973 *Yom Kippur* War, and the Kahan Commission, which dealt with the massacre in the Sabra and Shatila refugee camps in Lebanon.[41]

Although the activities of the armed services are regulated by law, there is no clear statutory definition of the army's powers. For example, there is no list of duties that the government may impose on the army or specific guidance as to the extent to which the army may be employed to serve goals that are not directly related to the protection of state security.

According to the Law and Administration Ordinance (amended in 1995), the government may use the army for the attainment of its national security goals. In this context, one of the most interesting constitutional questions raised during the Israeli withdrawal (disengagement) from the Gaza Strip in 2005 was whether the military was permitted to take part in the implementation of the disengagement plan within the borders of Israel. Since the evacuees were Israeli citizens, it was unclear whether the use of the army to evacuate them was legal. The move was legally based on the Evacuation-Compensation Law, which prescribed the guidelines for the evacuees' compensation. The disengagement opponents concurrently waged a legal battle. They petitioned the HCJ against almost every government decision dealing with the disengagement in a seemingly desperate attempt to forestall what they regarded as the 'evil decree'. The HCJ thus became an active partner every step of the way. Following the government's decision to use the army in the disengagement plan, a petition was filed with the HCJ, arguing that law enforcement actions performed within the state boundaries are the exclusive responsibility of the Israel police and that unleashing the IDF against civilians for the preservation of public order contradicted the very essence of the army.[42]

---

[41] We shall discuss these commissions of enquiry in ch 6.

[42] HCJ 7455/05 *The Legal Forum for the Land of Israel v The Government of Israel* (handed down on 22 August 2005).

Answering the petition, President Barak emphasised that, like any other administrative authority, the IDF acts according to the principle of legality, and all of its actions must be anchored in the law, primarily Basic Law: The Army. Under the Law and Administration Ordinance (amended in 1995), the IDF is allowed to take all measures required for the protection of national security goals. The implementation of the disengagement plan required keeping public order and preventing illegal entry into the Gaza Strip. In the circumstances, these tasks exceeded the capacity of the police and there was therefore an urgent need to use the army for the realisation of these goals. Therefore, the use of the army in that event was well within the scope of actions that the army was permitted to perform. The petition was rejected.

THE CIVIL SERVICE

Public service in Israel is considered professional, neutral and non-political. State employees are appointed on the basis of their merits and skills, and must implement the current government policies regardless of their personal political opinions. This view is reflected in the Civil Service (Appointments) Law (1959), which states that civil servants must be recruited through public tenders for specific functions as approved by the Civil Service Commission. Candidates must pass an examination, after which a professional and objective committee selects the most qualified personnel. Thus, the civil service in Israel serves whichever government is in power – much like the UK civil service, but unlike the so-called 'spoils system' in the US.

Yet, the fact that professional and non-political civil servants are appointed on merit does not mean that the government has no influence on the appointment process of civil servants. To some extent, we may say that Israel has developed a 'mixed system' in which the majority of public offices are staffed by public tender and with civil servants that receive tenure, but certain positions are exempt from tender and are filled at the will of the political leadership.[43] For example, general directors of government ministries, ministers' assistants, advisers and other positions of trust may be appointed at will by ministers and by other senior public officials. For other special positions, also exempt from

[43] Shmuel Hollander, 'Basic Principles and Rules of Public Service' (The Civil Service Commission, 2008) 25 (Hebrew).

public tender, candidates are requested to appear before a committee, presided over by a former Supreme Court judge, which interviews them and then recommends the most suitable candidate to the minister or the government. The committee's recommendations are not binding, but the government usually appoints nominees recommended by it.

The civil service in Israel is managed by the Civil Service Commission and is headed by the commissioner appointed by the government. The Commission is appointed to implement the government's policies in the fields of management and human resources. It is responsible for the approval of the organisational structure, the distribution of responsibilities between government units, the approval of permanent positions in ministries, the appointment of employees, qualifying and training employees, and so on.

The Commission's powers have been determined by various laws relating to civil servants' codes of conduct and discipline, in particular the Civil Service Regulations. The commissioner has broad responsibility not only for the recruitment process, but also for the discipline of civil servants.

A proper working relationship between the public service and the government is a key factor for effective governance. Government members have often claimed that the rule of bureaucrats and legal advisers makes it impossible for them to implement policies. This issue has often featured on the public agenda in the context of social protests concerning the high cost of living, and even more so in the context of bureaucratic barriers that impact the state's social welfare policy. Pundits and politicians wondered whether the civil service should blindly follow government policies or, rather, should defend the public's interests. The civil service's challenge seems to lie in finding the delicate balance between policies as determined by the political leadership and the way in which they are applied in practice, which should make for effective governance.

The Israeli civil service is overburdened with bureaucracy, which makes it inefficient and thus fails to fully perform its duties and meet citizens' needs. Bureaucracy impacts the hiring process too. For example, it takes an average of nine months to hire a civil service employee: five months to select a candidate through a public tender process and another four months before the person actually starts work.[44] There is a

---

[44] From the conclusions and recommendations of the Committee for the Civil Service Reform (2013).

need for managerial reform, as is evident from the fact that ministers tend to increasingly hire their own special and political advisers.

A reform plan for the civil service has recently been approved by the government following a committee report drafted by the Civil Service commissioner. According to this plan, which is based on what has elsewhere been termed 'New Public Management', civil servants would not be given tenure or rises in salary automatically due to seniority, as is the current situation. These benefits will instead result from performance reports, and tenure will be granted only after a minimum of five years, instead of the current two. The committee asserted that these reforms will not only influence the quality of the public service, but could also boost Israel's productivity, while making the public sector more efficient and service-oriented.

LOCAL GOVERNMENT

The Israeli government system is highly centralised. Although there are more than 200 local authorities in Israel, political power rests mainly in the hands of the central government. This is not just a byproduct of the state's small geophysical dimensions, but also of the circumstances of its establishment and of the military and social challenges that confronted the state immediately upon its establishment, which required a strong central government.

The structure of local government in Israel follows the concepts established in Palestine under the British Mandate. This framework was based on a number of local governing units that were consolidated through legal formulations such as the Municipalities Ordinance of 1934 and the Local Councils Ordinance of 1940. When the state was established, the leaders of Israel decided to preserve the existing structure of local government. The fact that the population of Palestine comprised a variety of ethnic groups, religions and nationalities intensified the urgency of preserving these structures. Furthermore, the various villages, cooperative settlements and *Kibbutzim* also reflected a broad spectrum of political-ideological positions, and constituted self-contained and homogeneous political units.[45] In fact, the local authorities were the

---

[45] David Newman, 'Creating Homogenous Space: The Evolution of Israel's Regional Councils' in Selwyn Iban Troen and Noah Lucas (eds), *Israel: The First Decade of Independence* (Albany, NY, SUNY Press, 1995) 495–96.

natural outgrowth of political communities that preceded the establishment of the state.

Upon the establishment of the State of Israel, local government was
regarded as the executive arm of the central government that required
local branches for the efficient provision of services to the state's residents. Local authorities were viewed as mere branches or extensions of
the central government, formed exclusively for administrative conveni-
ence and efficiency, were not autonomous or sovereign in their domains
and had no power to perform any action other than those matters specifically and explicitly delegated to them by the central government.[46]

In Israel today there are more than 260 local authorities, ranging from
the large cities whose populations exceed 200,000 to small settlements
of fewer than 2,000 people. There are two categories of local authorities: municipal and rural. The municipalities are each governed by a
mayor and a council, both elected directly by the residents. The council
is the municipal legislature while the mayor is the executive branch. The
Centre for Local Government in Israel is a body that consolidates and
unifies all of the local authorities and deals with the representation of
the local authorities in their contact with state bodies such as the Knesset
and the government.

Local governments' responsibilities pertain to everyday life and include
the infrastructure of the cities, local roads, planning and building within
the cities, sanitary services and water, as well as social infrastructure,
meaning social services such as education, culture and sport. But the powers of local governments in these areas are not without their limits. For
example, although local government is responsible for the education system, this power is subordinate to the Ministry of Education in relation to
the number of students in classrooms, teachers and the curriculum. Local
government has no powers concerning internal security and public order,
and has only limited powers in planning matters relating to land.

Under the law, central government is vested with powers of supervision over local government, and the Ministry of Interior is empowered to cancel any decision made by a local authority, and may even
arrogate its powers and act in its place. A local authority is a 'contractor'
or an 'agent' of the central government and is absolutely subordinated

---

[46] Ishay Rozen-Zvi, 'The Place of Justice: The Law of Local Government and
Social Injustice' (2004) 28(2) *Y'unei Mishpat* 417 (Hebrew). See also Ishay Rozen-Zvi,
'Taking Space Seriously: Law Space and Society' (2004) *Contemporary Israel* 23–27.

to the authority of the Ministry of Interior, who has exclusive powers to establish or abolish a local authority, unify several local authorities into one, annex their territories and redefine their boundaries. The Ministry of Interior also approves the local authorities' budgets and loans they take, and may even rule on the rates of municipal taxes and the level of deductions and exemptions. Local governments have particularly limited discretion in relation to such matters.

The principle of legality further requires that the local government act only within the framework of powers explicitly conferred by law, and any action that has not been explicitly authorised is null and void by power of the ultra vires doctrine. This doctrine was applied for the first time in the 1951 case of *Chet v Haifa*.[47] In this case, the HCJ stated: 'A municipality is a body created by law, having no existence other than by force of law. The scope of its powers is defined by law and any matter outside its legal boundaries is null and void [ultra vires]. When considering whether a particular matter exceeds the council's power of not, the criteria is whether it is permitted at all. In other words, it is not enough to state that a certain matter is not forbidden; it must be actually permitted to be valid in the eyes of the law. The law does not leave a vacuum to be filled at will.'[48]

Since the establishment of the State of Israel, the Supreme Court has annulled decisions by local authorities that were made without explicit legislative authority. For example, in *ShZM v Jerusalem Municipality*,[49] the latter refused to grant the petitioners a licence to open a sex shop, citing the 'wishes of the local residents'. The municipality claimed that Jerusalem is a unique city, characterised by a variety of population groups and high cultural tensions. It argued that this kind of business would gravely offend the lifestyles of the religious Muslims, the Christians and the religious Jews, an offence which they were incapable of sustaining without severe harm to their own well-being and the public peace in general. The Court ruled that the municipality's decision was unlawful because there was no explicit provision in the laws of businesses registration empowering it to deny a licence on such grounds. In its verdict, it emphasised that though it sympathised with the commendable and desirable motivations of the Jerusalem Municipal Council, the

---

[47] HCJ 36/51 *Chet v Haifa Municipality*, 5 PD 1553 (1951).
[48] ibid 1557.
[49] HCJ 230/73 *ShZM v Jerusalem Municipality*, 28(2) PD 113 (1950).

municipality (or any other local authority for that matter) is not the institution charged by the legislature as the custodian of public feelings.

Although the central government has broad supervisory powers over local governments, the overall degree of government supervision of local authorities is, in fact, negligible. Paradoxically, it is the formal legal structure that confers the central government with numerous supervisory powers, which is one of the factors responsible for the absence of actual supervision. Many government ministries have powers in this realm, and their lack of coordination frequently enables local governments to exceed the formal boundaries of their power and to prevent the central government from exercising effective supervision over the local authorities.[50] It has been stated that, at least in certain areas, Israel has been experiencing a steadily increasing 'de facto decentralisation' of powers since the 1980s. This decentralisation can be seen in the expanding powers of local planning and construction authorities, in the transition to independent financing of the local authorities and in shrinking government participation in the activities of local authorities.[51] Since the 1980s, the budgetary structure of local authorities has been revolutionised, budgets have risen considerably and there has been a parallel dramatic decrease in government participation. These changes have increased the independence of a number of the authorities that have become less dependent upon government participation in their budgets.

A reform in the structure and powers of local governments has been the subject of discussion by the government for several years now, but the plan is still incomplete. The evolution of local government in response to the population's modern needs will almost certainly lead to the re-allocation of centralised powers to a more local level in Israel, following the example of countries such as the UK, Italy and Spain.

CONCLUSION

Basic Law: The Government states that the government consists of the Prime Minister and other ministers. This minimal description does not

---

[50] Rozen-Zvi (n 47).

[51] Between 1980 and 1993, governmental participation in the activities of local authorities decreased by 25 per cent in real terms. See Yishai Blank, 'The Place of Local Government: The Law of Local Government, Decentralization, and Inequality in the Expanses of Israel' (2004) 34 *Mishpatim* 197 at 229 (Hebrew).

adequately reflect Israel's political reality. Despite the common perception that, formally, the Prime Minister is first among equals, in practice the office holder exercises enormous power. Once appointed by the President to form a government, a Prime Minister not only has the authority to appoint ministers and dismiss them, but he is also held responsible for domestic policy, national security and foreign affairs. A Prime Minister also has the potential choice of dissolving the Knesset. Although the basic law grants powers to the government, in practice these are carried out by the Prime Minister. Government decisions are often taken by the Cabinet. The decision to form a Cabinet and the ministers that comprise it fall within the ambit of the Prime Minister's discretion. In an attempt to relieve the Prime Minister's office from political constraints and to strengthen its power, mainly vis-a-vis scale-tipping parties, a reform to the Israeli parliamentary system was introduced in the 1990s. However, this reform was revoked in 2001. As a consequence, the Prime Minister's office has unrivalled status and remains very powerful.

It will also be apparent from this discussion that political power lies mainly in the hands of central government, despite a layer of elected local government. Furthermore, central government is responsible for national security and the army. All other security departments are placed under central governmental authority. Parliamentary oversight exists, but it is rather limited, as are other constitutional safeguards. In later chapters we will see that the Supreme Court has adopted a restrained approach towards the government's political decisions, despite the fact that such decisions are routinely contested before the Court. Finally, the civil service is mainly professional and non-political, although the government has influence over the appointment to many of its positions. In other respects, there have been attempts to reform and modernise what has been perceived to be a highly bureaucratic civil service with a view to introducing the disciplines associated with New Public Management. However, this task is yet to be completed.

FURTHER READING

Arian, Asher and Shamir, Michal, 'Two Reversals: Why 1992 Was Not 1977' in Asher Arian and Michal Shamir (eds), *The Elections in Israel 1992* (New York, University of New York Press, 1995).

Bracha, Baruch, 'The Constitutional Position, the Pardoning Power and other Powers of the President of the State of Israel' (1979) 9 *Israel Yearbook of Human Rights* 190.

Brichta, Abraham, *Political Reform in Israel: The Quest for Stable and Effective Government* (Brighton, Sussex Academic Press, 2001).

Diskin, Abraham, 'The Politics of Electoral Reform in Israel' (1995) 16(1) *International Political Science Review* 31.

Doron, Gideon, Naor, Arye and Meydani, Assaf (eds), *Law and Government in Israel* (New York, Routledge, 2010).

Doron, Gideon and Harris, Michael (eds), *Public Policy and Electoral Reform: The Case of Israel* (Maryland, Lexington Books, 2000).

Galnoor, Itzhak, *Public Management in Israel: Development, Structure, Functions, and Reforms* (New York, Routledge, 2011).

Hazan, Reuven, 'Presidential Parliamentarism: Direct Popular Election of the Prime Minister – Israel's New Election and Political System' (1996) 15 *Electoral Studies* 21.

Klein, Claude, 'Direct Election of the Prime Minister in Israel: The Basic Law in its First Year' (1997) 3 *European Public Law* 301.

Mahler, Gregory S, *Politics and Government in Israel: The Maturation of a Modern State* (Plymouth, Rowman & Littlefield, 2011).

Rahat, Gideon, 'The Politics of Electoral Reform Abolition: The Informed Process of Israel's Return to its Previous System' (2006) 54(1) *Political Studies* 43.

Razin, Eran, 'Needs and Impediments for Local Government Reform: Lessons from Israel' (2004) 26(5) *Journal of Urban Affairs* 623.

Vigoda, Eran, 'From Responsiveness to Collaboration: Governance, Citizens, and the Next Generation of Public Administration' (2002) 62 *Public Administration Review* 527

Weill, Rivka, 'Constitutional Transition: The Role of Lameducks and Caretakers' (2011) *Utah Law Review* 1087.

6

Watchdog Agencies

———●◆●———

Introduction – The Attorney General – The State Comptroller and Ombudsman – Commissions of Inquiry – The Media – NGOs – Conclusion

INTRODUCTION

THIS CHAPTER DEALS with the contribution of Israeli 'watchdogs' in a constitutional context. It begins with discussion of the Attorney General, who occupies a unique position in Israeli law, particularly vis-a-vis the government and the public. Basic laws offer no clear definitions of the role of the Attorney General and, following historical developments, this position has evolved into one of the main guardians of the rule of law. Later on, we will discuss the role of the State Comptroller and commissions of inquiry. Particular attention is devoted to the role of the media in Israel, which enjoys a large degree of freedom despite the existing legal restrictions, in particular those related to national security. This chapter concludes by describing the importance of the activities of NGOs, as they wield significant political and legal power in Israel. As we shall see, the Israeli courts have played a central role in the development of NGO activities, and NGOs are responsible for many of the petitions brought before the HCJ, mainly in cases dealing with human rights.

THE ATTORNEY GENERAL

Yitzhak Zamir, former Attorney General and Justice of the Supreme Court, once said that, when defending the rule of law and proper governing practices in Israel, the HCJ serves as the second line of defence while the advanced post – the first and main line of defence – is the Attorney General.[1] It is one of the most important government bodies and one of the most powerful public posts, yet it is not mentioned in any constitutional text. Surprisingly, no basic law applies to the office of the Attorney General and its broad powers are not prescribed in a single statute.[2]

The Attorney General (in Hebrew, the government's legal adviser) is Israel's chief prosecutor and has the power to file criminal charges, represents the state in judicial cases, serves as legal adviser to government authorities and is viewed as the authorised interpreter of the law for the government and whose legal opinions are binding. According to the HCJ rulings, the Attorney General's legal opinion is binding and the government cannot act contrary to it, otherwise the Attorney General would not appear in court on behalf of the government and could not protect government decisions in court when an appeal against such decisions is filed. Furthermore, the Attorney General protects public interests and may step in as a party to pending court cases in order to do so if he believes the public interest requires it. This multitude of key powers renders the office of the Attorney General's of central importance to the government as well as to the public, and very powerful. Consequently, calls have been made over the years to split up the Attorney General's roles and to redistribute his powers, which today are held by a single individual.[3]

The majority of the world's democratic states (some two-thirds) distinguish between the institution of 'the government's legal adviser' and

---

[1] Yitzhak Zamir, 'The Attorney General at Times of Crisis: The *Shin Bet* Affair', in Aharon Barak and Tina Shapnitz (eds), *The Uri Yadin Book* (Bnei Brak, Bursi, 2000) (Hebrew); Dina Zilber, *In the Name of Law* (Or-Yehuda, Kinneret Zmora-Bitan Dvir, 2012) (Hebrew).

[2] In fact, the Attorney General's powers are listed in some 140 different laws; see Gad Barzilai and David Nahmias, *The Attorney General: Powers and Responsibility – The Attorney General and Prosecutor General (State Attorney) Institutions: Principles, Comparative Analysis, Critique, and Reform Recommendations*, (The Israel Democracy Institute, 1997) (Hebrew).

[3] Between 1999 and 2007, nine bills were filed that referred to the AG. Some suggested that the role be split into chief prosecutor and government's legal adviser, while others suggested that the AG's election be anchored in a law following the recommendations of the Shamgar Committee. None of those suggestions materialized.

the state prosecutor.[4] Thus, in Israel, the general criminal prosecution is a separate and independent authority while the legal adviser is generally a unit of the justice ministry that acts as the government's consultant on legal matters and represents the state on civil matters. The fact that the Israeli Attorney General holds so many diverse powers is due to historical developments and the strong personalities of AGs over time.

Originally, Israel's new regime followed the model of the British Mandate government, in which the Attorney General (or chief prosecutor) was a Cabinet member. Accordingly, the position of Attorney General was a political position in which the Attorney General served as both head of the criminal prosecution department and as the government's legal adviser, representing the Crown in civil suits too. David Ben-Gurion, Israel's first Prime Minister and Defense Minister, wanted the position to be filled by a person who could counterbalance the Justice Minister, who was not a member of Ben-Gurion's ruling party at the time. He appointed his associate, Attorney Yaakov Shimshon Shapira, who soon became autonomous and separate from the Justice Minister. Over the years, the Attorney General's office has become independent, particularly when deciding whether or not to press criminal charges against suspects. Subsequently, prominent AGs such as Haim Cohen, Meir Shamgar, Professor Aharon Barak and Professor Itzhak Zamir (all of whom served as HCJ judges after completing their tours as Attorney General s) further established the independent nature of this office. Thus, although Israel was meant to follow the British tradition, right from the outset, the Attorney General and the Minister of Justice were not the same person. The key departure from the British tradition derived from the decision to separate the political role of the Minister of Justice from criminal prosecutions.

As mentioned above, even though the Attorney General has numerous powers, these powers have never been defined by legislation. The Shamgar Committee, which was established in the late 1990s, suggested that the Attorney General be chosen and appointed by an independent public committee[5] to prevent the politicisation of the position. The

---

[4] Barzilai and Nahmias (n 2).

[5] The Public Committee for the Examination of Ways to Appoint an Attorney General (aka the Shamgar Committee) issued a report in 1988, which was preceded by a Committee of Legal Experts on the Attorney General's Powers (the Agranat Committee) whose report was published in 1962.

government passed a resolution adopting some of the recommendations made by the Shamgar Committee.

The Attorney General maintains a unique and complex relationship with the Cabinet. After all, he advises the Cabinet and the ministers on the legality of their operations, but at the same time has the authority to order a police investigation and press charges against them, including the Prime Minister. Although in the early years, the position was held by politically affiliated individuals, a tradition has evolved since the 1960s whereby the Attorney General should have no political affiliations and, as a result, mainly judges or academics have held the post. It was further established that the Attorney General's term is not completed when one government is replaced by another, which renders him a neutral entity like any other civil servant, rather than a political nomination. Presently, the government appoints the Attorney General, but a public committee locates and screens candidates, and then makes recommendations to the Justice Minister. The government may only appoint one of the committee's candidates. Although the Attorney General's term in office has not been prescribed by law, the Shamgar Committee recommended terms of six years.

As noted above, the Attorney General serves as Israel's chief criminal prosecutor and has the power to decide whether or not to press charges, stay proceedings, close police investigations and file appeals. In Israel, the role of Director of Public Prosecution is called the State Attorney and is held by another person, but the Attorney General is hierarchically superior to the State Attorney and therefore the final decision to prosecute rests with him. His decisions on these matters are semi-judicial, which means that judicial review is limited. As a result, the Attorney General's office is relatively immune from judicial intervention. In principle, an Attorney General's decision not to file charges against a person should be subject to the standards of reasonableness – that is, subject to judicial review on a reasonableness standard – but the Supreme Court's position in the early years was that it would intervene in the Attorney General's considerations only in extreme cases where that decision was found to be lacking in bona fides or integrity rather not just 'unreasonable'.[6] On the basis of this position, every petition filed on such matters has thus far been rejected. The first time that the Supreme Court decided to address a motion filed against the Attorney General

---

[6] HCJ 156/56 *Shor v Attorney General*, ver 11, 285 (1957) 300.

was in the 1980s. It ordered the Attorney General to launch criminal proceedings against a person that he earlier decided not to investigate, stating that his decision was 'extremely unreasonable'.[7]

Nevertheless, the Court has generally abstained from intervening when the Attorney General has decided not to press charges due to insufficient evidence to convict. This position remains because 'this is a clear matter of factual and judicial estimation which, due to its very nature, may be disputed. Exercising his discretion on such matters, the Attorney General relies on his knowledge, experience, and professionalism to estimate the probable results of a legal proceeding that he may initiate. It is because of these qualities that he had been given the most important power to decide whether or not to indict. Thus, the Attorney General's spectrum of consideration is very wide'.[8]

In 1962, the basic principles of the Attorney General's powers were determined after the first public (Agranat) committee examined the issue.[9] It established that the Attorney General has exclusive powers to decide whether or not to initiate criminal proceedings, having examined both the evidence and whether the public interest justifies an indictment. Generally, the government or the Minister of Justice does not intervene in the way the Attorney General exercises this power, but history has shown that the government can actually 'dismiss' the Attorney General. The single most prominent example of such an occurrence was in the aftermath of what is known as the *Shin Bet* (or *Bus No 300*) case.

In 1984, four Palestinian terrorists hijacked a southbound passenger bus (bus 300). The Israeli security forces intercepted the bus and stormed in. The media reported that all four terrorists were killed when the security forces seized the bus, but later a newspaper published a picture showing two of the terrorists alive after the attack ended. The public storm that erupted forced the authorities to establish a commission of inquiry, which later determined that two of the four terrorists were not killed while exchanging fire with the security forces, but rather were killed later by blows to their heads. Nobody was found to be responsible for the killings.

It soon turned out that some of testimonies given to the commission of inquiry were false. The then Attorney General Yitzhak Zamir obtained

---

[7] HCJ 935/89 *Ganor v Attorney General*, ver 42, 485 (1990).
[8] HCJ 2534/97 *Yahav v State Attorney's Office*, ver 51(3), 1 (1997).
[9] See n 5 above.

information that *Shin Bet* (the General Security Service, Israel's domestic intelligence service) agents were involved in the terrorists' deaths, contrary to service members' testimony before the commission. He stated that there was enough evidence to indict the *Shin Bet* agents, but Prime Minister Shimon Peres and his deputy Yitzhak Shamir strongly opposed the idea. Subsequently, Attorney General Zamir was replaced by Yosef Harish and the *Shin Bet* agents who were involved in the affair were pardoned by the President and were never tried.[10] This gave rise to a very rare question: can a person be pardoned before he is convicted? The HCJ considered this question and concluded that the President has the power to render a 'preemptive' pardon. The HCJ's decision was endorsed by a majority of two judges, with Justice Aharon Barak dissenting.

This example reveals that in very rare cases, when the government wishes to overrule the Attorney General's decisions, it can do so by either pardoning suspects or offenders (which requires the President's consent, as was the case in the *Shin Bet* affair) or theoretically by submitting bills to the Knesset that restrict the Attorney General's scope of discretion.[11]

Given that the powers of the Knesset and the government to restrict the actions of the Attorney General are quite limited, it seems necessary to increase the control and supervision of his decisions, and particularly his power to prosecute. The HCJ may judicially review the Attorney General's decisions as to the head of state's prosecution, but, thus far, it has never intervened in a decision not to indict 'due to insufficient evidence'. One example of the reluctance to judicially review the acts of the Attorney General was the decision not to file criminal charges against Prime Minister Ariel Sharon, who was suspected of bribery. In this case, the Attorney General rejected the State Attorney's opinion that Prime Minister Sharon should be charged. The Attorney General ruled that there was insufficient evidence to put the Prime Minister on trial and

---

[10] The *Shin Bet* case produced two milestone verdicts in Israel's constitutional law, one dealing with the President's pardoning powers and whether he may pardon suspects before trial (see HCJ 428/86 *Barzilai v Israel's Government*, ver 39(3), 141 (1986)); and the other (HCJ 6163/92 *Eisenberg v Minister of Construction and Housing*, ver 47(2), 229 (1993)) dealing with the question of whether the government may appoint a person who was involved in the *Shin Bet* case as director general of a ministry, as that person had no criminal record only because he was never tried for his actions, having been pardoned by the President.

[11] Amnon Rubinstein and Barak Medina, *The Constitutional Law of the State of Israel*, 6th edn (Jerusalem/Tel Aviv, Shoken, 2005) (Hebrew).

decided to close the case. A petition was filed against this decision, but the HCJ chose not to intervene. Although it hinted that 'a different decision' could have been made, the HCJ rejected the petition because the Attorney General's decision was 'reasonable'.[12]

A further case in which the HCJ examined an Attorney General's decision on criminal charges was the *Katzav* case discussed earlier. The petitions in this case mainly challenged the reasonableness of the weak plea bargain that the Attorney General had offered the former President. The majority of the expanded HCJ five-judge panel rejected the petition. Interestingly, the two minority judges were willing to intervene in the Attorney General's decision to make a plea-bargain deal due to the insufficient evidence available. This reflected a certain shift in the Court's traditional stance, even though the petitions were ultimately rejected.

Another key role of the Attorney General is serving as the guardian of the rule of law. The AG must ascertain that the government and its agencies abide by the law, and must prevent them from taking illegal action. Experience has shown that this is a crucial role in defending the rule of law. The Attorney General's published opinions are binding on the government when the law is clear and undisputed. When alternative legal views exist, the Attorney General must present these options to the government so that it can choose the most suitable. An HCJ ruling acknowledged the Attorney General as the government's authorised interpreter of the law, stating that these interpretations reflect and represent the state's authorised interpretation of the law for as long as the Court has not ruled otherwise. The Court stated: 'The Attorney General has the power to interpret the law for the executive, which is bound by that interpretation.'[13] Nevertheless, the duty of the executive to follow the Attorney General's interpretation of the law is not anchored in the law. Formally, therefore, the government is under no obligation to heed the Attorney General's opinions, but in practice, since administrative authorities are committed to the rule of the law, they must follow the interpretation of the law as presented by the Attorney General. A key issue, however, remains unresolved. In a situation where the government feels that the Attorney General's position is legally erroneous,

---

[12] HCJ 5675/04 *The Movement for Government Quality in Israel v Attorney General* (published by NEVO on 19 August 2004).
[13] HCJ 73/85 *The KAKH Faction v The Knesset Speaker*, ver 29(3), 141 (1985) 152.

would it be in a position to retain a private attorney to argue for it in opposition to the Attorney General's position? In seeking to answer this question, it should be remembered that when involved in legal proceedings, the Attorney General must present the court with his view as to the proper course of action to be adopted, even if this view does not correspond with that of the government. This requirement means that the Attorney General may refuse to represent the government in court or may even argue that the action of the government is illegal. This was the case, for example, when petitions were filed arguing that the Prime Minister must depose a minister and a deputy minister because charge sheets had been filed against the two. In this case, the Attorney General sided with the petitioners, contrary to the view of the Prime Minister.[14]

In recent years, the number of political issues and questions presented to the Attorney General has expanded considerably. It seems that almost every issue on the public agenda is submitted for the Attorney General to review, and he must take a position on each one. This situation has reached a point where it seems that no political, economic or security resolution can be implemented before the Attorney General rules on its legality. This is one of the outcomes of the extensive legal expansion, resulting in almost every aspect of life being subject to legalistic interpretation and judicial review by the HCJ.

In summary, the Attorney General holds substantial power and exercises an important public role. He acts as head of the general prosecution authority while also having the power to advise and even commit the government to follow his views. In addition, the Attorney General is subject to minimal oversight or supervision by the legislature or the executive as his rulings are only subject to judicial review by the judiciary. Some argue that the concentration of such extensive powers in the hands of a single person, or even a single institution, impairs the principle of the separation of powers and the system of checks and balances that is necessary for the existence of a modern democracy.[15] Various suggestions have been made to distribute the Attorney General's powers to other bodies. Although the issue is on the public agenda and has been extensively discussed by various public committees and academic forums, no solution has been found.

---

[14] HCJ 5675/04 *The Movement for Government Quality in Israel v Israeli Government*, ver 47(5), 404 (1993).

[15] This is, for example, the view of the former Minister of Justice, Professor Daniel Friedmann.

The advocates of the splitting-up of the Attorney General's powers argue that there should not be such a direct link between the authority that gives the Cabinet legal advice and maintains ongoing contacts with government authorities, and the authority that decides whether or not to file charges against the same office holders. These are two essentially different roles which may conflict with one other. Furthermore, it is undesirable that a decision to file charges by the Attorney General may appear to be affected by the fact that he is the government's legal adviser (even if this is not the case). This issue first surfaced when the Attorney General decided to close the case against former Prime Minister Ariel Sharon for insufficient evidence. At the very least, the functions of the Attorney General should be anchored in a law that should attempt to address the various problems created by the multitude of the Attorney General's roles. The separation of the two main functions of the Attorney General – as head of prosecutions and as the legal adviser of the government – has been the main focus of debate in Israel, but so far has not produced any tangible results.

THE STATE COMPTROLLER AND OMBUDSMAN

The State of Israel has an active State Comptroller whose powers and duties are set out under Basic Law: The State Comptroller and in the State Comptroller Law (1958). The State Comptroller performs his duties on behalf of the Knesset, to which he is exclusively accountable, and is thus independent of the government. As well as acting as State Comptroller, it is also important to note that this office holder has come to assume the role of Ombudsman. The Knesset elects the State Comptroller in a secret vote for a seven-year term[16] and he is the first to receive the audit reports.

The State Comptroller and his office constitute an independent and apolitical office whose members' activities during and even after their terms are severely restricted. The State Comptroller may not be politically

[16] The State Comptroller Act was amended recently to allow outgoing State Comptroller Micha Lindenstrauss complete a report he had been working on for months that dealt, among other things, with the relationship between the defense minister and the previous Chief of Staff. Section 8c of the amendment gives an SC whose term ended another three months to complete a report or opinion that had been in process, provided that the audited parties are presented with a draft report or opinion at least three months before the SC's term ends.

active, an active member of or candidate for a local council or the Knesset, serve on the board of a profit-seeking organisation and he cannot join an organisation that the State Comptroller had audited for a period of three years after his term ends.

The State Comptroller's Office (SCO) audits a broad spectrum of bodies, including government ministries, state institutions, local authorities and government-sponsored organisations. According to section 2(a) of Basic Law: The State Comptroller, the SCO 'may audit the economy, the property, the finances, the obligations, and the administration of the state, of government ministries, of all enterprises, institutions, or corporations of the state, of local authorities, and of bodies or other institutions which were defined by law as subject to audit by the state comptroller'. In fact, the SCO may further inspect whether these and other bodies maintain proper management, observe the law, respond to public complaints, work efficiently, respond to and implement findings of previous State Comptroller reports, maintain integrity and honesty, and any other issues it considers appropriate.

To effectively perform these duties, the State Comptroller has been granted quite extensive powers that resemble the powers assigned to commissions of inquiry. Thus, audited bodies are obligated to present the SCO with their annual financial reports, surveys of their activities and any other information that the State Comptroller may require. Furthermore, he has the power to conduct investigations, which includes the right to subpoena any individual and demand that they testify and divulge any information they may have. In other words, the State Comptroller has equivalent powers to a national commission of inquiry.

In practice, the State Comptroller's work resembles that of a continental investigating judge. In addition, given that the Israeli legal system is principally adversarial, the nature of the SC's work departs from Israel's customary procedures for judicial decision making. The State Comptroller conducts investigations and reaches conclusions in a way that does not include reciprocal processes, cross-examinations or two-way debates to find the truth. The fact that the State Comptroller both investigates and passes judgment grants the office holder substantial power, which is why he must strictly observe norms of decency and integrity, and needs to consider the damage that a person or a group might suffer when a report and findings are published.

The State Comptroller's annual and special reports are submitted to the Knesset State Control Committee and to the Prime Minister. Audit findings are first discussed by this committee, which then presents its conclusions to the Knesset. The committee may order the establishment of a national commission of inquiry to further investigate an issue raised by the State Comptroller in his reports. When the audit findings include suspicions of illegal or criminal activity, the State Comptroller must present these findings to the Attorney General, who must then inform the State Comptroller and the Knesset State Control Committee of how he plans to handle the matter.

Customarily, the Supreme Court refrains from judicially reviewing State Comptroller findings, leaving this task to the Knesset. In the *Turner* case,[17] the HCJ established: 'reservations and appeals [against State Comptroller findings] should either be discussed as part of the audited parties' right to respond to the findings; or presented before the Knesset State Control Committee, where every report is thoroughly discussed'. If applied, judicial review is restricted to the formal aspects of the SCO's work, mainly the rights of individuals who might be harmed by the audit findings.

Recently, the SCO has increasingly deviated from a more traditional policy of issuing reports without naming people involved and now explicitly states the names of audited individuals, particularly when the findings indicate potential blame for abuse of power or irregular conduct. Currently, it is believed that publishing these reports is the State Comptroller's main enforcement tool. Even the HCJ referred to 'the public stigmatisation of a position holder whose integrity is questioned by an authority such as the state comptroller and the extensive public attention his assertions receive'[18] as a form of punishment, though SCO findings bear no normatively binding status because the SCO has no enforcement powers.

The SCO's powers and status developed gradually, and presently the Israeli public has great confidence in the State Comptroller. In particular, the State Comptroller's reports and rulings are covered extensively by the media, which creates public pressure on the authorities. The State Comptroller has become central and dominant in the public arena thanks mainly to the prominent personality of Justice Lindenstrauss who served as State Comptroller between 2005 and 2012. Lindenstrauss greatly expanded his auditing duties and pursued a policy of fighting

[17] HCJ 4914/94 *Turner v State Comptroller*, ver 49(3), 771 (1995).
[18] ibid 791.

government corruption. For example, he investigated the personal conduct of Prime Minister Ehud Olmert and his reports served as grounds
for a criminal investigation against the former Prime Minister, which
resulted in charge sheets and a trial. As a rule, Lindenstrauss consciously
used the media to promote his activities and, precisely because the SCO
has no legal whip to use, the public arena often acts as a substitute for
judicial sanctions.

In recent practice, State Comptrollers have split their annual reports
into chapters that they file several times a year. They also investigate and
file special reports on topical issues. At the same time, the public has supported attempts to reinforce the binding status of the State Comptroller
reports. Nevertheless, the courts are not yet ready to order audited bodies
to correct flaws pointed out in State Comptroller reports. In certain cases,
the courts have held that an audited body must take the State Comptroller
recommendations under consideration or must offer reasoned arguments
as to why they may not do so. In this spirit, the Supreme Court stated that
'for proper management practices, substantial State Comptroller criticism
of a body he may audit should not remain a dead letter'.[19]

Although this might prove to be problematic, the State Comptroller
has the power to inspect operations still in progress. Such intervention
in ongoing operations is likely to occur in relation to bodies which
would normally be audited when it is suspected that the completion or
continuation of the operation might give rise to grave and irreversible
damage. One such example was the investigation of the army's distribution of protective kits to civilians.[20] State Comptroller Miriam Ben-Porat
audited the system in real time and issued warnings even while the army
was at war.[21] There was concern that the way in which the process had
been managed might cause irreversible damage. In recent years, the
State Comptroller has examined Israel's domestic preparedness for war
(following forecasts that the population might be attacked in a missile
war) and the conduct of a candidate for the post of chief of staff, in the
wake of which that person was not appointed. Furthermore, the
Knesset has introduced an amendment to the State Comptroller Law to

[19] HCJ 766/87 *Zucker v The Tel Aviv-Yafo Mayor*, ver 42(2), 610 (1988) 619.
[20] State Comptroller, Annual Report 41, part B, for 1990 and FY 1989 –
Protective Kits for the Civilian Population, 971–87 (1991).
[21] Miriam Ben-Porat, *Basic Law: The State Comptroller* (Jerusalem, The Harry and
Michael Sacher Institutte for Legislative Research and Comparative Law, the Hebrew
University of Jerusalem, 2005) 9 (Hebrew).

allow an extra 90 days in which to complete reports already started. This amendment followed an inspection of the Ministry of Defense and the IDF that involved the Defense Minister and the Chief of Staff.[22]

When it becomes apparent that individuals might be harmed by an State Comptroller report, the State Comptroller is obliged to present the audited person with a draft of his findings before the report is completed and published or submitted to the Knesset, which grants that person the right to respond, argue his case and explain the audited flaw or complaint. The rule is that the more a person is made vulnerable by a future report, the broader the scope of his right to be heard.

The State Comptroller Law as introduced in 1949 did not address the position of the Ombudsman, which rarely existed in Western democracies at that time. As the role of the State Comptroller developed over time, the Ombudsman's powers were added later. Many civilians filed their complaints with the SC and thus de facto recognised his power to act as Ombudsman even before he was statutorily authorised to act as such. In 1966, a special Knesset committee examined whether the roles of Ombudsman and State Comptroller should be split and assigned to two persons and bodies or consolidated, and concluded that both powers should be exclusively assigned to the State Comptroller.[23] Thus, in 1971, amendment 5 was added to the law, acknowledging the State Comptroller's authority to serve as Ombudsman. In fact, the State of Israel is unique in assigning both roles to a single person. The advantage of this arrangement is that the State Comptroller may use materials in his role as State Comptroller which he collected as Ombudsman. This increases the effectiveness of the office by circumventing problems concerning jurisdictional limits, the distribution of powers and conflicting findings.

In Israel, citizens may approach the Ombudsman with issues that can also be taken to court and are thus subject to judicial review. The position differs from most other countries where the Ombudsman may be used only with respect to complaints that are not subject to judicial review.[24] In Israel, the fact that the Ombudsman addresses a complaint does not prevent the complainant from seeking a remedy in court, and the court does not have to follow the Ombudsman's decisions. At the

---

[22] See n 16 above.

[23] Ben-Porat (n 21) 27.

[24] HCJ 453/84 *Iturit Communication Services Ltd v Communication Minister et al*, ver 38(4), 617 (1985) 622.

same time, the Ombudsman may enquire into an issue that is pending in court or on which a court has already ruled.

The Ombudsman was granted extensive powers that were meant to protect 'whistleblower' civil servants who complain about corruption that takes place in the organisation for which they work. Dealing with such cases, the Ombudsman may issue any order he considers appropriate and just, including interim orders, to protect the complainant's rights. This is meant to prevent a situation in which a whistleblower who warns about his superiors' misconduct is dismissed or punished by them. Furthermore, the Ombudsman may order the nullification of such a dismissal and the dismissed individual may be awarded special financial compensation. Alternatively, the Ombudsman may rule that the complaining civil servant be assigned to another duty under the same employer. The Ombudsman's recommendations and conclusions are not legally binding, but a moral obligation reinforced by public support for the office ensures that his recommendations are followed.[25]

COMMISSIONS OF INQUIRY

In Israel, commissions of inquiry serve as an important tool for supervising government agencies, investigating key events, fact-finding and making recommendations for the future, mainly on issues of public interest. In fact, almost every national disaster or failure in Israel's history has been investigated by a commission of inquiry. Despite the fact that they were conducted decades ago, two commissions of inquiry remain deeply engraved in the Israelis' collective memory.

The first memorable commission of inquiry was the Agranat Commission that was formed to examine the *Yom Kippur* War of October 1973. Its conclusions rocked the state as much as the war had done because they entailed personal changes to Israel's top military and political echelons, but were also met with popular disapproval because the Commission found that the military officers were almost exclusively responsible for the war failures, clearing the politicians of blame. The second commission of inquiry that left a mark on Israel's history was the Kahan Commission, which investigated the events that took place in Palestinian refugee camps in Beirut during the First Lebanon War of

---

[25] Rubinstein and Medina (n 11) 320.

1982. Its findings led to the resignations of then Defense Minister Ariel Sharon and Prime Minister Menahem Begin.

The government is the authority that establishes commissions of inquiry by the power of the Commissions of Inquiry Law (1968). Their composition is determined by the President of the Supreme Court and they are headed by a judge, usually from the Supreme Court, but other members are not necessarily legal experts. These commissions do not follow standard legal procedure or the rules of evidence. In addition, Israel has governmental inspection commissions which are also established under the Government Law, and parliamentary commissions of inquiry discussed in chapter four.

A national commission of inquiry is established, according to section 1 of the Commissions of Inquiry Law, when the government decides that a certain issue of vital public importance should be investigated. Commissions of inquiry are expected to study matters thoroughly and present the Cabinet with their findings and recommendations. The government has the power to establish such commissions, but a 1995 amendment provided that, having received an State Comptroller's report, the Knesset State Control Committee may also establish a commission to further investigate an issue.

The commission's powers are outlined in a letter of appointment issued by its establishing body. However, it has gradually become the custom that, while investigating the main issue it was created to examine, a committee may expand the scope of its inspection and also examine related issues, including government policies. Commissions of inquiry have also been employed to consult the government on the desired policy in a given area. One such commission of inquiry studied the *Shin Bet*'s interrogation methods in the wake of a significant incident. Another case was the *Bus No 300* case, which was discussed earlier. The commission of inquiry established to investigate the events of October 2000 in which Israeli civilians were killed by police fire also studied the state's treatment of the Arab minority.[26]

---

[26] The National Commission of Inquiry into the Clashes between the Security Forces and Israeli Citizens in October 2000 – Report (2003). The report introduction reads: 'Something happened in Israel in early October 2000: In a series of violent demonstrations and riots staged in several locations in Israel, mainly in the north, and in clashes between civilians and police forces, 14 people were killed (13 Israeli citizens and one Gaza Strip resident) and many were wounded . . . In the wake of the said events, the Israeli government initially established a fact-finding

Commissions of inquiry have wide-ranging investigative powers. They may subpoena anyone they wish to testify or to produce documents. They have equivalent powers of summons to civil courts and they have the power to impose punitive measures such as fines. Their deliberations are generally open to the public, as are the reports they issue, except when a commission decides not to publish all or parts of its report for reasons such as the state's security or foreign relations. The commissions are obliged to allow anyone who might be harmed by the inquiry to appear before it and argue his case. Similarly, anyone who feels that the commission's findings might cause him harm may appear before the commission and present his evidence and arguments. This includes the right to review evidence that has been collected.

A commission report should include all the facts that the commission has discovered in full detail, as well as recommendations for future action. The government must accept the facts, but it is under no automatic obligation to follow the recommendations. Nevertheless, it must carefully consider these recommendations, given that commissions of inquiry are independent bodies that the public holds in high esteem. Traditionally, governments have followed recommendations to dismiss those holding public positions who have failed in performing their duties.

Though commissions of inquiry serve as a particularly effective tool, governments have never rushed to establish them and, in some cases, did so only in response to mounting public pressure, having first tried to settle for other inspection teams.[27] Similarly, the Knesset may call upon the government to establish a commission of inquiry, but cannot force it to do so. So far, the Supreme Court has avoided ordering the government to either establish a commission of inquiry or to avoid forming one. It determined that this is one of the government's wide-ranging prerogatives and that it will intervene in Cabinet resolutions on this matter only in rare and irregular cases, 'which have not and probably never will be brought before this Court'.[28]

---

committee, but . . . following the recommendation of that committee's chairman, its work was terminated and on August 11, 2000, the Government decided to establish a commission of inquiry according to the said law.'

[27] For example, the Landau Committee for the Investigation of *Shin Bet* Interrogation Methods was established after several fact-finding committees failed to uncover the true facts concerning the *Bus No 300* case.

[28] HCJ 2624/97 *Ronel v Israeli Government*, ver 51(3), 79–80 (1997).

Whether or not the Cabinet may be obliged to establish a national commission of inquiry under certain circumstances is a complicated question. Petitions have been filed against the government, demanding that the HCJ order it to establish a commission, but all such petitions have been rejected. Still, when the government refuses to establish a commission, it may be criticised by the Knesset and the public.

An interesting, and at the same time important, example involved the Second Lebanon War, which demonstrates the difference between various commissions of inquiry. In July 2006, the Lebanese Hezbollah organisation started firing rockets at Israel's northern settlements in a coordinated attack. At the same time, in a ground operation, it abducted two IDF soldiers, killed eight and injured many soldiers and civilians. In an emergency Cabinet session, the Israeli government decided to retaliate with a military operation inside Lebanon. The operation turned into a full-blown war that lasted more than a month and ended with more than 150 Israeli fatalities. The war left the Israeli public feeling that the army had failed and that the entire campaign had been poorly managed. When the war ended, several public campaigns called on the government to establish a national commission of inquiry to investigate the war fiascos and the mismanagement of the home front, as well as demanding that the Prime Minister, the Defense Minister and the Chief of Staff resign.

The government deliberated on the issue at length and eventually decided to establish a so-called governmental inspection commission that was asked to examine the conduct of the political players during the war as well as some military issues. The commission was headed by a retired district court judge and its establishment was meant to appease the Israeli public and the international community. The latter was not fully familiar with the distinctions between the various Israeli fact-finding commissions. There are, however, substantive differences between a governmental inspection commission and a commission of inquiry. A governmental inspection commission is established by a Cabinet member who also appoints its members pursuant to section 8(a) of the Government Law (2001). Thus, the executive is directly involved in the composition of this commission. This is very different from the case of commissions of inquiry whose members are chosen by the Supreme Court President, as a member of the judiciary. The law does not state who may head a fact-finding or inspection commission, what its composition should be or that it must be headed by a judge.

Such commissions have neither legal power to subpoena witnesses nor other broad investigative powers that are assigned to commissions of inquiry. Yet, when such a commission is headed by a judge, the Minister of Justice may, with the Cabinet's consent, bestow it with legal powers similar to those of commissions of inquiry.

Justice Eliahu Winograd was appointed head of the governmental inspection commission of the Second Lebanon War. Although the letter of appointment granted the commission with powers equal to those of commissions of inquiry, the public and the media were very critical of this move and of the government's refusal to establish a 'real' inquiry commission. Many wondered whether the Cabinet could be 'forced' to follow the model of previous Cabinets and establish a commission of inquiry. Although the HCJ had ruled that it would intervene only in rare and irregular cases, some believed that, through the military failure Israel had suffered in Lebanon, the threshold had been reached to warrant such intervention.

Thus, soon after the Winograd Commission was established, a petition was filed asking the HCJ to authorise its disqualification.[29] The petitioners argued that the war in Lebanon was 'of vital public importance' and thus the proper tool of investigation in this case was a commission of inquiry. A four-judge majority of a seven-judge panel rejected the petition. Nevertheless, the judges stated that although the decision whether or not to establish such a commission is the Cabinet's prerogative, the Court's decision not to intervene does not necessarily mean that it favoured the Cabinet's choice, nor does it mean that the Court decided to legitimise the Cabinet's decision or to refer to it as being appropriate or good. The majority of judges merely ruled that the government decision 'was not illegal' to the extent that requires the Court's intervention. The minority opinion was that the commission's appointment was flawed to the extent that the decision to establish it should be reversed.

The Winograd Commission worked for months, while the Israeli public waited for its conclusions, because an interim report it issued had created the expectation that it might lead to a change of government. Surprisingly, the final report included no conclusions or recommendations concerning the incumbency of senior position holders who were involved in war failures, which greatly disappointed the public. Although

---

[29] HCJ 6728/06 *The Ometz Association (of Citizens form Proper Administration and Social Justice) v Prime Minister* (published by Nevo on 30 November 2006).

it was quite rigorous, the report did not analyse the personal responsibility of the three key officials involved (the Prime Minister, the Defense Minister and the Chief of Staff), despite the fact that the Israeli public was principally interested in this aspect of the matter.

The fact that the absence of 'personal recommendations' was such a disappointment for the Israeli public is associated with the Israeli political culture. Commissions of inquiry are viewed as prestigious legal bodies and their recommendations are considered legally binding. The public perception is that individuals named by such commissions as 'responsible parties' are 'guilty', while everyone else is not. Thus, while the Israeli public expected the Winograd Commission to assign blame, it chose to leave the final judgment to the public.

As was pointed out in the preceding chapter, it is worth reiterating at this point that only in very few cases in Israel's history have Cabinet members resigned in the wake of failures or misdeeds concerning issues within their responsibility. Various commissions of inquiry have concluded that ministers should resign because they failed to uphold their ministerial responsibilities, and governments have adopted these recommendations. Since the Winograd Commission made no such recommendations, no one resigned immediately after its report was published. In fact, it was many months before the Chief of Staff eventually resigned and the Defense Minister was replaced.

The HCJ's decision not to intervene in cases such as that of the Winograd Commission left the government almost totally immune from judicial review on all matters pertaining to decisions as to whether it should establish a fact-finding commission and, if so, which type it should establish. It seems that the court's abstention is anchored in the separation of powers principle and is due to the fact that the government has extensive discretion when dealing with these issues.

THE MEDIA

According to the Freedom House 2012 report: 'Israel enjoys a lively, pluralistic media environment in which press freedom is generally respected.'[30] The report adds: 'Some [newspapers] freely criticise government policies and aggressively pursue cases of official corruption.'

---

[30] See www.freedomhouse.org/report/freedom-press/2012/israel.

The media is an important watchdog and freedom of the press is strongly protected in Israel. While the basic laws on human right do not include freedom of speech, the Supreme Court has affirmed that freedom of expression is an essential component of human dignity, as we shall see in chapter eight. The legal status of the freedom of the press has also been reinforced by court rulings citing the principles laid out in the Declaration of Independence.

The publication of hate speech and/or praise of violence is prohibited in Israel and the 1948 Prevention of Terrorism Ordinance bans expressions of support for terrorist organisations or groups that call for the destruction of Israel. According to the Press Ordinance, which is still in effect from the period of British rule, publishers are required to obtain a licence from the Interior Ministry to operate a newspaper. This ordinance allows the Interior Minister to shut down a newspaper, but this power has not been applied since the 1980s. The Government Press Office (GPO) requires journalists operating in Israel to have proper accreditation to attend official press conferences, gain access to government buildings and cross Israeli military checkpoints.

The military censor has the power to shut down a newspaper, stop its printing or confiscate its printing machines, citing national security. Yet, according to an unofficial agreement between newspapers editors and the IDF (known as the 'Editors Committee'), journalists would voluntarily submit sensitive stories to the military censor who would abstain from exercising his powers. The agreement further stipulates that censorship would be limited to the coverage of military and security issues to prevent breaches of state security. This censorship agreement between the media and the military is still in place, and these powers are seldom used, meaning that the censor's role is quite limited. There is a good relationship between the Israeli media and the military censor, which is the result of HCJ rulings and mutual agreements.

According to the military censor report,[31] Israeli journalists tend to voluntarily employ stricter censorship than what is institutionally required. According to the report, between 2002 and 2011, censors edited 17–20 per cent of the texts that the media submitted annually (with the exception of 2004, where the rate stood at 25 per cent). During

---

[31] Published in *The Seventh Eye*, March 2012 (Hebrew). The statistics were published by the military censorship. See www.the7eye.org.il/wp-content/uploads/2012/03/110312_censor.pdf (Hebrew).

the 2006 Second Israel–Lebanon War, the intervention rate was 24–30 per cent. The majority of news material was submitted for the censor's review not necessarily because it contained sensitive information, but perhaps because journalists preferred to shift the responsibility to the authorities.

Israel also has a press council that ensures professional ethics and free access to information by overseeing complaints on matters of press ethics and conducting ethics tribunals. While the country's legal framework is predominantly protective of press freedom, it does include a number of restrictive elements that are sometimes used against journalists. For example, journalists can be threatened with libel suits.

Israelis are active news consumers. The print media include some 12 daily newspapers, a wide range of weekly newspapers and Internet news sites divided along religious, ethnic and language lines. The leading newspapers are independent and all newspapers are privately owned and provide a variety of political views. Israel has the region's highest rate of Internet usage and the government generally does not restrict Internet access.

In recent years, extensive debates about the freedom of the press have taken place in Israel. They have not so much concerned legal regulation, but rather have focused on the question of media ownership. Moshe Negbi, a leading legal journalist, argued in his book that media proprietors have gained enormous powers to control and restrict content published in newspapers or TV channels that they own, and they use their powers to censor, distort or conceal information and opinions that may harm them or their profits.[32] It is not easy and may even be unconstitutional to fight this kind of private censorship because it relates to property rights. However, Labour Court Judge Elisheva Barak warned that it is essential 'to prevent a situation where whoever financially controls the media also controls the opinions of the public'. She explained that 'for the public, the freedom of the press means that the public will not accept information from and hear views of only those who have the financial means to run a newspaper'.[33] This issue is still being discussed in the Knesset and in the public arena.

---

[32] Moshe Negbi, *Freedom of the Press and Freedom of Journalists in Israel* (The Open University, 2011) (Hebrew).
[33] Labor Court 1000-3 (Jerusalem) *Yehiel v Palestine Post* (rendered 25 April 1993).

NGOs

NGOs play a very significant role as watchdogs in Israel. They are highly active and visible participants in both the national and international debates on political and legal matters. They issue high-profile statements and reports, generate media publications and use the courts to advance their agendas. For example, local NGOs are responsible for a significant portion of the petitions filed with the HCJ, as reflected in the names of many cases, indicating that Israeli courts have become a central arena for engaging in contentious social and political issues.

Some NGOs are particularly visible in their opposition to the government, such as the Association for Civil Rights in Israel (ACRI), B'tselem and Adalah. ACRI is Israel's oldest and largest human rights organisation and it mainly addresses human rights violations committed by Israeli authorities in Israel and the occupied territories. It was also very successful in landmark cases in areas such as freedom of expression, the right to privacy, freedom of and from religion, and lesbian, gay, bisexual, transgender and intersex (LGBTI) rights. Adalah concentrates on promoting and protecting the rights of Palestinians and Arab citizens of Israel as well as Palestinians living in the occupied territories. It frequently appeals to the HCJ and argues the cases of minorities whose human rights have allegedly been violated.

Another leading NGO is the Israel Women's Network (IWN) that aims to improve the status of women and promote women's rights and equality in Israel. Ever since it was established, it has achieved numerous successes, including the initiation of laws such as the 1998 Sexual Harassment Prevention Law, and the 2005 law establishing a commission for equal employment opportunities. It also filed lawsuits against discrimination in the IDF. A few NGOs, such as the Hotline for Migrant Workers, deal with the rights of migrant workers and refugees. The leading NGO on public ethics is the Movement for Quality Government in Israel (MQG). Over the years, the MQG has become one of the leading watchdogs and a well-known public petitioner to the HCJ, advocating public accountability and the rule of law.

Since 2009, the Israeli public, media, the government and the Knesset have been conducting an intense debate concerning foreign governments' funding of political NGOs. It has been argued[34] that much of

---

[34] By right-wing politicians and by the Institute for Zionist Strategies, for example.

the funding of several Israeli NGOs comes from foreign sources – particularly European governments, including the European Commission – and therefore specific NGOs are able to promote particular political ideologies and to oppose government policy on many issues. The result of this debate was the enactment of the NGO Transparency Law in 2011.[35] This was introduced despite intense lobbying against it by foreign-funded NGOs and came into effect at the beginning of 2012, requiring NGOs to file quarterly reports outlining funds received from foreign governments and bodies.

In Israel, NGOs are responsible for a significant proportion of the petitions filed with the HCJ. As we will see in the next chapter, citizens, residents and even non-residents have standing in the HCJ without having to prove potential or actual injury. The HCJ does not screen the cases it deals with and hears almost every petition filed. Furthermore, it plays a central role in public policy making and is a central arena for engaging in contentious social and political issues. The willingness of the HCJ since the 1980s to hear cases filed by public petitioners was one of the main reasons for the intensification of the activity of NGOs in Israel.

CONCLUSION

The main focus in this chapter has been to consider how different watchdog agencies contribute to the constitutional system. In this context, the Attorney General holds one of the key roles in providing government oversight, mainly as the guardian of the rule of law. Among the many functions performed by the Attorney General, the office holder must ensure that the government and its agencies abide by the law, as well as preventing them from taking illegal action. Fierce debates are held from time to time – mainly in the media – as to the role of the Attorney General and the decisions he takes concerning certain government policies. Almost every controversial political decision is presented to the Attorney General for 'approval' of its legality. Failure to do so could lead to the matter being taken to the Supreme Court for final decision. The political and social discourse in Israel has mainly been focused in recent years on the 'legal' aspects of government decisions. This

---

[35] The Law on Disclosure Requirements for Groups Supported by a Foreign Governmental Body.

much-criticised tendency has been referred to as the 'legalisation of politics' and it will be further explored in the next chapter.

The SC's powers have developed in a rather different way over the past few years. We have seen that even without the capacity to enforce a remedy, the SC has an important oversight function. This effectiveness is frequently amplified by the intense media coverage devoted to the SC's reports, which create public pressure on the government to correct the deficiencies that have been identified. In the cases of both the Attorney General and the SC, a great deal depends on the force of personality of the office holder performing their allocated functions.

In general, the broadcast and print media, as well as the activism of other NGOs, perform an important watchdog role. Not only do they operate as powerful political players, capable of changing government policies, but they also raise public awareness and demand that the government accounts for its actions. In order to pursue their own agendas, Israeli NGOs frequently launch campaigns in the media. At the same time, they provide social services outside government and serve as providers of alternative sources of information. As a result of such activism, decisions about funding NGOs and other forms of support are discussed in a public forum. Recently, their activities have been made subject to legal control as NGOs are now required to disclose any funding from foreign governments. NGOs are responsible for drafting a significant proportion of the petitions filed with the HCJ. In the next chapter, we will see that one of the main reasons for the proliferation of NGOs in Israeli society has been the willingness of the Supreme Court since the 1980s to hear cases filed by public petitioners.

FURTHER READING

Friedberg, Asher, Geist, Benjamin, Mizrahi, Nissim and Sharkansky, Ira, (eds), *Studies in State Audit* (Jerusalem, The State Comptroller and Ombudsman, 1995) available at: http://old.mevaker.gov.il/serve/site/english/studies.asp

Gavison, Ruth, 'Custom in Law Enforcement: The Power of the Attorney General to Stay Criminal Proceedings' (1986) 21 *Israel Law Review* 333.

Klein, Claude, 'Constitutional Scandal and its Legal Treatment: The Appointment of the Attorney-General' (1998) 4 *European Public Law* 441.

Navot, Suzie, *The Constitutional Law of Israel* (Alphen aan den Rijn, Kluwer, 2007).

Navot, Suzie, 'The Governmental Commission of Inquiry for the Second Lebanon War' (2009) 15 *European Public Law* 17.

Rabin, Yoram and Peled, Roy, 'Between FOI Law and FOI Culture: The Israeli Experience' (2005) 1 *Open Government: Journal on Freedom of Information* 41.

7

The Constitutional Role of Courts

Introduction – The Court System – The High Court of Justice –
Judicial Review and Political Response – Standing and Justiciability
– Judicial Activism – Conclusion

INTRODUCTION

THIS CHAPTER BEGINS by discussing the main features of the judicial system in Israel. The focus will be on the Supreme Court acting as the HCJ. Historical reasons allowed for the creation of this administrative court that deals with citizens' petitions against administrative authorities, in which the HCJ functions as the court of both the first and last instance. Israel drew upon common law principles of legal interpretation, the principle of stare decisis, the status of judges and the overall structure of the legal system. This common law conception of the judicial role was particularly significant in the evolution of constitutional law.

The development of the powers of the court will be revealed from the discussion of the judicial review of laws and the reactions of the Israeli parliament. During the 1980s, the court dramatically changed its position regarding the doctrines of justiciability and standing. These changes reduced the scope of issues considered non-justiciable, and petitions that were previously rejected were then dealt with by the HCJ and decided on their merits. The results of these changes relating to the Court's discretion as to whether and how to intervene, and the Court's relationship with other state branches will be discussed in the next section. This chapter closely observes the current lively public debate on judicial activism and ends with an attempt to show the gap between the alleged judicial activism of the HCJ and the actual situation where almost all the petitions against government decisions are dismissed.

THE COURT SYSTEM

The Israeli judicial structure was greatly influenced by the British system, which was introduced in Palestine with the British Mandate in 1917. Israel's judiciary is autonomous, independent and trusted by the public. The court system is set out, according to Basic Law: The Judiciary and the Courts Law, as comprising three levels: magistrates' courts, six district courts and the Supreme Court. There is a magistrates' court in almost every major city in Israel and these courts may hear criminal cases for which the maximum penalty stipulated by law is a seven-year prison term. In addition, these courts hear civil matters and financial lawsuits up to a specified value that is adjusted periodically, as well as serving as family courts.

Israel's six district courts serve as the courts of first instance for issues they are empowered to hear by specific legislation. These courts deal with matters over which magistrates' courts do not have jurisdiction and hear appeals against the verdicts of magistrates' courts. These courts mainly employ the adversarial method, in which the parties determine how the trial is to be conducted. Nevertheless, judges are part of the discussion, steering and directing it. Israeli judges routinely intervene in arguments, cut them short and pose questions for clarification. A presiding judge is in charge of managing the trial, determines which questions may and may not be asked, and what evidence is admissible. Though the involvement of judges seems to be increasing over time, the main burden is still borne by the parties.

The Supreme Court is the highest court in the State of Israel and it too plays two roles: it is the court of final resort for appeals against verdicts handed down by district courts and thus rules on civil, administrative and criminal matters. In addition, it sits as the HCJ and hears petitions against state authorities and other tribunals. Fifteen judges serve on the Supreme Court, which generally hears cases in panels of three, unless the court president decides to expand the panel. Supreme Court rulings are final, but the Courts Law offers the Supreme Court President an option to schedule another hearing of a tried (civil, criminal or HCJ) case with an extended panel when the issue at hand might have broad public or legal implications, or when the original verdict deviates from a previous ruling whose importance requires another hearing. In more exceptional cases, the President may order a retrial of criminal cases.

In addition to these three courts, the Israeli judicial system includes particular tribunals whose jurisdiction is limited to certain issues or individuals. These include religious tribunals with powers to rule on mainly matrimonial issues, labour tribunals that rule on labour-related matters, military tribunals that deal with issues concerning people in the military and others.

A judicial appointment for all courts is 'for life' and in practice until the age of 70. Once appointed, a judge's position can generally only be terminated if he resigns. Although judges may be dismissed, following a decision of the Judges' Disciplinary Tribunal or a decision by the Judges' Election Committee, this occurrence is very rare.

The judiciary has an Ombudsman's office for public complaints against judges. The Ombudsman is empowered to recommend disciplinary proceedings against a judge and even issue a recommendation – to the Judges Election Committee – to terminate the judge's tenure. The Ombudsman submits an annual report surveying the overall functioning of the judges, an arrangement that actually gives this office a certain degree of supervision over the judges without impairing the independence of the judiciary.

The judges' salaries and other payments are prescribed by the Knesset's Finance Committee. In order to minimise the possible influence of the legislature over the judiciary on this issue, Basic Law: The Judiciary prohibits a decision to cut only the judges' salaries, meaning that any reduction of judges' salaries must be linked to a similar reduction in the salary of another sector.

The institutional independence of the judiciary is problematic. The judiciary is not administratively autonomous, but is a unit of the Ministry of Justice. The law grants the Minister of Justice extensive powers in the administration of the courts, and the judiciary has only partial powers over staffing, the maintenance of court buildings and the budget. The Minister of Justice also chairs the Judges Election Committee. These arrangements mean that institutional independence is not guaranteed by law, although the tradition that has developed over the years, and which was endorsed by almost all Ministers of Justice, has been to refrain from interference in the administration of the courts.

THE HIGH COURT OF JUSTICE

The HCJ resulted from an historical, accidental and unplanned process that created an unusual situation in which certain complaints (administrative grievances of individuals harmed by government authorities) are filed directly with the Supreme Court. During the British Mandate, the lower courts (magistrates' and district courts) were presided over by local judges, Jews or Arabs, while the Supreme Court was exclusively composed of British judges. The policy was that local judges should handle ordinary civil and criminal issues, but disputes that pertained to the Mandate authorities should be heard, from beginning to end, by judges from the British establishment.[1] Thus, it was determined that the Supreme Court should address administrative disputes.

After Israel was established, this structure was no longer needed, but the judicial situation did not change as the newly founded state decided to keep the British Mandate's administrative and legal structures in place. Accordingly, the HCJ kept operating as it had done previously, only presided over by Israeli judges. Soon it became central to the development of justice and basic principles of democracy – mainly the rule of law. Over the years, the HCJ has proven its willingness to confront the government, including on security-related issues. It became a powerful key player among government authorities and plays a vital role in Israel's public life, as is evident in almost every chapter in this book. In the absence of a written constitution, the HCJ's interpretative power created what has become known as the 'Judicial Bill of Rights', which is elaborated on in the next chapter.

Complaints against the government are filed directly with the HCJ, which serves as the first, last, and only instance of judicial review. Thus, when a citizen feels harmed by or has a grievance in relation to the government, he goes directly to the highest judicial body in the state. This is an almost entirely unique situation from a comparative perspective.

Before 2000, the HCJ was in charge of dealing with administrative issues. In 2000, the Knesset introduced the Administrative Affairs Courts Law, which authorised district courts to sit as administrative courts and address such issues. The law was intended to reduce the HCJ

---

[1] Ruth Gavison, Mordechai Kremnitzer and Yoav Dotan, *Judicial Activism: For and Against* (Jerusalem, Yediot Hahronot and Magnes, 2000) 5–7 (Hebrew).

workload as both an administrative court and a criminal and civil appeals court. The administrative courts were mainly assigned cases that do not deal with authorities' infringements of human rights (which has always been the key issue in the HCJ), but which address issues such as local taxes, education, religious councils, public tenders, associations, business licensing, local authorities, tourism, planning and construction, public housing, transportation, political parties and so on. District court judges trained in administrative law preside over such cases.

HCJ procedures differ from other courts. It does not hear oral testimonies or question witnesses. Its hearings are meant to provide an immediate remedy. According to section 15(c) of Basic Law: The Judiciary, the HCJ may extend 'relief for the sake of justice' in every matter that is outside the jurisdiction of all other courts. The HCJ is explicitly authorised to issue habeas corpus and mandamus, ban orders of lawful holders of public positions, and even issue orders to other courts and to other bodies and individuals with judicial or semi-judicial powers. The boundaries of the HCJ's powers are broadly and vaguely defined, and the fact that it is easily accessible and its proceedings simple and quick has turned it into the forum of main redress for civilians who feel offended by government action. As such, it has acquired significant prestige, importance, and power over the years.

HCJ judges have extensively applied the 'relief for the sake of justice' section of Basic Law: The Judiciary, expanding the scope of their control of state authorities. Trends in the HCJ's decisions in recent years indicate that, at least from the judges' point of view, the court's jurisdiction has no boundaries. There is almost no record of the HCJ ever rejecting petitions because it was not authorised to discuss the issues raised in them. When it does reject petitions or refers them to another court, it does so only after exercising its discretion and stating that it does so because it would rather employ a cautious approach and self-restraint, despite having the power to discuss the issue. The feeling is that the HCJ is almost in absolute control over the scope of its powers. This has opened up judicial review of questions that used to be regarded as non-justiciable. For example, the HCJ has increased its involvement in internal Knesset affairs, political questions and military decisions, and has expanded the application of constitutional rules (such as the equality principle) to bodies that are not government agencies, including government-owned companies or semi-public bodies. HCJ decrees and verdicts are obeyed by all governmental bodies and public authorities.

This is evident from the fact that it is very unusual for contempt of court sentences to be issued against such bodies.

To quote Alexander Hamilton, HCJ judges have 'no influence over either the sword or the purse',[2] only the public's trust in them. The HCJ judges' willingness to intervene in issues that would be viewed as unjustifiable in other countries and the fact that it may judicially review legislation, coupled with its activist image, have placed it at the centre of Israel's public and political discourse in recent years.

JUDICIAL REVIEW AND THE POLITICAL RESPONSE

Judicial review of all government agencies, and mainly of laws, has long been one of the most disputed issues in Israeli society and has often generated serious public controversy. The disputes follow from the fact that Israel lacks broad national consensus on fundamental issues such as the place of religion, the nature of the state, the status of the occupied territories, the scope and status of human rights and so on. Many believe that decisions on these issues should be political, that is, made by the parliament, based on majority views, and not made by the courts.[3]

After the enactment of the two basic laws on human rights in 1992, the Supreme Court acknowledged its own power to judicially review laws in the *Bank Hamizrahi* case, (discussed in chapter one). President Aharon Barak cited the American case of *Marbury v Madison*, in which the US Supreme Court interpreted the US Constitution as empowering it to enforce the supremacy of the Constitution over all other laws. According to Barak, 'this was the central contribution of American constitutional concepts to the universal constitutional concept'.[4] His approach – whereby the Israeli legal tradition, as in many other democracies, requires that an extra-parliamentary body, in the form of the court, rules on the limitations imposed on the Knesset by basic laws – has been the prevailing approach in Israel since 1995. However,

---

[2] Alexander Hamilton, *The Federalist Papers*, No 78, 28 May 1788.
[3] Amnon Rubinstein and Barak Medina, *The Constitutional Law of the State of Israel Law*, 6th edn (Jerusalem/Tel Aviv, Shoken, 2005) 173 (Hebrew).
[4] CA 6821/93 *United Hamizrahi Bank v Migdal Cooperative Village* 49(4) PD 221 (1995) 443.

this approach has been severely criticised by the Knesset and in academia.[5]

In the absence of an explicit constitutional norm, the acknowledgement of the Court's judicial review powers was received with mixed political reactions. The Knesset did not react to the *Bank Hamizrahi* verdict with new legislation. While the Knesset absorbed the constitutional process that some MKs believed was imposed upon it, it did not rise to the challenge with which the Court presented it in that monumental verdict. The Court chose to leave an array of unresolved constitutional questions for the legislature, but the Knesset failed to answer them. It did not complete the constitution and it failed to introduce Basic Law: Legislation, which was supposed to establish the basic laws' normative constitutional status and the Supreme Court's judicial review powers. The constitutional process was halted as the Knesset introduced no new basic laws, and the Israeli constitution remained incomplete. The fundamental question of the body authorised to quash laws, on which most democracies are clear, remained unresolved. This outcome appears to have been due to political reasons attributable to a coalition government. Unable to resolve key political issues, in particular those concerning state and religion-related matters, the Knesset often found it convenient to defer them to the Supreme Court. This way, problematic questions were eventually answered and the Knesset had, at the same time, someone else to blame.

The Court, however, did not mirror the Knesset's silence. Upon examination of the nearly 20 years of experience since the constitutional revolution, the Supreme Court's judicial review appears to have been and to have remained quite restrained. The Knesset is aware of the HCJ's ability to intervene and therefore conducts its own constitutional inspections within the legislative process.

The Supreme Court has nullified some 10 laws (mainly specific sections) over the past 18 years, all following judicial rulings that these laws

---

[5] See, for example, Ruth Gavison, 'The Role of Courts in Rifted Democracies' (1999) 33 *Israel Law Review* 216; Michael Mandel, 'Democracy and the New Constitutionalism in Israel' (1999) 33 *Israel Law Review* 25; Moshe Landau, 'A Constitution as Supreme Law for Israel?' (1981) 27 *Hapraklit* 30 (Hebrew); Moshe Landau, 'A Constitution for Israel – When, if At All' (1981) 11 *Iyuney Mishpat* 27 (Hebrew); Gary Jeffrey Jacobsohn, 'After the Revolution' (2000) 34 *Israel Law Review* 139; Gideon Sapir, *The Constitutional Revolution – Past, Present, Future* (Tel Aviv, Miskal and Hemed Books, 2010) (Hebrew).

disproportionately impaired rights listed in the basic laws. Judicial review is very restrained. However, this trend seems to be shifting in recent years. Since the legislature failed to complete a constitutional bill of rights, the Court's interpretations expanded the right to dignity, allowing for judicial review of laws that disproportionately harm rights that are not listed in basic laws. New petitions filed with the HCJ asked the Court to invalidate laws that were inconsistent with unwritten rights, such as the right to equality. First, the Court acknowledged its right to nullify such laws in principle, but did not actually do so. Thus, in the *Tal Law* case,[6] petitioners argued that the law that exempts *yeshiva* students from military service violated the principle of equality. The HCJ determined that the right to dignity, as it appears in Basic Law: Human Dignity and Liberty, includes several aspects of the right to equality, and eventually decided to nullify the *Tal* Law because it disproportionately harmed the right to equality.[7] The same reasoning was applied in the *Adalah* case.[8] The petitioners argued that the law harms basic rights to equality and family life, even though these rights were not listed in any basic law. The Court rejected the petition itself (by a slim majority of six to five), but established that the right to human dignity includes aspects of the right to equality. The rights to due process and freedom of expression were similarly acknowledged as part of Basic Law: Human Dignity and Liberty. Thus, constitutional interpretation of Basic Law: Human Dignity and Liberty allowed the Court to expand the principle of dignity and include unwritten rights.

The Knesset has reacted to this expansion in adjudication in a variety of ways. First, it decided to increase the number of Supreme Court judges from 14 to 15[9] and ruled that to be elected as a Supreme Court judge, candidates must win at least seven votes from the nine members of the elections committee (when a regular majority sufficed before). It also attempted to intervene in the election of the President of the Court. It should be noted that Supreme Court Presidents are nominated according to their seniority. Traditionally, there was no election process

---

[6] HCJ 6427/02 *Movement for Government Quality v The Knesset*, ver 61(1), 619 (2006).
[7] HCJ 6298/07 *Ressler v The Knesset* (published by Nevo on 21 December 2012).
[8] HCJ 7052/03 *Adalah v The Interior Minister*, ver 71(2), 202 (2006).
[9] Over the years, the number of judges went up from seven when the Court was founded (although only five judges served then) to 15 in 2012. In 1959, the number was raised to nine judges and in 1963 to 10, while in 1992, it was raised again to 12 and in 1994 to 14.

and the committee simply approved the nomination of the next judge in order of seniority. A 2009 law restricted this method, stating that only judges with at least three years of tenure remaining may be elected president. When President Dorit Beinisch retired, she was to be succeeded by Justice Miriam Naor, but the Knesset introduced a law in 2012 that removed the restriction in order to guarantee that Justice Asher Grunis assumed the post (although he had less than three years of his tenure left to serve).

The introduction of 'temporary laws' is another response to the Supreme Court's approach to judicial review. Recently, the Knesset has been naming new laws 'temporary provisions' – particularly when the laws in question had been argued to violate human rights. Such ad hoc, temporary legislation is the Knesset's way of signalling that it is aware of the harm that this legislation may cause to human rights, but since the law is provisional, that harm should be viewed as proportional. Referring to this phenomenon in the first *Adalah* case, Justice Arbel remarked: 'The fact that basic rights are harmed by a temporary provision due to ad hoc needs can indeed indicate the proportionality of that harm. That the harm is temporary, since the legislation is a temporary provision, reflects on our appreciation of the might, depth, and extend of the harm caused to a basic right.'[10] Indeed, most petitions against such temporary provisions have been rejected. The Court has refrained from quashing them because it recognises the proportionality entailed in their temporality. Nevertheless, when a temporary provision was extended again and again (as was the case of the *Tal* Law that exempted ultra-Orthodox students from military service), the Court did not hesitate to invalidate it. It would seem that at least some of the Supreme Court judges view such frequent extensions with suspicion, feeling that the Knesset might be trying to institutionalise complicated and sensitive issues, while simultaneously skipping over the need to conduct an orderly public debate and attempting to ignore the meaning of offensive legislation as part of Israeli law.

While the Knesset kept silent on constitutional matters, the Supreme Court further addressed some of the issues that had remained unresolved since the *Bank Hamizrahi* case. One of those issues is the supremacy of basic laws. The basic laws on human rights include a limitation clause that allows the legislator to harm these rights through legislation. This limitation clause reflects the recognition that rights are not absolute

---

[10] *Adalah* (n 8).

and may be deviated from in certain circumstances. At the same time, other basic laws that deal with government institutions do not include a limitation clause; that is, the conditions in which they may be 'harmed' by an 'ordinary' law have not been explicitly determined. The approach that the Supreme Court seems to be taking is that these basic laws should be viewed as if they do contain a limitation clause, actually creating 'judicial limitation clauses' that allow for the review of laws that impair institutional basic laws. For example, Section 4 of Basic Law: The Knesset states that elections in Israel must, among other things, be 'equal'. The basic law does not include an explicit limitation clause. The Court established that equality in elections is a central value that deserves maximum protection in the same fashion as basic human rights. For this reason, it may state that harming the equal opportunities principle in the context of the Knesset elections fails to comply with the limitation clause of Basic Law: Human Dignity and Liberty.[11] Some believe that 'exporting the limitation clause to institutional basic laws constitutes a second constitutional revolution'.[12] At the very least, it reflects a trend in which the Court is expanding the rules of judicial review of the laws in Israel.

At the same time, instead of treating basic laws as Israel's solid constitution, the Knesset seems to be increasingly inclined to amend them, sometimes for very specific purposes and with relative ease (as mentioned in chapter one). For example, Basic Law: The Knesset was enacted in 1958 and in 34 years, until 1992, was amended 15 times; from 1992 onwards – it was amended another 24 times. Enacted in 1964, Basic Law: The President of the State was amended twice in 28 years, and over the 20 years between 1992 and 2012, it was amended on five additional occasions.[13]

---

[11] HCJ 3434/96 *Hoffnung v The Knesset Speaker*, ver 50(3), 57, 70 (1996).

[12] Ariel Bendor, 'Four Constitutional Revolutions' (2003) 6 *Mishpat Umimshal* 305 (Hebrew); A Reichmann, 'This is No Way to Build a Constitution' (2003) 35 *Orech Hadin* 42 (Hebrew); A Klagsbald, 'Conflicts with Basic Laws' (2005–06) 48 *Hapraklit* 293 (Hebrew); Hillel Sommer, 'From Childhood to Adulthood: Open Issues in the Implementation of the Constitutional Revolution' (2004) 59 *Mishpat vaAsakim A* 59 (Hebrew).

[13] Similarly, amendments of other, newer basic laws were all made after 1992; for example, Basic Law: The Judiciary, which was enacted in 1984, was amended twice. Basic Law: Jerusalem Capital of Israel, enacted in 1980, was amended once, while Basic Law: The State Comptroller, enacted in 1988, was amended twice. See Suzie Navot, 'Israel' in Dawn Oliver and Carlo Fusaro (eds), *How Constitutions Change – A Comparative Study* (Oxford, Hart Publishing, 2011) 191–209.

Over the past few years, the Knesset has also tended to make personal or *ad casum* amendments to basic laws. These amendments are usually adopted against the backdrop of political events that required the Knesset's immediate attention, but it has chosen the path of constitutional legislation rather than regular legislation. This was the case for the amendment to Basic Law: The Knesset, which added new rationales for the disqualification of parties. A further example was the decision on the biennial budget, which was introduced in the form of a temporary basic law, as discussed in the *Bar-On* case.

The *Bar-On* case prompted an interesting case of judicial review and Knesset reaction. The Knesset knew it was following a problematic legislative procedure (because it employed its constituent power to temporarily amend the constitution), but felt that it was authorised to do so. For its part, the HCJ felt that, in principle, it could expand its judicial review powers to apply to basic laws too, according to supra-constitutional principles that can be found in its earlier adjudication. But it had never before used this pretext to quash a law. It rejected the petition in the *Bar-On* case and it did not nullify the temporary amendment. However, the fact that the possibility was discussed indicated that the Court acknowledged its power to do so and did not deny its prerogative to judicially review even amendments of basic laws by a constituent power.

The procedure for judicial review of the constitutionality of laws takes two basic forms:

1. Direct judicial review by the HCJ: any person alleging a violation of his protected rights may file a 'direct' petition with the HCJ, challenging the constitutionality of that violation. Direct petitions may be private – protesting the violation of a personal right – or public – where the petitioner represents a group and argues that harm has been suffered by an entire population sector. Initially, the HCJ would not acknowledge *actio popularis* petitions, but attempts were made in the early 1980s to persuade it to adjudicate 'public' issues. Subsequently, it expanded the scope of its judicial review and eventually accepted *actio popularis* petitions. It has no filtering procedure and conducts no abstract judicial review.

2. Indirect judicial review in all courts: in the absence of provisions to the contrary, theoretically, the power to examine the constitutionality of laws resides with any judge as part of the legal proceeding over which that judge presides. For example, in a criminal proceeding

where the accused claims that his indictment is based on a law that violates the provisions of a basic law, the presiding judge may adjudicate the constitutionality of that law. This, however, has only happened once, when a magistrates' court judge invalidated a section of the Income Tax Ordinance.[14] This was the only (and exceptional) case of indirect judicial review by a magistrates' court. It is generally accepted that the only court authorised to nullify laws is the Supreme Court sitting as the HCJ. Therefore, petitions requesting judicial review are brought before it and are discussed by an extended panel of nine or 11 judges.

The procedures for judicial review of laws are not anchored in statute. Although the HCJ has been judicially reviewing laws for more than two decades, the very legitimacy and implementation of judicial review is the subject of a lively and often acrimonious political and public debate. As a result, the annulment of laws by the Supreme Court is particularly restrained, and though many petitions for judicial review have been filed, most of these petitions have been dismissed. At the same time, groups that oppose the Supreme Court's activism have occasionally suggested the establishment of a constitutional court in Israel. They argue that the Supreme Court should be stripped of its power to judicially review laws, which should be assigned to a constitutional court comprising representatives of the various sectors of the Israeli population.

This proposal has been raised primarily by the circles that regard the Supreme Court and its liberal rulings as threatening the Jewish nature of the state (mainly ultra-Orthodox MKs). It was raised because some groups in Israel have been increasingly rejecting the Supreme Court's legitimacy and right to judicially review laws or refusing to accept its rulings when they conflict with their own views. A decade-long sociological study[15] revealed that ultra-Orthodox Jews have little to no confidence

---

[14] MC (TA) 4696/01 *The State of Israel v Hendelman* (published by Nevo on 14 April 2003). This decision was later criticised by the District Court: 'Though this case was not presented before us, I wish to remark that the Magistrates Court should have exercised restraint and instead of hurriedly nullifying Section 236B1(b), it could have found a better solution for the alleged harm caused to the freedom of occupation right by appropriately interpreting the section': DC(TA) 70597/04 *Hendelman v The State of Israel* (published by Nevo on 12 January 2005), Judge Shnitzer's verdict at [17].

[15] Arye Rattner, *The Culture of Law – The Legal and Justice System as Viewed by Israel's Society (A Longitudinal Study 2000–2009)* (Jerusalem, The Shasha Centre for Strategic Research, The Hebrew University in Jerusalem, 2009) (Hebrew).

in the Court. In 2011, for example, some 100,000 of them demonstrated in protest after Supreme Court Justice Edmund Levi approved a prison sentence meted out to parents who would not send their daughters to the same class as girls of a different Jewish background. This was after the Supreme Court ruled that separate classes were discriminatory and therefore forbidden.[16] The demonstrators chanted: 'Yes to the *Torah*. No to the HCJ.'

In summary, judicial review of laws, as opposed to constitutional interpretation, has been restrained. The number of cases in which the HCJ has actually nullified laws is very small. It is believed that 'the Court's power to nullify laws is similar to the power of nonconventional weapons . . . and the Court should use it only when a basic right or value is prominently and substantively harmed'.[17] This trend of restraint is primarily expressed by the rules of interpretation applied by the HCJ when claims are made that basic rights have been harmed. All laws are presumptively constitutionally valid and people who argue that a law should be nullified must show that the law harms a basic right and that this harm is disproportional. Furthermore, the Court usually avoids nullifying temporary provisions, even if they do harm basic rights. With respect to remedies, after concluding that a certain law is unconstitutional, the HCJ sometimes 'suspends nullification', which postpones the verdict's application. This remedy prevents the formation of a 'legislative vacuum' and gives the Knesset time to introduce a different legal arrangement.

STANDING AND JUSTICIABILITY

No ordinary or basic law prescribes preconditions that must be met before the HCJ can exercise its powers. As noted above, section 15(c) of Basic Law: The Judiciary allows the HCJ to grant 'relief for the sake of justice' and issue orders that bind public position holders, irrespective of who initiated the process. Traditionally, however, the HCJ made the threshold requirement of 'standing' a precondition for hearing a petition. Thus, only petitioners who were personally affected by a government act could file an appeal against it with the HCJ. The Court applies

---

[16] HCJ 1067/08 *No'ar Kh'halacha org v Minister of Education* (rendered on 6 August 2009).

[17] HCJ 7111/95 *Local Government Centre v The Knesset*, ver 50(3), 485 (1995) 496.

this requirement more strictly when the issue in question is a public or even a political matter, demanding that the appellant show real harm to gain standing.[18]

Gradually, particularly since the 1980s, the HCJ has become more amenable when a public issue is deemed important and has been willing to intervene even if the appellant has showed no personal damage.[19] For example, the HCJ agreed to intervene in a petition filed against the President of the State of Israel's decision to pardon officers who were involved in the *Bus No 300* case, even though none of the petitioners was personally harmed by that decision. The petitioners argued that pardoning people before they are tried and convicted violates the rule of law. Ever since then, the right to standing has been rarely mentioned in the Court's adjudication. This inevitably led to the creation of numerous public associations that file petitions with the HCJ whenever anything appears wrong to them. Justice Cheshin cynically described this in a verdict: 'By way of exaggeration, we could say that today, people pick up a newspaper and, skimming through the items, find something they disapprove of and call to their friends: "Let us make pilgrimage to the Supreme Court." They then write the petition in the car.'[20]

This trend has impacted on Israeli society. Despite the fact that the HCJ did not have the powers to oversee all government and legislative decisions granted by the constitution, the public have used the court to obtain public policy decisions that could not be obtained through any other means. This phenomenon gradually enhanced and strengthened the Court's position as a key political player, which may be seen as creating a new balance of power between the branches of the state. The Court transitioned from its position as the protector of personal rights to the body whose task it is to ensure the realisation of public values. The new doctrines of standing and justiciability, which are more tolerant of 'public' action, allowed for public petitioners and NGOs to present the Court with questions of human rights, Palestinians' rights and minority rights. These were the issues that political institutions were quite unable to resolve, if not reluctant to deal with at all. This broad view of standing proved to be a powerful mechanism for the Court to protect the rule of law and the legality of government. As for justiciabil-

---

[18] HCJ 40/70 *Becker v The Defense Minister*, ver 24(1), 238 (1970) 246–47.
[19] HCJ 428/86 *Barzilay v Israel's Government*, ver 40(3), 505 (1986).
[20] HCJ 2148/94 *Gelbert v Hon Supreme Court President*, ver 48(3), 573 (1994).

ity, Israeli judges have generally rejected the non-justiciability claim regarding political issues, choosing to adopt a more flexible arrangement that confers considerable discretion on the Court, thereby enabling judicial intervention in political issues.

Judicial review of sensitive political questions may be treated in several ways, spanning an imaginary continuum where a constitutional barrier at one end prevents any kind of judicial intervention, while at the other end permitting ordinary judicial review of all political issues. Only rarely do states and their judiciaries position themselves clearly at these two conflicting ends. Nonetheless, examples of both approaches may be observed, namely, the approach that constitutionally negates the possibility of judicial review of political issues, such as that adopted in the US with the doctrine of 'political questions', and the approach that regards political issues as legal questions that lend themselves to judicial review, as is the case in Spain.[21]

Between these two extremes, there are intermediate approaches. Each country has its own particular response to the 'political question' doctrine, determining its place on the judicial review continuum[22] based on its own balancing formula and the outcomes of country-specific considerations. These variables include the status of the constitutional court, its relative position in the system of state authorities, its power and its degree of independence, as well as custom and political culture. On a formal level, the relevant approach is also determined by normative and constitutional arrangements, which occasionally exclude defined areas from the court's jurisdiction.

According to one of the potential intermediate approaches, when there is no constitutional barrier to judicial intervention, it is incumbent upon judges to establish mechanisms that enable them to avoid adjudicating political questions. This model is very close to the end of the spectrum that prevents judicial intervention in political questions and may be called the 'non-justiciability approach'.

Another approach, closer to the position of endorsing regular judicial review, allows the judges to establish criteria for intervention in political

---

[21] See, for example, Juan José Diaz Sanchez, 'El Control Jurisdiccional de los Actos del Gobierno y de los Consejos de Gobierno' (2012) 26 *Revista jurídica de Castilla y Leon* 45; Nuria Garrido Cuenca, *El acto de gobierno, un análisis de los ordenamientos Francés y Español* (Barcelona, Cedecs, 1998).

[22] The idea of a 'continuum' is taken from Justice Barak's article 'The Parliament and the Supreme Court – Towards the Future' (2000) 45 *Hapraklit* 5, 8 (Hebrew).

issues, although these criteria differ from those applied to the judicial review of acts by other branches of government. This approach does not necessarily preclude judicial review of political issues, but is more 'restrained' and is rarely exercised.

In this context, the Israeli model is particularly interesting. It may be said that it simply moved along the length of the scale from non-justiciability and non-intervention in certain areas to a reserved approach of restraint, often extending all the way to unconstrained judicial review. Justice Barak described it well: 'I observe the doctrine of non-justiciability of political issues with great suspicion. As much as it is possible, I would rather examine every argument on its merits and address it on the level of its cause – that is, whether the government authority adhered to or violated the law – and not on the level of its non-justiciability.'[23]

Furthermore, the Israeli adjudication discussed the distinction between 'normative' and 'institutional' justiciability. Normative justiciability addresses the question of the legal means for dealing with a dispute. A dispute is normatively justiciable if legal standards for its resolution exist. Such legal standards exist where there is a legal norm and therefore, as Barak stated, the disputed issue is justiciable. To establish institutional justiciability, the Court must decide whether it should rule in relation to a dispute or whether it is best left for other branches of government to handle. Normative justiciability is the threshold requirement, while institutional justiciability, which is more demanding, deals with the question of whether the law and the courts constitute the proper framework for dispute resolution.

Pursuant to the traditional approach, an issue is deemed non-justiciable if the Court has no legal tools to address it and the task of its resolution is assigned to the political bodies in charge of the issue. Presently, the political aspect of any action is irrelevant and the Court's mission is to preserve the rule of law by ensuring that all branches of government act within their law boundaries. In the 1980s, Justice Barak refused to place political issues outside the scope of judicial review, and his ruling soon became known for its simple motto: 'everything is justiciable'.[24] Yet, although the

---

[23] Aharon Barak, *A Judge in a Democratic Society* (Jerusalem, Nevo, 2004) 275 (Hebrew). For a further interesting discussion of the issue, see Dafna Barak-Erez, 'The Justiciability Revolution – A Situation Assessment' (2008) 50 *Hapraklit* 3 (Hebrew).
[24] HCJ 910/86 *Ressler v The Defense Minister*, ver 43(2), 441 (1988).

political nature of an act does not cancel out its legal nature, the legal nature of the executing body does impact on the nature of the rules applied by the Court.[25]

The HCJ decided that it has the power to supervise Knesset proceedings and examine decisions by the Knesset Speaker and committees, and political coalition agreements, but whether it actually does this and the extent of its intervention naturally depends on the body it audits. Dealing with the Knesset, for example, the Supreme Court exercises restraint. In the *Weiss* case, Supreme Court President Barak decided to reject a petition against the transitional government's right to continue negotiations with the PA. Among other things, Barak stated: 'intervention on such issues should be reserved to irregular situations . . . Such issues – whose primary components are political, and which are a major bone of contention for the Israeli society – should be addressed by political discourse, by the Knesset's organs, or by popular vote'.[26]

The HCJ judicially reviews decisions based on military considerations, but also approaches such issues with caution and restraint. Nevertheless, HCJ rulings on military issues have been criticised by the public and the Knesset. A famous case was *Plonim*, in which a petitioner challenged the legality of the Israeli practice of holding foreign nationals in custody as 'bargaining chips' used for the extraction of information about IDF missing soldiers and prisoners of war (POWs).[27] The Supreme Court ruled that this practice was illegal. This was a controversial decision and was the subject of animated discussion in the public arena.

An outstanding example of this approach was the Supreme Court's involvement in the disengagement from the Gaza Strip.[28] The Court

---

[25] Justice Barak, for example, addressed this issue as follows: 'Conceivably, the decision to go to war or to make peace is not subject to normal rules governing administrative discretion. In these exceptional cases, petitions will be dismissed not because of the absence of a legal norm, but due to the absence of a prohibitive norm and the existence of a permitting norm; in other words, due to lack of grounds. The act is not non-justiciable, but rather justiciable and legal.' ibid.

[26] HCJ 5167/00 *Weiss v Israel's Prime Minister*, ver 55(2), 455 (2001) 472, President Barak's verdict at [14].

[27] ACH (additional criminal hearing) 7048/97 *Plonim v The Defense Minister*, ver 54(1), 721 (2000).

[28] The withdrawal (disengagement) from the Gaza Strip, including the dismantling of Jewish settlements and the evacuation of Jewish settlers, was the main policy of the Israeli government in 2004–05. The disengagement plan sharply departed from the platform of the ruling *Likud* party.

examined the substance of all the petitions relating to the disengagement. It exercised close and ongoing supervision of the process, confirmed and legitimised all of the government decisions, and was a full and active partner in the execution of the disengagement plan, defending both its legality and its constitutionality at all stages. Courts in other constitutional systems may have declined to intervene or even judicially consider this kind of national-political decision, which was also the source of serious public controversy. The Court, however, chose to be a full and leading partner in the entire plan.

Its political nature notwithstanding, the disengagement plan could not have been executed without the legal backing of the Supreme Court. At the very beginning of the process, the HCJ rejected the claim that the question of the constitutionality of the Evacuation-Compensation Law[29] was non-justiciable due to its political nature. This law and other necessary government acts were approved by the HCJ (only one section concerning the amount of compensation was declared void) after substantive and comprehensive deliberations. The dismissal of all the petitions concerning the disengagement plan after dealing with the cases on their merits created a semblance of legal approval for the different government decisions. The HCJ affirmed the government's decisions, but only after (and subject to) its examination of them on a substantive level. The Court heard the case on its merits, examined the questions raised and only then dismissed the appeal.

Prima facie, the exercise of either doctrine – non-justiciability or judicial self-restraint – may ultimately produce the same result: the Supreme Court refrains from intervening. However, limiting this examination to outcomes could be misleading. Under the non-justiciability doctrine, the Court's non-intervention means that the decision itself is not examined on its merits. Yet, when a petition is rejected due to judicial self-restraint, the Court generally examines it on a substantive level, after which it decides not to intervene. The Court's decision is therefore conceived by the public as approving of the government's policy, which gives the Court the power to make the final decision: government policy may not be implemented before the Court says it can be.

---

[29] The Disengagement Plan (Implementation) Law (otherwise known as the Evacuation-Compensation Law) prescribed guidelines for the compensation of evacuees.

This is a fine illustration of the approach endorsed in Israel. Acting within its own discretion, the Supreme Court may or may not intervene in political questions. The result is that the Court confirms decisions by government authorities after examining them on their merits. Thus, it is occasionally regarded as the body that grants the final 'approval' of political decisions. Clearly, this lays the ground for, and offers an incentive to, filing appeals against almost every political decision, which is one of the most notable shortcomings of this approach.

Although the Supreme Court is always reluctant to judicially review sensitive political questions, they are justiciable in Israel and anyone can challenge them in court. This is one of the reasons why the Supreme Court of Israel has been considered, at least for the past two decades, a very activist court.

JUDICIAL ACTIVISM

A sharp debate over the issue of judicial activism was and still is conducted in the Israeli adjudication and constitutional literature. This has been influenced by many comparative scholarly papers on the issue.[30] The concept itself has never been properly defined and remains vague,[31] but the one thing that the various definitions have in common is an understanding that the more the HCJ intervenes in the policies of various government bodies, the more activist it is.

Perhaps the starting point is to recognise that the Israeli Supreme Court is internationally known for its activism. Having operated without a constitutional framework since the State of Israel was founded, it has developed numerous tools for intervention in government decisions over the years, expanding the rules of justiciability up to the point where the Court has, in many respects, turned into a supervising and criticising

---

[30] There is not enough space here to cite the extensive literature on judicial activism or self-restraint. I shall just mention a few approaches that appear in the basic works of the following: Robert H Bork, *Coercing Virtue: The Worldwide Rule of Judges* (Washington DC, Aei Press, 2003); Richard A Posner, *The Federal Courts: Challenges and Reform* (Cambridge, MA, Harvard University Press, 1999); Kent Roach, *The Supreme Court on Trial: Judicial Activism or Democratic Dialogue* (Toronto, Irwin Law, 2001); Stephen Halpern and Charles Lamb, *Supreme Court Activism and Restraint* (Lexington, MA, Lexington Books, 1982).

[31] Aharon Barak, 'On a Worldview re Justice and Judicial Activism' (1993) 17 *Iyuney Mishpat* 475 (Hebrew).

authority. Social processes further influenced the HCJ's willingness to intervene in areas that the judiciary ordinarily does not address.

In the early years, still under the influence of the British tradition, Israeli adjudication was typically formalistic. The written word was of paramount importance and solutions for legal issues were mostly found in the texts of laws. The Supreme Court adhered to the strict separation of powers, particularly in its relationship with the Knesset. The absence of a formal, written constitution prevented the judicial review of laws, which left the Court with a merely interpretative role. Nonetheless, the HCJ became a central defender of democratic values very early on. As we shall see in the next chapter, defending human rights in the early years of Israel, even before these rights were anchored in a constitutional document, the HCJ has always been viewed as particularly activist. HCJ rulings created the unwritten Israeli bill of rights, which serves as an alternative to the constitution.[32]

The traditional, formalistic approach began changing in the mid-1980s as these arguments lost power and value-based arguments and considerations gained ground gradually but steadily, following the profound cultural and political changes that took place in Israel from the late 1970s onwards. This phase was analysed in a fascinating book by Menahem Mautner, who dubbed it 'the transition from formalism to activism'.[33] Justice Aharon Barak, who was appointed Supreme Court judge in 1979 and served until 2006, including as Court President, extensively contributed to this transition. The fact that the HCJ was willing to forgo preconditions such as standing resulted in its examination of general issues and resolutions that affected no one in particular. Minimising the non-justiciability doctrine further helped the HCJ address sensitive political and military issues.

Israel came under the direct influence of US culture in the 1970s and 1980s, and social values such as individualism and liberalism started to have an impact on the world of law as well. Since the 1980s, Israeli legal education has been greatly Americanised. US law became more influential. This American influence was eventually reflected in academic papers

---

[32] Gavison, Kremnitzer, Dotan, *Judicial Activism: For and Against* (Jerusalem, Yediot Hahronot and Magnes, Jerusalem, 2000) 6 (Hebrew).

[33] Menachem Mautner, 'The Decline of Formalism and the Rise of Values in Israeli Law' (1993) 17 *Iyuney Mishpat* 503 (Hebrew). For English coverage, see Menachem Mautner, *Law and the Culture of Israel* (Oxford, Oxford University Press, 2011).

authored in Israel and in the adjudication of the HCJ.[34] This coincided with political changes that took place in Israel. The Labour Party lost its position at the government's helm, parties as a whole lost power, and extremist and fundamentalist groups gained strength, while the Arab minority started rebelling. This state of affairs sparked extensive debates about the cultural nature of the State of Israel, and the Court was often called upon to intervene and preserve Israel's democratic nature.

After the constitutional changes of 1992, judicial activism climaxed in the *Bank Hamizrahi* case, in which the Court held that it has the power to judicially review laws. Stating that basic laws have constitutional status, and thus that the Court may nullify Knesset legislation that conflicts with these basic laws, was perhaps the apex of the Supreme Court's activist period.

Similarly, a new style of reasoning evolved, addressing the laws' normative meaning. The earlier formalistic application of the law to the facts of each case was replaced by attempts to find a balance between conflicting values. The new justiciability approach went hand in hand with the Supreme Court's use of reasonableness as its primary instrument for the purpose of supervising government and administrative decisions.[35] The purpose of the norm, not its language, became paramount. Concepts such as 'the purpose of the law', 'the spirit of the law' and 'the legislator's intention' replaced the dry legislative letter. Judges started indulging in more creativity in their judicial activities, feeling free to seek creative solutions in an attempt to attain just, moral and value-based judicial results. The HCJ expanded the scope of its intervention and even criticised the values and acts of public position holders. Thus, HCJ rulings started shaping policies and even determining general norms.

There are many and diverse examples of Israeli activist adjudication. Particularly prominent were cases that sought the enforcement of ethical norms in relation to public officials, mainly in the 1990s. In terms of comparative law, the HCJ's intervention in issues such as public ethics, government culture and proper administration is quite unique. For example, the Court ordered the Prime Minister to dismiss a minister who had been

---

[34] Suzie Navot, 'Israel: Creating a Constitution' – The Use of Foreign Precedents by the Supreme Court (1994–2010)' in Tania Groppi and Marie-Claire Ponthoreau (eds), *The Use of Foreign Precedents by Constitutional Judges* (Oxford, Hart Publishing, 2013).

[35] Mautner, *Law and the Culture of Israel* (n 33) 60.

formally charged, although he was under no legal obligation to do so.[36] Ruling in a petition against the appointment of a person involved in the *Bus No 300* case as a ministry director general, the Court stated it is 'unreasonable' to appoint a person who committed grave crimes as a senior civil servant. This ruling was based on the idea that 'a civil servant is the public's trustee', which later served as grounds for determining that coalition agreements must be made public,[37] a duty that was later anchored in law.

Furthermore, the HCJ's willingness to control internal Knesset proceedings is also unique, considering that many other comparative judicial systems are of the view that parliamentary activities and resolutions are not to be questioned by the courts. Initially, the HCJ was extremely cautious about reviewing parliamentary proceedings and ruled that it would only intervene if the Knesset should deviate from its authority in quasi-judicial Knesset proceedings, but it was not long before this approach changed. In 1981, in the *Sarid* case, Justice Barak ruled that there is a need to find a balance between the principle of separation of powers (stating that the general procedures of the parliament are its own internal affair) and the principle of the rule of law. He held that the balancing test for intervention was 'the potential damage of a Knesset act or decision to parliamentary life, and the extent of its influence on the foundations of the constitutional structure'.[38] Over the past few years, the Court has stated that judicial review of internal parliamentary proceedings is not so different from judicial review of general administrative decisions. Nevertheless, de facto intervention in internal parliamentary proceedings remained a rarity, as the Court intervened in only a few cases since the 1980s. The Court still maintains a distinction between intervening in Knesset acts and the work of other administrative authorities, but when they make semi-judicial resolutions, the Court's intervention is considered normal. The HCJ established that the Knesset enjoys a special status and distinguished between its willingness to intervene in Knesset and government resolutions by acting with explicit restraint towards the former.

---

[36] HCJ 3094/93 *The Movement for Government Quality in Israel v Israel's Government*, ver 47(5), 422 (1993).
[37] HCJ 1601/90 *Shalit v MK Peres et al*, ver 44(3), 404 (1990).
[38] HCJ 652/81 *Sarid v Speaker of the Knesset*, ver 36(2), 197 (1981) 202.

Many scholars have argued that the Israeli Supreme Court was extremely activist in the 1980s and 1990s.[39] Richard Posner wrote of the Supreme Court led by President Barak that:

> What Barak created out of whole cloth was a degree of judicial power undreamed of even by our most aggressive Supreme Court justices . . . A court can forbid the government to appoint an official who had committed a crime . . . or is otherwise ethically challenged and can order the dismissal of a cabinet minister because he faces criminal proceedings; that in the name of 'human dignity' a court can compel the government to alleviate homelessness and poverty; and that a court can countermand military orders, decide 'whether to prevent the release of a terrorist within the framework of a political "package deal"', and direct the government to move the security wall that keeps suicide bombers from entering Israel from the West Bank . . . In Barak's conception of the separation of powers, the judicial power is unlimited.[40]

Amnon Rubinstein, a renowned professor of constitutional law and Israel Prize laureate, wrote that 'in fact, in many senses, under Barak's leadership, the Court has turned itself into an alternative government'.[41]

This judicial activism has taken its toll on the Supreme Court as it transformed into a dominant and effective body intervening in the performance of other government authorities. Members of academia and the public have criticised the Court's role in shaping norms. It has been argued that the Court imposes its values on the political system, intensifying public antagonism against, and damaging the public's trust in, the judiciary. Critics of the Court rejected its willingness to examine every issue on its merits, based on the standards of 'reasonableness' and 'proportionality'. They have argued that judges should not deal with legislation, which should be reserved as the domain of elected parliamentarians, and that some of the Court's rulings were completely illegitimate. Furthermore, legal discussions of political, military and public issues seem to have become entangled with political debates, so that even if the Court does not offer a final ruling, the

---

[39] Former Supreme Court President Moshe Landau, Professor Gad Barzilai, Professor Yoav Dotan, Professor Ruth Gavison and Professor Gideon Sapir to name just a few.

[40] Richard Posner, 'Enlightened Despot', *New Republic*, 23 April 2007, available at: http://www.tnr.com/section/enlightened-despot.

[41] Mautner, *Law and the Culture of Israel* (n 33) 56.

fact that it has discussed an issue pushes it further up the order of public priorities.[42]

The Supreme Court has been particularly criticised by politicians, although the fact that the political system would not make final decisions on topical issues served as a catalyst for the multitude of petitions filed with the HCJ by and on behalf of MKs, which reflects the weakness of the political culture and bolstered the position of the Court. Referring to this phenomenon, Justice Menahem Elon said: 'The excessive number of petitioners and petitions follows from the weak political culture that has recently afflicted the political system, which may have declined absolutely.'[43] Judicial norms have become central to public debates, replacing government ethics. It seems that in the modern Israeli reality, every issue with a political dimension – from the decision on the number of terrorists that should be released in a POW exchange deal to a decision on the next Israel Award laureate – is sooner or later placed on the Court's desk. This process has been labelled 'the judicialisation of the government'.[44] Thus, when the Court rejects a petition against the legality of a political resolution, the public perceives it as if the HCJ had stated that the policy were correct and just, even though this is a misconception and the Court eventually chose not to intervene in the other authority's discretion.

In fact, the claim that Israel's public life has undergone judicialisation is unfounded. Most of the key social decisions are still made by political institutions and not by the Supreme Court, although the latter is sometimes forced to engage in issues that the legislature avoided. In certain respects, the Court's very willingness to intervene weakens the political body it reviews. Though theoretically this willingness applies to a wide range of issues, reality has shown that the Court has actually intervened very little and Israeli politics are still conducted within government corridors.[45] When addressing Knesset internal affairs, the Court feels authorised to intervene, but rarely does so. It would seem that the general impression that the Court 'interferes in everything' is a mere myth.

---

[42] See Posner (n 40); Barak Medina, 'Four Myths of Judicial Review: A Response to Richard Posner's Criticism of Aharon Barak's Judicial Activism', June 2007, available at: http://ssrn.com/abstract=992972.

[43] HCJ 1635/90 *Zerzhewsky v The Prime Minister*, ver 45(1), 749 (1991) 760–61.

[44] See Itzhak Gal-Nur, 'The Judicialization of the Public Sphere in Israel' (2004) 7 *Mishpat u'Mimshal* 355 (Hebrew).

[45] Daphne Barak-Erez, 'Judicial Review of Politics: The Israeli Case' (2002) 29 *Journal of Law & Society* 611.

The same applies to judicial activism. The Supreme Court appeared activist when it overruled the decisions of other authorities, but alleging that it was actually engaged in activism would require a thorough inspection of its adjudication patterns, and no such study has been conducted. It is true that the Court is willing to examine every issue presented before it on its merits, but a detailed examination of its judicial control of government activities shows that it has almost always in practice confirmed government decisions, expansively citing reasonableness, which has left the government with almost unlimited discretion. Most petitions filed on such matters were dismissed accordingly.

One example of the gap between the alleged judicial activism of the HCJ and the reality will be discussed in the next and final chapter of this book. The Court has been willing to discuss almost every petition filed against IDF activities in the occupied territories, examining whether the means in question were 'proportionally' employed, but it has nearly accepted almost every decision that the IDF has made as part of its 'war on terrorism', which we shall discuss in the next chapter.

CONCLUSION

This chapter discussed the crucial role of the Supreme Court in Israel's constitutional context. Recent decades have seen a shifting of power, mainly from elected politicians to unelected judges. In turn, the constitutional revolution and the change in the Court's position regarding the doctrines of justiciability and standing, the readiness of the Court to examine petitions on their merits, along with the difficulties of the political branch deciding on controversial issues, have all impacted on the role of the Court. At the same time, the Court has become a dominant and effective oversight body. In this capacity, a new more expansive view of standing has proved a powerful mechanism for the Court to protect the rule of law and to ensure the legality of government authorities.

By way of contrast, the Knesset has remained largely silent on constitutional matters, leaving the task of completing the human rights revolution almost entirely to the Supreme Court, which further addressed some of the issues that remained unresolved since the *Bank Hamizrahi* case. The dominance of the Court has resulted in a phenomenon called the 'judicialisation of politics' or the 'constitutionalisation of public life'. It seems that in Israel, almost every political decision involves the

Court. This position has been strongly criticised by politicians as well as the media and members of academia, who argue that the outcome is that judges undermine the legitimacy of decisions made by democratically elected politicians. The debate over judicial activism is still very much alive in Israel and is conducted both in the public arena as well as in the academic literature.[46]

This impression of judicial activism may be rather deceptive. Most of the key social decisions are still made by political institutions and not by courts. The judiciary is sometimes forced to engage in issues that were avoided by the legislature. The Court perhaps appears activist because it is ready to hear and deal with every petition, but, in practice, it frequently confirms decisions made by governmental bodies. One of the most effective ways of dismissing political petitions has been the flexible application of reasonableness and proportionality, which has left the government with almost unlimited discretion. Indeed, the Supreme Court has a crucial role within Israel's constitution, but the argument that it has become an alternative government seems exaggerated. Detailed examinations of its decisions show that most petitions filed on political matters are dismissed.

[46] There is not enough space here to cite the extensive literature on judicial activism in Israel. I shall just mention a few examples: Daniel Friedmann, *The Purse and the Sword: The Trials of the Israeli Legal Revolution* (Tel Aviv, Yedioth Books, 2013) (Hebrew); Gavison, Kremnitzer, Dotan, *Judicial Activism: For and Against* (n 1); Mautner, *Law and the Culture of Israel* (n 33); Assaf Meydani, *The Israeli Supreme Court and the Human Rights Revolution: Courts as Agenda Setters* (Cambridge, Cambridge University Press, 2011); Avinoma Ya'ari, 'Judicial Activism and its Influence on the Israeli Army' in Dvora Cohen and Moshe Lisk (eds), *Key Affairs in Israel* (Ben Gurion Centre for the Research of Zionism, the Negev University, 2010) (Hebrew); Zeev Segal 'Judicial Activism vis-a-vis Judicial Restraint: An Israeli Viewpoint' (2011) 47(2) *Tulsa Law Review* 319; Yigal Mersel, 'On Aharon Barak's Activist Image' (2011) 47(2) *Tulsa Law Review* 339; Margit Cohn and Mordechai Kremnitzer, 'Judicial Activism: A Multidimensional Model' (2005) 18(2) *Canadian Journal of Law and Jurisprudence* 333; Eli Salzberger, 'Judicial Activism in Israel: Sources, Forms and Manifestations' (2007), available at: http://papers.ssrn.com/sol3/papers. cfm?abstract_id=957849; Ariel Bendor, 'Are There Any Limits to Justiciability?' (1997) 7 *Indiana International & Comparative Law Review* 311; Moshe Landau, 'Judicial Activism' (2002) 7 *Hamishpat* 535. A special issue of the Israeli law journal *Iunei Mishpat* was devoted to the issues of judicial activism in 1993, among many others the articles by Aharon Barak and Itzhak Zamir: Aharon Barak, 'On the Philosophy of Law and Judging and Judicial Activism' (1993) 17 *Iuniei Mishpat* 475 (Hebrew); Ytzhak Zamir, 'Judicial Activism – A Decision to Decide' (1993) 17 *Iuniei Mishpat* 647 (Hebrew).

FURTHER READING

Barak, Aharon, 'Foreword: A Judge on Judging: The Role of a Supreme Court in a Democracy' (2002) 116 *Harvard Law Review* 16.

Barak, Aharon, *The Judge in a Democracy* (Princeton, Princeton University Press, 2006).

Barak-Erez, Daphne, 'Judicial Review of Politics: The Israeli Case' (2002) 29 *Journal of Law & Society* 611.

Barak-Erez, Daphne, 'Broadening the Scope of Judicial Review in Israel: Between Activism and Restraint' (2009) 3 *Indiana Journal of Constitutional Law* 119.

Bendor, Ariel, 'The Relevance of the Judicial Activism vs. Judicial Restraint Discourse' (2011) 47 *Tulsa Law Review* 331.

Carmi, Guy E, 'A Constitutional Court in the Absence of a Formal Constitution? On the Ramifications of Appointing the Israeli Supreme Court as the Only Tribunal for Judicial Review' (2005) 21 *Connecticut Journal of International Law* 67.

Dotan, Yoav, 'Judicial Review and Political Accountability: The Case of the High Court of Justice in Israel' (1998) 32 *Israel Law Review* 448.

Gavison, Ruth, 'The Role of Courts in Rifted Democracies' (1999) 33 *Israel Law Review* 216.

Lahav, Pnina, 'Israel's Supreme Court' in Robert Freedman (ed), *Contemporary Israel: Domestic Politics, Foreign Policy and Security Challenges* (Boulder, CO, Westview, 2008).

Mautner, Menahem, *Law and the Culture of Israel* (Oxford, Oxford University Press, 2011).

Medina, Barak, 'Four Myths of Judicial Review: A Response to Richard Posner's Critique of Aharon Barak's Judicial Activism', June 2007, available at: http://ssrn.com/abstract=992972.

Meydani, Assaf, *The Israeli Supreme Court and the Human Rights Revolution: Courts as Agenda Setters* (Cambridge, Cambridge University Press, 2011).

Navot, Suzie, 'More of the Same: Judicial Activism in Israel' (2001) 7 *European Public Law* 355.

Salzberger, Eli, 'Judicial Activism in Israel: Sources, Forms and Manifestations', available at: http://ssrn.com/abstract=984918.

Segal, Zeev, 'Judicial Activism vis-a-vis Judicial Restraint: An Israeli Viewpoint' (2011) 47 *Tulsa Law Review* 319.

Segev, Joshua, 'The Changing Role of the Israeli Supreme Court and the Question of Legitimacy' (2006) 20 *Temple International and Comparative Law Journal*. 1.

Shetreet, Shimon, *Justice in Israel: A Study of the Israeli Judiciary* (Leiden, Martinus Nijhoff, 1994).

Shetreet, Shimon, 'Resolving the Controversy over the Form and Legitimacy of Constitutional Adjudication in Israel: A Blueprint for Redefining the Role of the Supreme Court and the Knesset' (2003) 77 *Tulane Law Review* 659.

Weill, Rivka, 'Hybrid Constitutionalism: The Israeli Case for Judicial Review and Why We Should Care' (2012) 30 *Berkeley Journal of International Law* 349.

Zamir, Itzhak and Zysblat, Allen, *Public Law in Israel* (Oxford, Oxford University Press, 1996).

8

Human Rights

Introduction

Part I : Human Rights – Foundations – Constitutional Rights and their Limitations – The Limitation Clause – Equality – Gender – Discrimination on Grounds of Sexual Orientation – The Arab Minority (Israeli Palestinians) – Recent Developments in Human Rights: From the Knesset to the Court

Part II: The Occupied Territories and the War on Terror – An Unresolved Conflict – The Supreme Court and National Security – Conclusion

INTRODUCTION

THE FINAL CHAPTER of this book discusses the development of human rights protection in Israel's constitutional law before and after the enactment of the 1992 basic laws, focusing on key issues of relevance in Israel. Fundamental liberties such as freedom of expression and the right to equality have not yet been constitutionally acknowledged. While the Knesset refrains from completing the human rights chapter, the Supreme Court is noted for its expansion of rights and generous interpretation of the rights listed in the basic laws – particularly human dignity – that have allowed for the inclusion and protection of new rights in Israel's incomplete constitution. The second part of this chapter focuses on Israel's war on terror, which has demanded a delicate balance between the protection of human rights and the need to provide security for Israeli citizens.

PART I: HUMAN RIGHTS

FOUNDATIONS

As discussed earlier, the State of Israel did not finalise a constitution when it was established, but opted for a gradual introduction of a 'constitution by chapters', known as the Harari Resolution. Although it includes references to basic human rights, Israel's Declaration of Independence was not accorded constitutional status and was considered valid only for the purposes of interpretation, which is why it may not be used as a basis for nullifying Knesset legislation that conflicts with it. At the same time, the protection of human rights in Israel did not start with the *Bank Hamizrahi* case, nor did it emerge when the 1992 basic laws were enacted. Human rights were protected in Israel from the outset; the 1992 basic laws only granted rights special statutory status.

The absence of a written constitution and the fact that the Israeli legal system was based on and linked with the British system created the 'supremacy of the Knesset' principle. Attempts to grant legal status to the Declaration of Independence – which specified a series of basic rights such as the freedom of worship and absolute social and political equality of all citizens – failed. Upon the establishment of the State of Israel, the Knesset anchored certain human rights in state laws. For example, the 1951 Women's Equal Rights Law established that 'the same laws and legal actions shall apply to both men and women'. Later, it enacted the Defamation Law, the Privacy Protection Law and the 1988 Equal Work Opportunities Law, which prohibits discrimination against labourers due to their gender, sexual orientation, marital status, race, religion, nationality and so on. Israel, however, never endorsed a bill of rights, despite many political attempts over the years to do so. In recent years, it seems that the bill of rights is no longer on the political agenda. It has almost disappeared from parties' political platforms and was not an issue in the most recent or the previous elections. The completion of a human rights bill for Israel still seems remote.

The absence of constitutional human rights supposedly allows parliament to harm them without legal constraint. It would seem, therefore, that the Knesset's sovereign power in this respect is unlimited, but history has shown that from the very beginning, the Knesset has respected human rights and has restrained its own powers in relation to them. Very few laws that explicitly harm human rights have been enacted, and the Knesset has rarely abused its sovereign power. Interestingly, legislation that departs from human rights has only surfaced on the Knesset agenda in recent years, particularly after the constitutional revolution of the 1990s.

The first human rights cases followed from the Israeli decision to keep British Mandate legislation entirely in place. Some of these Mandatory laws granted the government extensive powers to abridge human rights. It is therefore not surprising that many human rights-related verdicts from the early 1950s addressed the use of powers that followed from Mandatory orders.

In view of this, the Supreme Court's significant contribution to the protection of human rights is perhaps the most prominent and unique feature of Israel's constitutional law. Acting as the HCJ, the Supreme Court undertook to defend these rights and created what was to be known as the Bill of Judicial Rights – a set of human rights acknowledged and protected by HCJ verdicts – customary rights that feature only in HCJ adjudication, which, by virtue of stare decisis, have turned into binding legal norms in Israel. Thus, long before Basic Law: Human Dignity and Liberty was introduced, rights that were later enshrined in this law were protected by the Court, despite lacking any normative, constitutional or legal foundation. It is important to recognise that rights protection has arisen from the decisions of the Supreme Court.

In the early days of the new state, the HCJ ruled that the executive may not restrict human rights without relying on explicit legislation that permits it to do so. With this seemingly simple interpretative rule – 'no individual right may be impaired without the explicit consent of the chief legislator' – HCJ verdicts restricted the powers of the government and public administration, and established that human rights may only be denied with the explicit consent of the legislature through legislation.

The HCJ expanded on this position, defending human rights in a series of rulings. In the 1950 *Shayeb* case,[1] the petitioner claimed that the Defense Minister would not let him practise his profession as a teacher due to his political views, arguing that the minister's decision conflicted with 'the principle of the rule of law' and violated his freedom of occupation. Shayeb argued that only laws may restrict basic liberties and

---

[1] HCJ 144/50 *Shayeb v The Defense Minister*, ver 5(1) 399 (1950).

since there is no law that makes a person's ability to work and make a living conditional upon his political views, the authorities may not restrict his freedom to find employment as a teacher. The Supreme Court ruled: 'Even if a citizen holds misguided and wrong views, his life and blood are not forfeit . . . his occupation may not be restricted, nor should he be harassed, if only administratively.' This judicial norm, which has often been repeated in HCJ rulings, means that human rights may not be denied or restricted by a Cabinet member or other civil servants only because they believe, even if correctly, that this could benefit the state. It is worth remembering that this rule was established soon after the State of Israel was founded, when the executive was still extremely powerful. Referring to this case, Elyakim Rubinstein (future Attorney General and Justice of the Supreme Court) wrote: 'This verdict was one of the first in which the Supreme Court stood up in principle against dangerous government trends. It appears to be an important step toward further democratization, and should be viewed as a move that established the rule of law in this country by curbing illegal operations by the executive.'[2]

This trend continued in the famous 1953 *Kol Ha'am* case,[3] whose verdict laid the foundations of the freedom of speech principle in Israel's constitutional law. The case started when the Interior Minister decided to close a newspaper named *Kol Ha'am* (The People's Voice) that published a series of articles against government policies for 10 days. A 1919 Mandatory order that remained in effect was the source of the minister's prerogative to close a newspaper 'if it published material that is likely to threaten public order'. The newspaper appealed to the HCJ, which reversed the minister's decision. Justice Agranat, future Supreme Court President, stated that the minister's decision did not adequately consider the status of freedom of expression in Israel. The Court deduced the existence of this liberty from the Declaration of Independence, stating that, even if not legally binding, laws should be interpreted in the spirit of protecting this right. The State of Israel is a democracy, Justice Agranat wrote, and democratic regimes cannot exist when the judiciary does not acknowledge freedom of speech. Although laws that restrict rights may not be nullified (because Israel does not have a constitution), the Court would interpret laws in a manner which

---

[2] Elyakim Rubinstein, *Judges of the Land* (Jerusalem, Shoken, 1980) (Hebrew).
[3] HCJ 73/53 *Kol Ha'am v Minister of Interior*, ver 7(2), 871 (1953).

is consistent with and protects freedom of speech. The judge remarked that the Interior Minister should employ a 'balancing test' and weigh state security interests against the freedom of expression, considering the latter's importance. This right, he stated, may be restricted if it is highly probable that public order might be seriously and severely harmed.

In this case, the Court defended a civil right primarily by using an interpretative tool. Another guiding principle established through adjudication refers to the application of a minimalistic interpretation to laws that harm human rights. The HCJ established that when a law may be interpreted in more than one way, it should be interpreted in a way that best serves human rights, and laws that directly impair human rights should be interpreted narrowly. In *Kol Ha'am*, the HCJ employed these interpretative tools: examining the 1919 Press Order, it narrowly interpreted the word 'likely' to mean 'imminent probability' and not merely a 'bad tendency'. It further adopted a rule that applies to every administrative authority, namely, that human rights may only be harmed by the power of an explicit legal authorisation. Interestingly, it did not refer to other constitutional systems or international law – at least not in the early stages – in order to 'import' the list of human rights. Justice Agranat wrote about freedom of speech as being one of the basic principles of a democratic state.

The introduction of the balancing test and the *Kol Ha'am* decision had a dramatic impact on the Israeli justice system. The latter judgment has since been extensively cited and has greatly contributed to the recognition of human rights in Irael. The verdict created a probability-balancing test for cases in which civil rights conflict with other interests. This rule has been further developed over the years, leading to additional balancing formulae for the various rights.

Since the early days, the HCJ has addressed almost every basic human right, including political rights such as the right to vote or stand for elections. Yet when the Knesset decided to explicitly restrict political rights, the laws it introduced could not be nullified, due to the Knesset's sovereignty principle. Nevertheless, the HCJ stepped up and restricted the scope of legal harm. For example, it offered a minimalistic interpretation of the amendment to Basic Law: The Knesset that allowed for the disqualification of political parties on the basis of their views. Yet, when Rabbi Meir Kahana (whose *Kakh* movement was disqualified due to its racist platform) appealed against the decision and argued that the amendment was undemocratic and should be declared null and void, the HCJ stated that it could not judicially review the law, but the law's interpretation would be restricted.[4]

Another example of how the Supreme Court has promoted human rights is the *Katalan* case.[5] The Court was asked to rule on whether the Prison Service could order that an enema be performed on a prisoner against his will to recover drugs that he had supposedly ingested. The law allowed this violation of bodily integrity, but the Court established that in Israel, every person has the right to maintain his dignity and bodily integrity, and that this right applies to everyone, including prisoners and detainees. Performing an enema on a prisoner – against his will and not for medical purposes – violates this right. Justice Barak added that the source of this human right is the Declaration of Independence and thus no administrative authority may violate it without an explicit legal authorisation.

The judiciary's elaboration on human rights and the application of the balancing formulae was part of an important endeavour that further developed Israel's constitutional law. Despite the fact that the young State of Israel encountered numerous hardships – including wars, terror attacks and other serious security issues, absorption of waves of immigrant, economic upheavals and social tensions – the infrastructure for the solid protection of human rights had been laid. In the absence of a constitutional bill of rights, it was up to the Supreme Court to acknowledge human rights as endorsed by modern democracies worldwide. This acknowledgement, however, was limited. In the *Rogozinsky* case,[6] for example, the HCJ established that: 'The law of the state – which assigned all matrimonial issues of Israel's Jewish citizens and residents to the Rabbinical Courts, ordering that marriages and divorces be conducted according to the *Torah* – precedes the freedom of conscience.' Yet, in the absence of clear, unequivocal and explicit laws, legal interpretations provided for an appropriate human rights regime.

The legal status of human rights changed dramatically in 1992 with the introduction of two basic laws dealing with human rights, which restricted the Knesset's ability to violate them.

---

[4] EA (Elections Appeal) 2-3/84 *Neiman v Central Elections Committee Chairman*, ver 39(2), 225 (1984).

[5] HCJ 355/79 *Katalan v The Prisons Service*, ver 34(3), 294 (1979) 298.

[6] CA 450/70 *Rogozinsky v The State of Israel*, ver 26(1), 129 (1970).

CONSTITUTIONAL RIGHTS AND THEIR LIMITATIONS

The constitutional revolution started in Israel with the enactment of two basic laws on human rights in March 1992 – Basic Law: Freedom of Occupation and Basic Law: Human Dignity and Liberty – that changed the constitutional status and the Court's view of those rights. These basic laws not only acknowledged the rights, but also established that, in certain conditions, they may be undermined. The constitutional revolution, however, profoundly changed the Israeli legal system by granting constitutional status to human rights such as freedom of occupation; the right to preserve a life, human dignity and bodily integrity; the right to property; freedom from detention, arrest and extradition; free movement in and out of Israel; and the right to privacy. Furthermore, the Knesset's ability to restrict these human rights is restricted by limiting terms, as specified in these basic laws. Thus, a law that violates human rights in a manner inconsistent with the limitation clause is an unconstitutional law, and therefore the Court may declare it null and void. This is the root of the constitutional change. The key change is not the rights or their extent of coverage (human rights had previously been endorsed by the Supreme Court and acknowledged as 'judicial' rights), but the new power of judicial review.

Basic Law: Human Dignity and Liberty – which is the main law defending human rights – includes this instruction: 'This basic law shall not restrict the validity of any law that preceded its enactment.' This clause was meant to uphold the validity of older laws that do not meet the requirements of the basic laws' limitation clauses and protect them from judicial review. President Barak explained that this situation was the result of political compromises that followed disagreements on state and religious issues.[7]

Ever since 1992, the HCJ has been following a three-stage procedure when examining the validity of laws that infringe human rights (the *Bank Hamizrahi* verdict laid the foundations for this procedure). In the *first stage*, it examines whether a new law violates a constitutional right by answering several secondary questions. For example, has the right in question been acknowledged in Israel? Does that right have a constitutional status – that

---

[7] Aharon Barak, *Proportionality: Constitutional Rights and their Limitations* (Cambridge, Cambridge University Press, 2012) 26.

is, does it feature in an existing basic law? Does the new law harm that constitutional right? In the *second stage*, it examines whether the constitutional right is damaged legally and whether it coincides with every component of the limitation clause (discussed below), mainly the proportionality principle. If the extent of harm to a constitutional right is proportional, the law remains valid. If the Court established that the harm in question is not proportional, it moves on to the *third stage*, where it examines the potential results of the law's unconstitutionality. This is the remedy stage, at which the Court determines whether the law is to be nullified, either completely or partially.[8]

Ever since 1992, constitutional adjudication has closely observed these stages of examination and the principle established in *Bank Hamizrahi*, whereby if the Court concludes that a law does not comply with the limitation clause, it may quash it. It should be noted that the question about the level of court (that is, any court or only the Supreme Court) that may judicially review laws has not yet been clearly answered, but as a rule, petitions arguing that a law is unconstitutional are examined by an extended panel of the Supreme Court.

THE LIMITATION CLAUSE

Following the Canadian model,[9] the Israeli legislature established a legislative balancing test known as the limitation clause, according to which human rights may be harmed if this is done for appropriate reasons and according to the instructions of the clause. It reads: 'There shall be no infringement of rights under this Basic Law except by a law befitting the values of the State of Israel, enacted for a proper purpose, and to an extent no greater than is required.' This clause plays a dual role: it defends human rights, but also permits their limitation. It expresses the idea that these rights are not absolute and exist within a social framework which must also accommodate public and national goals.

The first part of the limitation clause requires that the impairment be 'by law'. The limit must be 'prescribed by law' if it is to benefit from the limitation clause, a demand which reflects the desire to allow only deliberative democratic institutions – not officials – to abridge rights. When

---

[8] ibid 222.
[9] See the limitation clause in s 1 of the Canadian Charter of Rights and Freedoms.

that chain of authorisation is lacking, harm is deemed disproportionate. The second part of the limitation clause requires that the impairment be legitimate. It is based on values and refers to the justification for harming a constitutional right. The law should match the values of the State of Israel, should serve a proper cause and must not be excessive, or rather it must be proportionate.

In recent years, Israel's constitutional discourse has focused on proportionality, which is the key element of the limitation clause. Every constitutional verdict that addresses the constitutionality of a law includes an analysis and a discussion of the issue of proportionality. The proportionality issue has crossed the boundaries of states and judiciaries. It is a key factor of constitutional law in almost every Western country, and the amount of literature covering it is enormous.

The limitation clause requires that the law in question is consistent with the values of the State of Israel as a Jewish and democratic state. It refers to Zionist and traditional aspects and, on the democratic scale, such laws must acknowledge fundamental values such as the rule of law, the separation of powers and basic human rights.

The limitation clause further requires that the restrictive law be enacted for a proper purpose. To determine this, two secondary questions must be addressed: what is the nature of the purpose that justifies the violation of human rights?; and how essential is that purpose, and does it justify violating human rights? The first question focuses on the content of a proper purpose. It has been established that a proper purpose is one that 'was designed to attain social goals that generally coincide with the state's values and are specifically sensitive to the importance of human rights in the comprehensive social setup'.[10] The second question is meant to clarify why attaining that purpose is urgent or essential because the fact that the cause is 'proper' does not, in itself, justify harming a constitutional right.

The Supreme Court established that the extent to which the attainment of the purpose is necessary depends on the nature of the infringed right and of the relevant infringement. When the right harmed is important and pivotal, the purpose of the law could justify the infringement if it intends to attain some essential social goal or resolve a pressing social issue. In general, constitutional democracies are characterised by the

---

[10] HCJ 7052/03 *Adalah v The Interior Minister* (handed down on 14 May 2006), President Barak's verdict at [52].

concept that not all means may be used to attain a proper end. An appropriate balance has to be maintained between attaining a proper goal and harming a right, namely, harm must be proportional. The phrase 'to an extent no greater than is required' was interpreted by the HCJ as the requirement of proportionality. In a broad sense, this involves the weighing the right against the purposes of the law and the means used to attain that purpose. Proportionality is determined by three sub-tests: *suitability*, or rational connection; *necessity*, or the application of less restrictive means; and the appropriate balance between the benefits of attaining the purpose and the harm done to a specific right, which is *proportionality* in the strictest sense (*stricto senso*), or the value-based test. Israeli adjudication has established that all three sub-tests must be met.

The suitability or rational connection test requires that the means used by the limiting law must fit its purpose, that is, the means chosen for the law should match the desired end. No 'absolute certainty' is required, but slim chances do not suffice either. The second proportionality test considers the necessity of the law and has also been dubbed 'the test of the less restrictive means'. Here, the legislator needs to choose – from all the means that could be used to attain the purpose of the restrictive law – the one that least harms human rights. This test examines whether the purpose of the law could be attained by less harmful means (or by existing laws) and if one is found, the law in question must be deemed redundant. In other words, the legislator should choose the least harmful means from the selection of means that can be employed for the attainment of the legislative purpose.

The third sub-test is 'proportionality *stricto senso*', whereby harm to a constitutional right may be justified by an appropriate balance between the benefits of attaining the law's purpose and the harm it might cause to human rights. This, therefore, is the test of benefit versus harm, which weighs the positive impact of the law's goals against the negative impact of harm to the constitutional right. Ruling in the *Adalah* case, for example, President Barak wrote that:

> A proper purpose, a rational connection between the statute's purpose while using the least restrictive means which can still achieve the proper purposes – are all necessary conditions for the constitutionality of the limitation of human rights. These are insufficient conditions. A constitutional regime seeking to realize a regime of human rights cannot suffice with these. Rather, it also draws a line of human-rights protection that the legislator may not

cross. It requires that the fulfilment of the proper purpose – by rational means that are least restrictive in achieving the purpose – cannot lead to disproportional limitation to human rights.[11]

The first and second sub-tests are essentially different from the third sub-test. The first two – rational connection and minimal harm – focus on the means to an end. Thus, when the two tests show a rational connection between the attainment of a purpose and the legislative means chosen, and that there are no other, less harmful means of attaining the purpose, then it is proportional, according to the first and second sub-tests. The third sub-test considers the harm caused to human rights and acknowledges that not all means – including those that maintain rational connection and are less harmful – may be used to attain a worthy end. This sub-test expresses the notion that there is a value barrier that democracies may not cross even if the purpose intended to be served by the legislature was worthy.[12] Furthermore, the Supreme Court has acknowledged a 'proportionality spectrum' enjoyed by the Knesset. Thus, there is a scope of discretion when choosing the means to the end and there may be several solutions or means that meet the proportionality test: 'Any choice of means or combination thereof within the spectrum upholds the requirements of the limitation clause. The legislator has leeway in that spectrum, from which he may choose at his own discretion.'[13]

To demonstrate the workings of the limitation clause with its various components and proportionality tests, we shall return to the *Adalah* case, in which the HCJ examined the constitutionality of a highly controversial law: an amendment to the Citizenship Act, restricting the entry of residents of the West Bank and the Gaza Strip to the State of Israel. Among other things, restrictions were imposed on the reunion of married couples when one is an Israeli Arab and the other resides in PA territories. Dubbed 'family reunion prevention', the amendment was based on the desire to prevent the risk (which had materialised previously) that the option of settling in Israel might be abused through the settlers' involvement in terrorist acts. The basic assumption of the security forces was that the freedom of movement accorded to Palestinian spouses who acquire a legal standing in Israel through family reunion might significantly threaten Israel's residents and citizens.

[11] ibid [75].
[12] ibid [30].
[13] ibid [77].

The amendment was introduced as a temporary provision for one year, with an option for extension, but it has been in effect ever since because it has been continually extended. Over the past several years, the Supreme Court has been asked to examine this law's legality on two occasions, in cases known as the first and second *Adalah* cases. Both petitions were examined by an extended panel of 11 judges and both were eventually rejected by a majority of one (six to five), which in itself reflects the inherent complexity of this issue.

In the first *Adalah* case, the majority, led by Justice Cheshin, concluded that although the law was inconsistent with human rights, it met the terms of the limitation clause and was therefore valid. The minority under President Barak maintained that the law did not meet the limitation clause terms. Both blocs provided in-depth analysis of the limitation clause tests. The Court accepted the state's argument that security is the basic purpose of the amendment that was intended to minimise the risk posed to the state's citizens and residents, and that this is a proper purpose.

Examining the issue of proportionality, the judges agreed on the first sub-test and determined that the comprehensive ban on the entry of spouses into Israel indeed prevented the security risk that such an entry might pose, thus establishing that 'a rational connection' exists between the means chosen and the purpose of the law. The judges also agreed on the second test. In relation to the test of necessity or less restrictive means, even dissenting President Barak stated that, although a general restriction as a means is always suspected of disproportionality, in this case it was more effective in terms of minimising the security threat and thus met the 'necessity' test. Naturally, the majority judges shared this conclusion.

The judges were therefore in disagreement as to the third test – proportionality *stricto senso*. The minority view was that the law should be nullified because the additional level of security attained by the general ban it imposes is not proportional with the harm it inflicts on family life and the equality between Palestinian and Israeli couples. The majority disagreed, believing that individually examining every family reunion request would not appropriately guarantee the public's safety. Justice Cheshin explained: 'Restricting the right to maintain family life in Israel does harm Israel's citizens, but that harm is minimal and is overruled by the Israeli citizens' and residents' right to live security.'[14] Justice Cheshin stressed that when the right to family life is weighed

---

[14] ibid [121].

against the right to safe and secure life of all who reside in Israel, the latter takes precedence.

Five years later, when the temporary provision was extended again, the Court was asked to re-examine its legality and once again rejected the petition as six of the 11-judge panel (which included judges who were not on the original panel) stated that it passed the tests imposed by the limitation clause, citing arguments from the previous judgment. The disagreement between the majority and minority judges on the third sub-test also remained.

In conclusion, the *Adalah* case is not only a good example of how the limitation clause tests are applied in practice, it also offers some insight into the Supreme Court's view of the legislature in the constitutional context. Some judges are reluctant to interfere with security policy issues and so permit the legislature to choose from a wide range of purposes and means in order to achieve ends related to national security. A ruling of unconstitutionality is regarded as the last resort. Judicial review is conducted very cautiously, as is indicated by the figures that, between 1992 and early 2012, less than a dozen laws (many of them merely specific sections) were declared unconstitutional.

EQUALITY

The equality principle is a cornerstone of every democracy and yet Israel is one of the few democracies that has not constitutionalised the right to equality, probably because this is the most problematic right in the Israeli context.

The Jewish tradition held the equality principle – as in equality before the law – in high regard. The Bible, as the oldest Jewish law, stated: 'One law and one manner shall be for you and for the stranger that sojourneth with you' (Numbers 15:16) and 'Ye shall have one manner of law, as well for the stranger, as for one of your own country' (Leviticus 24:22). In the Mandate Letter, the British law of Palestine pledged to avoid discrimination for racial, religious or linguistic reasons. The British government expressed this position in an important legislative instrument in 1922, which defined the legislative powers of the High Commissioner in Palestine.

When Israel was established, the equality principle was explicitly stated in its Declaration of Independence: 'The State of Israel . . . will

ensure complete equality of social and political rights to all its inhabitants irrespective of religion, race, or sex.' Over the years, certain aspects
of this principle have been specifically and legislatively addressed. In
acknowledgment of the equality of the genders, for example, the
Knesset introduced the Women's Equal Rights Law in 1951. Labour-
related laws stated that equal opportunities in the workplace should be
maintained regardless of the applicants' gender, age, sexual preferences,
race, religion, nationality or country of origin. Another important law
that aimed at eliminating discrimination in the public realm is the Law
against Discrimination in Products, Services and Entry to Public or
Entertainment Places (2000), which banned discrimination for any reason when supplying goods or public services, or when operating a public site. These and similar legislative items, however, have not been
assigned constitutional or entrenched status, which is why the Knesset
may deviate from them in later legislation.

In the absence of a constitutional or general proclamation of the
equality principle, the Supreme Court has served as the body that has
ordered government agencies to treat all citizens equally. In a series of
judgments, the Court has established that 'it ought to be assumed' that
the purpose of all legislation is to promote and protect equality and
thus, if this assumption is to be contradicted by a law, the law must
explicitly say so.[15] Following its rulings on human rights issues, the Court
established that when a given law could be interpreted in more than one
way, the interpretation that upholds everyone's equality before the law
shall always be chosen.

It seems, however, that the constitutional revolution skipped over the
equality principle. The 1992 basic laws did not include it. This was
chiefly because such a constitutional norm might impact religious laws.
Politically, the Knesset stopped the constitutionalisation process and
thus the equality principle was never explicitly anchored in constitutional laws. Nevertheless, when these basic laws were introduced,
Supreme Court judges opined that even though the equality principle is
not mentioned in them as such, the principle nevertheless has constitutional status. 'From now on', Professor Barak wrote, 'equality is a supra-
legal . . . and a central constitutional principle.'[16] This view is based on a

---

[15] HCJ 104/87 *Nevo v The National Labour Court*, ver 44(4), 749 (1990) 764.
[16] Aharon Barak, *Interpretation in Law – Vol III: Constitutional Interpretation* (Jerusalem,
Nevo, 1994) 423 (Hebrew).

broad interpretation of 'human dignity'. Clearly, the adoption of this view by the Court means that legislation limiting the right to equality will have to meet the terms set forth in the limitation clause.

In recent years, this approach was actually upheld by the Supreme Court, which was willing to acknowledge that certain aspects of the equality principle are included in the scope of the right to dignity, and thus have been accorded constitutional status. Therefore, laws that violate the right to equality, while failing to comply with the terms of the limitation clause, may be nullified. This dramatic development is surely a revolution in itself and has been received with mixed feelings. It seems that most members of the public do not fully understand the legal implications of these HCJ decisions and do not understand the entire constitutional system. Public knowledge of the constitutional status of human rights is vague. The idea of judicial review is well established and therefore Israelis know that the Court may judicially review any law passed by the Knesset. The specific grounds for this review – the question of whether the right of equality is part of the right to dignity – are beyond common knowledge. On the other hand, the Knesset is well aware of this new constitutional development and, as we have previously noted, is increasingly using temporary provisions for problematic laws in an attempt to avoid judicial review. Below we shall examine several areas in which inequality still prevails in Israel.

GENDER

Although numerous laws ban the prioritisation of men over women in the workplace and elsewhere, and although some affirmative action has been taken, it is hard to say that there is gender equality in Israel. Unequal status is expressed in various laws, mainly those pertaining to matrimonial issues[17] – in which men have more rights than women – and are 'supported' by the clause that prevents judicial review of laws passed prior to the enactment of the 1992 basic laws. As may be recalled, Israel has never truly separated state and religion, which is why numerous religious edicts have the power of state laws. Rabbinical courts enjoy a unique judicial power over all matrimonial issues pertaining to the marriage and divorce

---

[17] Gila Stopler, 'Countenancing the Oppression of Women: How Liberals Tolerate Religious and Cultural Practices that Discriminate against Women' (2003) 12 *Columbia Journal of Gender and Law* 154, 171.

of Israel's Jewish citizens and residents. The same applies to Muslims, Druzes and Christians. Rabbinical and different religious courts rule according to religious laws, pursuant to which spouses are not equal before the law.[18]

Here too, the Supreme Court made a unique and crucial contribution to promoting gender equality, and was even willing to intervene in issues that had been considered non-justiciable, such as training in military professions. A case in point is the famous *Miller* case,[19] which marked a breakthrough in women's equality. Ms Miller filed a petition with the HCJ against the military practice of not letting women take pilots' courses. Addressing this question, the Court held that, even though training women to be pilots costs more than training men – because they serve relatively shorter periods – the army should bear this extra expense in the name of equality. Justice Mazza determined that budgetary considerations, which were presented as the reason why the IDF would not let women take pilots' courses, cannot take precedence when the issue in question is a demand for the realisation of a fundamental right such as the right to equality. In the absence of evidence that establishes that permitting women to serve as pilots would be extremely and unreasonably costly, the army may not keep women out of this profession. In her verdict, Justice Strasberg-Cohen also discussed the extra cost of letting women take the pilots' course, but noted that resources should be allocated to create an equal starting point for both genders. This verdict had extensive implications for the military, and many other professions that had traditionally been viewed as 'men's professions' have since become available to women as well.

Equality in the workplace is also problematic. For example, according to several studies, women advance to and hold some 20–30 per cent of middle management positions, while their advancement to senior management positions is prohibited by the 'glass ceiling'. Further, despite their abilities and experience, women constitute only some two per cent of senior managers. This unequal representation is manifested in both

---

[18] Ruth Halperin-Kaddari, 'Colonizing Women: Ethical and Legal Issues Surrounding Systematic Gender and Race Discrimination, in Women, Religion and Multi-Culturalism in Israel' (2001) 5 *UCLA Journal of International Law & Foreign Affairs* 339, 348. Matrimonial inequality in Israel is seen in, for example, the fact that at the wedding, the husband 'acquires' his wife; in addition, men 'grant' a divorce, which women cannot obtain otherwise.

[19] HCJ 4541/94 *Miller v The Defense Minister*, ver 49(4), 94 (1994).

management positions and in the military. In Israel, the representation of women in the Knesset, the government and municipal authorities is very low by comparison with other democracies, and advancement has been slow since the state was founded. The maximum representation of female members in the Knesset was 22 per cent in 2012. The number of women in government is even lower, between 6 and 18 per cent. Very few women have been appointed as the senior ministers of defense, foreign affairs or education. Nevertheless, in the 1970s, a woman (Golda Meir) served as Prime Minister. The fact that Israel had one of the first female heads of state in the West and that she was one of the key political figures in Israel's history is important, but it is an exception to the rule.

The Supreme Court has also acknowledged the right of women to hold public positions associated with religious services and to take seats on bodies that elect chief municipal rabbis and religious councils. Ruling on these matters, the Court tried to minimise the impact of religious laws on discrimination against women. Nevertheless, as noted above, women are still underrepresented. It seems that this situation will change only when the State of Israel introduces an alternative structure, according to which people may marry and divorce through Western civil institutions. Yet, even if such a law is enacted, the extent to which a law can create social change is not clear. Due to its unique position as a developing democracy and a state with a special cultural tradition and religious identity, Israel has so far failed to adopt a single national standard for women.[20]

As in many other countries, Israeli adjudication has extensively addressed the principle of affirmative action. Here too, questions have been raised as to whether this principle violates the equality principle, as it does not ignore a person's gender, religion, nationality or physical disability, and even discriminates against others, or whether such practices are part of the equality principle and are a means of attaining substantive equality. Ruling in the *Israeli Women's Lobby* case, Justice Mazza determined that affirmative action is one of the necessary means and chief guarantees of the attainment of equality. The affirmative action policy is based on the fact that formal equality cannot in practice guarantee the implementation of equality. The Israeli legislature first officially endorsed the mechanism of affirmative action when it established that women should be appropriately represented on the executive boards of government-owned companies, and today Israeli law contains numerous provisions that were meant to promote appropriate gender representation. Nevertheless, the Supreme Court has played a major role in placing this doctrine on the public agenda and making the government accept it.

DISCRIMINATION ON GROUNDS OF SEXUAL ORIENTATION

The importance of the equality principle was further emphasised when the Supreme Court acknowledged the rights of same-sex couples. The crucial verdict in the *Danilovich* case[21] was handed down in 1994. Danilovich, an El Al flight attendant, sued the Israeli airliner after it refused to issue a free airline ticket for his male partner, which was a traditional perk given to employees' spouses. The Regional Labour Court stated that Danilovich was entitled to this benefit based on a 1992 amendment to the Equal Employment Opportunities Law, which for the first time explicitly banned discrimination on the basis of sexual orientation. The Labour Court rejected El Al's subsequent appeal and the airliner appealed to the HCJ, where the majority of judges further established that the refusal to grant the benefit constituted wrongful discrimination according to the Equal Employment Opportunities Law.

The *Danilovich* decision was a pivotal one, but also resulted in attacks by the religious lobby against the HCJ's perceived activism and particularly against its President, Aharon Barak. The decision cannot, however, be regarded an activist one. Justice Barak explicitly stated that he was applying a statutory provision, namely the 1992 amendment of the Equal Employment Opportunities Law, which prohibited employment discrimination due to sexual preference. However, he did not clarify whether he would have considered this discrimination illegal in the absence of the statutory provision. Justice Dorner's concurring judgment referred to the general constitutional principle. This verdict paved the way for additional judgments that upheld the rights of same-sex partners, particularly in relation to financial and property issues.

Another key ruling, setting an important precedent, was handed down in the *Yarus-Hakak* case,[22] in which the Supreme Court allowed a

---

[21] HCJ 721/94 *El Al Israeli Airlines v Danilovich*, ver 48(5), 749 (1994).
[22] CA 10280/01 *Tal Yarus-Hakak v The Attorney General*, ver 59(5), 64 (2005).

lesbian couple to adopt each other's biological children. Later, the Attorney General issued detailed instructions concerning same-sex adoptions that were even more advanced and flexible. Nevertheless, the public and legal struggle of same-sex couples is not over. No court verdict has ever explicitly stated that same-sex couples are equal to heterosexual couples in every respect. Verdicts on such issues are rarely handed down. Ruling on cases that address the rights of same-sex couples, the Supreme Court has repeatedly insisted that its decision does not acknowledge the validity of same-sex marriages. It left the issue of the legality of same-sex marriage unaddressed and unresolved, believing it to be a matter for the legislator. Although an HCJ decision ruled in favour of five same-sex Israeli couples who married in Canada and requested that their marriages be registered in Israel, same-sex marriages are not acknowledged. Nonetheless, the gay and lesbian community has politically, legally and culturally moved from the margins of Israeli society towards increased visibility and growing acceptance.

THE ARAB MINORITY (ISRAELI PALESTINIANS)

The equality principle creates serious problems in relation to Israeli Palestinians (or Arab citizens). These issues are not directly associated with classic cases of civil and minority rights, but with Israel's unique situation, characterised by the absence of peace between Israel and the Arab world, ongoing security problems and the natural identification of the majority of Israeli Palestinians with the national and cultural Arab heritage.

Israel's Declaration of Independence promised all of the state's citizens absolute equality in civil and political rights and rejected racial, religious or gender discrimination. The Declaration called on the Israeli Arabs to take part in building the state and to assume representative positions in its institutions. Yet, while equality was promised, the newly founded state defined itself as 'a Jewish state in the Land of Israel', which hints at a distinction between the statuses of Jews and non-Jews in Israel. In practice, it is impossible to speak of equality when Israeli Palestinians are exempt from the military and national service duty, and do not enjoy all the same civil rights as are required by the rules of full equality.[23]

---

[23] Sammy Samooha, Minority Status in an Ethnic Democracy: The Status of the Arab Minority in Israel' (1990) 13 *Ethnic & Racial Studies* 349.

The dual definition of Israel as a Jewish and a democratic state that is committed to equality creates constant tension between these principles. The 1950 Law of Return, for example, is the most tangible expression of Israel as a Jewish state. It is a legal expression of the fact that Zionism is a central concept on which the state was founded and reflects the everlasting link between Diaspora Jews and the State of Israel. The Law of Return acknowledges the right of all Jews, wherever they may be, to immigrate to Israel and become nationalised. It means that every Jew is a potential Israeli citizen who is automatically granted preferential treatment, while other residents who wish to settle in Israel must follow the nationalisation process outlined in the Citizenship Law. Although it may appear that the prioritised status of Jews is inconsistent with the equality principle, nationalisation and settlement rights are not subject to the equality principle, since the fundamental right of states to decide on and direct the composition and nature of their populations has been acknowledged internationally. This was explicitly stated in the International Covenant on the Elimination of Racial Discrimination adopted by the United Nations on 21 December 1965, which Israel signed and ratified.

Israeli Jews and Arabs are not equal in terms of their military service duties. The Security Service Law of 1986 imposes the duty of military service on every Israeli resident who turns 18. The standard term is three years for men and two years for women. After completing their tours of duty, all former members of the IDF are obliged to report annually for duty with the reserve forces. While the law makes no national or religious distinctions between residents, IDF recruiting officers may draft people or not at their own discretion. In most cases, the IDF has avoided drafting Israeli Palestinians, while Druze and Bedouins have been drafted since the late 1950s.

The official reason for exempting Arabs is that the state does not want to put them in a situation in which they must face the dilemma inherent in the confrontation or even use of weapons against members of their own nation. This means that while the vast majority of Israeli Jews are drafted, the vast majority of Israeli Palestinians are not. Consequently, certain state benefits accorded to army veterans are in practice not offered to Israeli Palestinians. Recently, Israeli officials seriously discussed the option of having Israeli Palestinians and ultra-Orthodox Jews – two undrafted population groups – volunteer for national service, believing that this would make the duty to serve the country and veterans' entitlement to state benefits more egalitarian. This project has, however, only recently started. Currently, everyone has an equal right to social benefits that are not conditional upon completion of military service. By law, everyone is entitled to the same university tuition fees, housing provisions and child allowances. Nevertheless, the state's basic commitment to full equality, as expressed in the Declaration of Independence, has never been fully realised and Israeli Palestinians still suffer from discrimination in many fields. They do realise their basic civil rights, but when it comes to sharing positions in, and benefits from, public establishments, or to the allocation of budgets for education, housing, settlement, social welfare, employment and local governments, there still are wide gaps between the positions of Jews and Arabs. Unequal resources are assigned to various public projects and government services, mainly for political and social reasons, as Israeli governments have consistently prioritised Jewish settlements.

Unlike in several other countries, Knesset laws do not determine the standards of public services such as health, sanitation, infrastructures and so on, to which the nation's citizens are entitled. These matters fall within the discretion of specific ministries, which determine their budgetary priorities and thus generally allocate resources to populations that are closest to the government and politically identify with its policies. Furthermore, since government allocations are not all arranged by comprehensive laws that determine fund distribution criteria, there are clear disparities between the various segments of the population.

The Supreme Court also chose to address this issue and, in a series of judgments over the past several years, it examined in great detail arguments about discriminatory budgets and even intervened in government decisions on these matters. For example, in one of these cases,[24] the plaintiffs argued that the Ministry of Labour and Social Affairs was acting in a discriminatory manner when it chose to allocate funds to help the needy in the lead-up to Passover, but does not do the same before Muslim holidays. The Ministry of Labour and Social Affairs acknowledged its duty to equally allocate funds to the needy regardless of their religion and amended its fund distribution criteria to apply to members

---

[24] HCJ 2422/98 *Adalah (The Legal Centre for Arab Minority Rights in Israel) v Minister of Labour and Social Affairs*, ver 98(2), 531 (1999).

of all denominations. In another case,[25] the plaintiffs argued that the Ministry of Religious Affairs has been ignoring its duty to earmark funds for the cemeteries of the Arab minority. The Court accepted the petition and ordered the ministry to distribute funds equally to all denominations.

The right to equality, and to equal distribution of funds, is currently recognised as a binding principle through legislation and adjudication, but it is not routinely upheld and Arab NGOs are forced to repeatedly ask the HCJ to order equal distribution. Furthermore, when the Court does accept the petitions, ordering that budgets be allocated in accordance with the equality principle, it only refers to future action and the subsequent budgetary year. Such remedies in practice often preserve existing gaps and insufficiently deter against discrimination.[26] It should be stressed, however, that the application of the equality principle to the distribution of funds between Jews and Arabs has significantly improved since the 1990s.

An interesting case in point addresses the allocation of state-owned lands. According to Basic Law: Israel Lands, such plots may not be sold or otherwise have their ownership transferred to another, and are managed by the Israel Land Authority (ILA). Ever since the State of Israel was established, hundreds of new Jewish settlements were built on state lands, yet – with the exception of Bedouin townships in the Negev and the recognition of several unacknowledged settlements – not a single settlement was built for the Arab minority on such lands.

The *Kaadan* case[27] concerned the legality of the manner in which the ILA allocated lands for an exclusively Jewish settlement. An Israeli Palestinian wished to purchase a house or a residential plot in the Katzir communal settlement, which was built on lands that the ILA had assigned to the Jewish Agency, which in turn assigned plots only to Jews. When the plaintiff's request was rejected by the Jewish Agency, he turned to the HCJ. The Court accepted the petition and established that the state has a constitutional duty to uphold the equality principle in the allocation of public goods. Finding no legal grounds for the state's discriminatory policy, President Barak declared that the state was not legally

---

[25] HCJ /1113/99 *Adalah (The Legal Centre for Arab Minority Rights in Israel) v Minister of Religious Affairs*, ver 54(2), 164 (2001).

[26] Y Rabin and M Lutzky, 'The Ongoing Budgetary Discrimination against the Arab Sector' (2002) 7 *Hamishpat* 505 (Hebrew).

[27] HCJ 6698/95 *Kaadan v ILA*, ver 54(1), 258 (handed down in 2000).

entitled to allocate lands to the Jewish Agency for the construction of the Katzir communal settlement based on the discrimination between Jews and non-Jews. Thus, for the first time ever, the Court determined that the state may not directly or indirectly discriminate between candidates for government allocations due to their national or religious identities. It pointed out that the state does not allocate lands for the construction of Arab communal settlements and the government has no policy that features the allocation of lands to Palestinian residents.[28]

In principle, the HCJ refused to acknowledge this case as an instance of the 'separate but equal' policy. Referring to the rationale behind the famous American case of *Brown v Board of Education*,[29] it stated that such a policy is inequitable by nature due to the majority seeking the separation. In this case, such a separation 'insults a minority group . . ., points at the way it is different from others, and instils a sense of social inferiority'.[30] It therefore ordered the state to 'reconsider' the plaintiff's request to purchase a plot and build a home in Katzir on the basis of the equality principle.

From a legal standpoint, the *Kaadan* case deals with the abolition of a discriminatory phenomenon, but it must also be read politically, as it revealed the disturbing fact that since the establishment of the State of Israel, plots have been allocated almost exclusively to Jews. Establishing a Jewish state on the Land of Israel implies building and developing settlements exclusively for Jews. Subsequently, Arab settlements have not been allocated lands for their own expansion for many years. A decision to allocate lands for the construction of a new Arab settlement was made only recently.

This case does not mean that Arabs will be admitted into new Jewish settlements from now on. The majority of the Israeli Palestinians do not

---

[28] Ruth Gavison, 'Does Equality Require Integration?: A Case Study' (2000) 3 *Democratic Culture* 36, 77–78.

[29] *Brown v Board of Education of Topeka* 347 US 438, 74 SCt 686 (1954)

[30] The Israeli adjudication accepted the separate but equal argument only once, in the case of HCJ 528/88 *Avitan v ILA*, in which a Jew asked the Court to let him lease a plot in a settlement that was allocated for the Bedouins. The Court rejected his petition, stating that 'there is a public interest in helping the Bedouins permanently settle in urban areas for reasons associated with the desire to offer them better public services . . . These interests, and the need to change traditions and customs that prevailed in the Bedouin sector for years, justify prioritizing them when granting subsidized plots in a settlement that was planned for them to take permanent residence'.

want this. There are very few mixed settlements in Israel, which is mostly because both population groups wish to preserve their own identities and ways of life. For Israeli Palestinians, this case means that the state may allocate lands for their development.

In 2012, the Knesset introduced the Admittance Committees Law, which created a way for communal and rural Jewish settlements in the Negev and the Galilee to refuse settlement candidates because, among other things, 'they do not match the social-cultural fabric'. Clearly introduced to counter the *Kaadan* verdict, this law in practice legalised screening processes that had been practised in those settlements primarily to refuse the entry of Israeli Arabs. A petition has been filed against this law, but the HCJ has not yet addressed the question of its constitutionality.

RECENT DEVELOPMENTS IN HUMAN RIGHTS: FROM THE KNESSET TO THE COURT

The constitutional discussion of human rights in which many in Israel have engaged over the past two decades did not take place in the Knesset. The constitutional revolution had some significant impact on the perception and status of human rights in the fields of education, politics, the media and the public arena, but the body primarily responsible for developments and progress in relation to these issues is the Supreme Court. This seems to be part of a process that the Israeli society is undergoing, which in many respects accords the Supreme Court with the 'final say' on almost every aspect of public life.

This process, and the Supreme Court's willingness to address issues that many countries view as non-justiciable, have been widely criticised, as we have seen. It should be remembered, however, as described in the previous chapters, that without this judicial activism, doubt exists as to whether other forms of remedy could have assisted in the protection of the rule of law, human rights and equality before the law. The legislature's silence on the status of rights that were omitted from the 1992 basic laws on human rights naturally motivated the Court's activism in developing these rights, while relieving the Knesset of the obligation to take strong stands on these disputed rights.

Nevertheless, it has been a slow process. After the 1992 basic laws and the 1995 *Bank Hamizrahi* case, petitions were filed asking the HCJ to judicially review laws that violated human rights listed in the basic laws.[31] The judicial review process was moderate and restrained. Very few laws were nullified in the first decade after the constitutional revolution and, in any event, most of the Court's verdicts were delivered formalistically, examining the limitation clause and its application to the facts.

Over the years, and while the legislature failed to complete the basic laws on human rights, attempts were made to convince the Court to interpret Basic Law: Human Dignity and Liberty as including human rights that had not been constitutionally anchored. When it started addressing petitions that sought the inclusion in the right to dignity of rights such as the equality principle, freedom of speech, the right to a family life, the right to due process and so on, the Court assumed that if the original basic law did not include these rights, it did not negate them either.

Yet, despite this expansionist approach, some of the attempts to acknowledge the constitutionality of unwritten rights have failed. For example, in the *Gilat Association* case, Justice Orr would not acknowledge the right to an education as being constitutional because no constitutional anchor has been found to permit the inclusion of this right in the basic law on human dignity.

In the *Adam, Teva v Din* case, President Barak stated that he could not see how the right to an appropriate living environment could be 'squeezed into' the right to dignity:

> Indeed, if the right to an appropriate living environment should be included within the right to dignity, it should include every other human, political, social, civil, and economic right. This is not the way to properly interpret a constitution. Truth be told, constitutional interpretation is not pedantic or legalistic . . . and indeed, constitutional interpretation takes a broader view of things, but it still is a legalistic interpretation, part of our interpretation, and even interpretation has a limited interpretational scope. Interpreting the law to mean that the right to an appropriate living environment is constitutional would exceed the limits of the interpretative view. Thus, those who want the right to an appropriate living environment to be part of our basic laws should convince the Knesset to do so.[32]

---

[31] The HCJ actually rejected the *Bank Hamizrahi* petition and did not nullify the law.

[32] HCJ 4128/02 *Adam, Teva v Din v Israel's Prime Minister* (handed down on 16 March 2004), President Barak's verdict at [18].

Although these two rights were not included in the right to dignity, other important rights were, precisely because the Supreme Court chose to interpret the right to dignity broadly. For example, it determined that a defendant's right to be present at his own trial is part of the right to due process, which is a constitutional right protected by Basic Law: Human Dignity and Liberty.

This process by which the Supreme Court completes the constitution – cautiously, with restraint, but steadily – is interesting. While the basic assumption is that certain rights (the right to equality or the freedom of expression) are implied by the human right to dignity, a complete bill of rights cannot be recognised under this limited right. Referring to this issue, President Barak said: 'When derivatively naming rights that are not explicitly listed in basic laws on human rights, but are included in the "human dignity" concept, it is not always possible to cover the full extent the "derived" rights would have had if they were individual and "named" rights.'[33]

This position means that the Supreme Court reserves the right to consider whether a certain aspect of equality, for example, should be acknowledged and constitutionally protected because it is closely associated with the right to dignity. Similarly, the Court may refuse to include another aspect of equality in the right to dignity and refuse to judicially review a law that impairs equality. Still, although it is all at the Court's discretion, some of its decisions to broadly interpret 'human dignity' and include rights that the legislature had explicitly chosen not to include in basic laws were criticised by several scholars.[34] These critics felt that it is not legitimate for the Court to grant certain rights a constitutional status before the legislature has done so, arguing further that it encourages the legislature to be 'lazy' when dealing with human rights.

One of the most far-reaching developments refers to the right to equality, as has been seen previously. When the legislature kept silent, the Supreme Court granted parts of the equality principle (not entirely – only certain aspects thereof) the constitutional status that allows judicial review of laws that disproportionately limit them.

---

[33] HCJ 366/03 *The Commitment to Peace Association v The Finance Minister* (handed down on 12 December 2005), President Barak's verdict at [15].

[34] Such as Professor Daniel Friedmann, Professor Gideon Sapir and Dr Hillel Sommer. See, for example, Hillel Sommer, 'The Unlisted Rights – On the Scope of the Constitutional Revolution' (1997) 28 *Mishpatim* 257 (Hebrew).

In an almost unprecedented move in 2012, this position led to the invalidation of a law that the Knesset introduced to exempt *yeshiva* students from military service. The grounds for the nullification were outlined in a previous verdict on the so-called *Tal* Law,[35] in which the HCJ ruled that certain aspects of equality are encompassed in the constitutional right to human dignity. In 2006, the Court stated that the harm caused by this law to the right of equality is proportional, acknowledging that the issue before it is socially complicated and sensitive, and that the desired change (drafting *yeshiva* students for civil or IDF service) must be attained gradually. Therefore, it concluded that five years needed to pass before a ruling could be made about the legality of the existing arrangement. After the arrangement was extended by a further five years, the HCJ was again asked to examine the constitutionality of the exemption and, in 2012, the majority of judges, led by President Beinisch, ruled that this time, the Court must declare the exemption arrangement unconstitutional.[36]

In the first *Adalah* case, which was discussed previously, it was argued that the law banning the reunion of Israeli Palestinians with their spouses from the PA violated their rights to equality and family life. These two rights are not included in Basic Law: Human Dignity and Liberty, but the appellants argued that they are covered by the constitutional right to human dignity. President Barak asserted that the right to human dignity is a 'framework' right from which 'daughter rights' could be derived, and that includes the right to family life.

Taking a different position, Vice President Cheshin stated that the constitutional right to human dignity does not cover the right of Israeli spouses to realise their right to family life with non-Israeli partners in Israel.[37] He thus opposed the entire process of including various rights within the right to human dignity: 'Stretching basic rights in every direction – up, down and sideways – might damage the constitutional discourse, which might eventually restrict the constitutional protection of human rights.' Justice Grunis was of the view that extensively expanding the scope of a constitutional right might create a real, practical problem in relation to the Court's ability to constantly deal with constitutional

---

[35] HCJ 6427/02 *Movement for Government Quality in Israel v The Knesset*, ver 61(1), 619 (2006).

[36] HCJ 6298/07 *Ressler v The Knesset* (published by Nevo on 21 February 2012).

[37] In the aforementioned *Adalah* case (n 10), Vice President Cheshin's verdict at [41].

allegations. Yet, despite these contradictory positions, and although the final decision did not quash the law, the majority endorsed President Barak's view as to the inclusion of the right to family life in the right to human dignity.

In another case, the HCJ ruled that the freedom of political expression is also tightly and nearly associated with the right to human dignity.[38]

The above discussion demonstrates that Israel lacks national agreement on certain fundamental issues, including basic rights. The political silence (or even paralysis) about completing the constitution has been replaced by supplementary constitutionalisation by the Supreme Court. It appears that, over time, the Court's 'novelties' have become part of Israel's common law and their legitimacy is no longer questioned, even though certain case outcomes suffered severe criticism. For example, the Court regularly reviews social and economic decisions with far-reaching budgetary implications. In 2003, it dealt with a government decision to reduce the financial support provided by the state to those in need. It dismissed the petition, but stated that it did not prove that the particular measures taken by the government were responsible for pushing the needy below the 'standard of dignified living'.[39] The Knesset held a special session on 'the latest HCJ interventions in the state's budget' and adopted a resolution (which is not binding, but demonstrates the level of criticism for HCJ rulings on these matters) stating that 'the Knesset views the Supreme Court's infiltrations into issues that unequivocally fall within the jurisdiction of the executive and legislative branches with concern'.[40] Still, while certain critics oppose the expansion of the right to human dignity to acknowledge the constitutionality of other rights, other critics maintain that the Court is not doing enough to promote social rights. Perhaps the fact that the criticism goes both ways (some complaining of undue restraint and others complaining of excessive activism) indicates that the Court actually deals with the human rights field quite carefully.

---

[38] HCJ 10203/03 *The National Census Ltd v Attorney General* (published by Nevo on 20 August 2008), Justice Naor's verdict at [26].

[39] HCJ 366/03 *Commitment to Peace and Social Justice v Ministry of Finance* (rendered 12 December 2005).

[40] Knesset minutes, 13 January 2004, taken from Menahem Mautner, *Law and the Culture of Israel* (Oxford, Oxford University Press, 2011) 66.

PART II: THE OCCUPIED TERRITORIES AND THE WAR ON
TERROR

AN UNRESOLVED CONFLICT

The State of Israel has been embroiled in a grave security situation ever
since its foundation. Some of its neighbour states have not yet accepted
its presence in the region. Furthermore, for the past two decades or so,
its citizens have been attacked by terrorists who came from PA territories that it occupied during the 1967 war. The Israeli–Palestinian conflict, which many believed was drawing to an end in the 1990s, assumed
a horrific new shape in the 2000s when Palestinian suicide bombers
exploded in Israeli cities, and curfews were routinely imposed on West
Bank cities. A sharp decrease in terrorist attacks has been experienced in
recent years, but the feeling of conflict that is still unresolved is part of
Israel's daily life. The Israeli–Palestinian conflict is rooted in a seemingly
intractable dispute over land claimed both by Jews as their Biblical birth-
right and by the Palestinians who seek self-definition. Despite repeated
attempts to end the conflict between the Israelis and the Palestinians,
there is no peace settlement in sight.

On the Israeli side, the Palestinian uprising (*Intifada*)[41] and Israel's
retaliatory and preventive operations during the 2000s gave rise to several serious questions as to how a balance might be struck between
defending human rights and meeting the security needs of the state during a time of war. Questions included the following: is collective punishment legitimate? May Israel demolish homes of suicide terrorists? What
legal instruments, if any, should courts use to review moves by security
forces? Should Israel legally open the door to more intensive military
operations? What should be the scope of judicial intervention when
dealing with anti-terrorist measures?

Many countries suffer from terror threats, and even the US had to
deal with them following the 9/11 attacks. These questions, therefore,
are not uniquely Israeli in nature and nations worldwide have discovered

---

[41] For a comprehensive description of the *al-Aksa Intifada*, see Orna Ben-Naftali
and Keren Michaeli, 'We Must Not Make a Scarecrow of the Law: A Legal Analysis
of the Israeli Policy of Targeted Killings' (2003) 36 *Cornell International Law Journal*
233.

the hard way that ordinary legal instruments that suit ordinary times may be lacking when counter-terrorist action is required. Clearly, traditional, time-consuming legislative steps fail when states require urgent legislative tools. Terrorism defies democracy and challenges democratic states, while naturally some of the means available to fight terrorism are illegal and unjustifiable according to democratic standards. The war on terrorism might require the reaching of decisions that are inconsistent with democratic values. In this war, the end might be confused with the means. Democracies must make difficult and delicate decisions on ways to balance national security and human rights, while employing emergency means to counter the threats.

Legally, Israel has been under 'a state of emergency' from day one. A government declaration on a state of emergency – enacted by the power of section 38 of Basic Law: The Government – provides the executive with particularly extensive powers. The government may introduce emergency regulations that can overrule ordinary Knesset legislation and even parts of other basic laws. This situation in practice allows for a series of legal arrangements that may only be employed in a state of emergency.

According to Basic Law: The Government, as amended in 1992, the Knesset may declare a state of emergency, which may remain in force for one year, after which it can renew the declaration if it sees fit to do so. Since 1992, the Knesset has renewed the state of emergency declaration annually. The fact that the state of emergency has not been withdrawn for more than 60 years since Israel was founded has been the subject of severe criticism. In 1999, a petition was filed with the HCJ by the Association for Civil Rights (ACRI), which requested that the Court order that the state of emergency be terminated, arguing that this ongoing situation is both unjustifiable and harms the rule of the law, the separation of powers and basic laws. In a unanimous ruling rendered more than 10 years later,[42] the Court held that the petition had 'run its course' because since the ACRI filed the petition, the state has slowly abolished several emergency laws. Justice Rubinstein said that while 'much work remains to be done' on the issue, the government should be allowed to complete the legislative process. The threats to Israel's existence still remain, Rubinstein added. Still, it was only to be expected that emer-

---

[42] HCJ 3091/99 *Association for Civil Rights v The Knesset* (published by Nevo on 8 May 2012).

gency legislation should match the 64-year-old democratic state, and this goal is achievable.

After the 1967 war, the HCJ became accessible to Palestinian residents of the occupied territories who believe they were harmed by the military government's actions. Ever since the *Intifada* started, many Palestinians have filed appeals against allegedly illegitimate actions undertaken by Israeli forces as part of their military operations. Petitions were filed during combat, including by suspected terrorists, which meant that decisions had to be made in real time. Supreme Court President Barak wrote:

> Is it proper for judges to review the legality of the war on terrorism? Many, on both extremes of the political spectrum, argue that courts should not become involved in these matters. Critics argue that judicial review undermines security, while others claim that judicial review unjustifiably legitimizes governments' actions against terrorism. Both arguments are unacceptable. Judicial review of the legality of the war on terrorism may make this war harder in the short run, but also fortifies and strengthens the people in the long run. The rule of law is a central element of national security.[43]

THE SUPREME COURT AND NATIONAL SECURITY

A central question in the war on terror is whether courts may intervene in the decisions of bodies whose duty it is to actually fight terrorism. As noted above, special legal tools are employed in times of emergency that might threaten the liberties of the population they are meant to defend, violate human rights and conflict with other democratic values. It has been argued that the courts should avoid intervening when decisions or laws are made to fight terror in times of emergency. Barak cited Cicero[44] to make his point:

> They say that when cannons roar, muses are silent. Cicero expressed a similar idea when he said *inter arma silent leges* (in times of war, the law is silent). These are regrettable statements. I hope they do not reflect democracies today. I know they do not reflect the way things should be. Every battle a country wages, against terrorists or any other enemy, follows rules and laws. There is always law, domestic or international, according to which the state

---

[43] Aharon Barak, 'A Judge on Judging: The Role of a Supreme Court in a Democracy' (2002) 16 *Harvard Law Review* 116, 158.

[44] Marcus Tullius Cicero. His actual wording was '*Silent enim leges inter arma*'.

must act. And the law needs Muses most urgently then when cannons roar. We need laws most in times of war.[45]

One of the clearest examples of how this concept is realised occurred on the eve of the First Gulf War of 1991. Concerned that Iraq might use non-conventional weapons against Israel, the Israeli Ministry of Defense decided to hand out protective kits in the occupied territories, but only to the Jewish settlers and not to the Palestinians. A Palestinian resident filed an urgent petition with the HCJ, arguing that this decision was discriminatory. The HCJ accepted the petition and ordered the IDF commander to issue protective kits to the Palestinians as well. Justice Barak wrote in his verdict that, even in times of war, 'the military commander must uphold the law. The power of a society to stand up against its enemies is based on its recognition that it is fighting for values that deserve protection. The rule of law is one of those values'.[46]

This verdict indicates that the HCJ would be willing to hear and sometimes even support petitions against military activities, even if they are filed during an actual war or in times of terror attacks. Clearly, Israeli adjudication in this field is characterised by HCJ judicial control. Neither arguments of standing nor claims that issues are non-justiciable prevented the Court from passing judgment on the IDF officers' decisions. Time and again, the HCJ has rejected claims that issues it has addressed were non-justiciable or should not be measured by legal criteria. Each and every case was reviewed on its merits, as the Court has insisted for many years that a balance must be struck between often-conflicting values, such as the need to protect the state and the security of its residents on the one hand, and the need to uphold human dignity and liberty on the other. In practice, the Court restricted the Executive's choice of means and tools in its response to terrorism. Justice Barak put it plainly in several cases, stating: 'A democracy must actually fight terror "with one hand tied behind its back" because the means that terrorists use cannot be employed by democracies.'

Following this approach, the HCJ delivered a long and impressive series of verdicts on the war on terror.[47] Below we discuss some of the

---

[45]   Barak (n 43).

[46]   HCJ 168/91 *Morcos v Minister of Defense*, ver 45(1), 467, (1991) 470–71.

[47]   Most of these verdicts were published in English on the Supreme Court's official website, under 'Fighting Terrorism Within the Law'. See: http://elyon1.Court. gov.il/VerdictsSearch/EnglishStaticVerdicts.html.

more prominent HCJ cases that show how the Supreme Court has dealt with the dilemmas that terrorist activities have created.

Suspect Interrogation Methods

The human right not to be subject to torture is as fundamental as the right to life and the ban on slavery, and is a key element of the human right to dignity. In December 1984, the UN issued a special convention prohibiting such practices.[48] This convention unequivocally bans the use of torture in any circumstances (Article 2(2)) and the countries that signed it must follow their signature with domestic legislative steps, including in criminal law, and set punishments that reflect the grave nature of such felonies. Israel ratified the convention in 1991. Generally, torture conflicts with Basic Law: Human Dignity and Liberty and with the provisions of the Israeli penal code.

Israel fights terrorism with numerous tools, including the GSS (General Security Service, or *Shin Bet*), the main body in charge of preventing hostile terror activities against Israel, which interrogates suspects of such activities. The Supreme Court had never addressed *Shin Bet* interrogation and investigation methods before Palestinian and Israeli human rights groups filed several petitions against these methods with the HCJ between 1994 and 1999. The HCJ handed down a verdict in September 1999 on which the nine-judge panel was unanimous: the GSS may conduct interrogations, but its physical interrogation techniques were declared illegal.[49]

The petitioners argued that the physical means employed by GSS investigators not only infringed the human dignity of suspects, but also constituted criminal offences. They claimed that these methods violate international law as they constitute acts of 'torture', which are explicitly banned. Furthermore, the 'necessity' defence constitutes an exceptional post factum argument, which is exclusively reserved for criminal proceedings against investigators who violate the new rules of interrogation. It

---

[48] Convention against Torture and Other Cruel, Inhuman, and Degrading Treatment or Punishment, UN GAOR, 39th Sess, 93rd mtg, art 2(1), UN Doc. A/Res/39/46 (1984).

[49] HCJ 5100/94 *Public Committee against Torture v The Government of Israel*, ver 56(4), 817 (1999). See also Matthew G St Amand, 'Public Committee against Torture in Israel, et al: Landmark Human Rights Decision by the Israeli High Court of Justice or Status Quo Maintained?'(2000) 25 *North Carolina Journal of International Law* 655.

does not provide GSS investigators with pre-emptory authorisation to torture suspects.

The HCJ ruled that a balancing test is necessary for dealing with interrogation rules. The balancing process resulted in a set of rules of reasonable interrogation. These rules are based on preserving the suspects' humanity while observing the classic IDF concept of 'purity of arms' during the interrogation. They reflect reasonableness, common sense and fairness. Democratic states need such rules because illegal investigations harm not only the suspects' dignity but also that of society. Thus, a reasonable interrogation is necessarily free from torture and other cruel, inhuman and degrading treatment of suspects – all of which are prohibited. There are no exceptions and there is no room for balancing. The Court stated that investigators who employ violent means might be held criminally liable.

Nevertheless, the Court assumed that if a GSS investigator is criminally indicted after applying physical interrogation methods while seeking life-saving information, the 'necessity' defence may be available in the right circumstances. The 'necessity' exception is likely to arise in cases known as 'ticking bombs',[50] when there is an immediate need to preserve human lives. However, this exception does not offer a priori approval to employ such wrongful means.

This judgment and the set of rules it produced significantly changed the GSS interrogation methods. Most of the physical interrogation methods are no longer applied, with very few and extreme exceptions. The Court's judgment further led to the introduction of the *Shin Bet* Law of 2002, which outlines the legal framework for the GSS, but does not deal with interrogations.

The Security Fence

In June 2002, the Israeli government decided to build a security fence to prevent terrorist infiltration from Palestinian territories into Israel. While there was broad public consensus in Israel about the need to construct a security fence, many disputed its route. The Israeli government did not wish to unilaterally delineate a political border since negotiations with the

---

[50] This term refers to a situation in which a suspect, arrested by the GSS, has information about an imminent and even evolving terrorist event that cannot be prevented without that information.

Palestinians – along whose border the line was to be demarcated – were always on the horizon. Israel therefore declared that the fence was only a security line and not a political borderline. In certain places along the chosen route, the fence violated the rights of local Palestinians: private land was seized, farmers were denied access to their fields, and roads to urban centres were blocked, denying access to medical and other essential services.[51] A petition against the legality of the chosen route, known as the *Beit Surik* case,[52] was filed with the HCJ in 2004.

A three-judge panel ruled against the security fence's route around Jerusalem because it was found to inflict too much damage on the Palestinian population. The HCJ also ruled that Israel has the right and the power to build a fence for security reasons, in practice legitimising this counter-terrorism operation, as the barrier is crucial to its self-defence. Drawing the route of the fence, the local military commander must weigh the security and military considerations and the state's defence against the human rights of the local Palestinian population. If the two issues clash, the commander must find a balance between them on the basis of the proportionality principle. Yet, the verdict left open the question about the very legality of the fence, which was not built along the Green Line.[53]

Two weeks after this verdict was published, the International Court of Justice (ICJ) in The Hague published an advisory opinion according to which building the fence (which it called 'a wall') for political reasons, and not along the Green Line, was illegal, violated international law and constituted an annexation of territory.[54]

---

[51] Emanuel Gross, 'Combating Terrorism: Does Self-Defence Include the Security Barrier? The Answer Depends on Who You Ask' (2005) 38 *Cornell International Law Journal* 569–82; Ruth Wedgwood, 'Agora: ICJ Advisory Opinion on Construction of a Wall in the Occupied Palestinian Territory: The ICJ Advisory Opinion on the Israeli Security Fence and the Limits of Self-Defence' (2005) 99 *American Journal of International Law* 52, 58–59.

[52] HCJ 2056/04 *Beit Surik Village Council et al v Government of Israel et al*, ver 58(5) 807 (2004).

[53] The 1949 Green Line is not a borderline, but refers to demarcation lines set out in an agreement between Israel and its neighboring countries (Egypt, Jordan, Lebanon and Syria) after the 1947–48 Arab–Israeli War. The Green Line also marks the line between Israel and the occupied territories.

[54] *Legal Consequences of the Construction of a Wall in the Occupied Palestinian Territory*, Advisory Opinion (9 July 2004). According to this opinion, the fence is not a temporary security measure, but rather a political attempt by Israel to draw new permanent borders.

This opinion, and the fact that the HCJ accepted the *Beit Surik* petition, encouraged many other Palestinians to file petitions against the fence route. The following famous case[55] concerned Alfe Menashe (an Israeli settlement in Samaria, some 4 km east of the Green Line), where the security fence created an enclave of several Palestinian villages on the Israeli side. Referring to the ICJ's opinion, the petitioners argued that the State of Israel had no legal right to build the fence because it served no security needs and because, by doing so, Israel de facto annexed Palestinian territories.

The outcome of the HCJ judgment in this new case was that the fence route in that specific location should be altered. A nine-judge panel unanimously produced one of the most important legal documents ever written in Israel, certainly for foreign readers. Containing nearly no novelties in Israeli law, the 80-page judgment predominantly constituted a dialogue with the ICJ opinion and the international legal community. It basically reiterated the principles established in the *Beit Surik* case. The HCJ again determined that the military commander may build a separation or protective fence in Judea and Samaria for security and military reasons, but that the current route of the fence seriously and disproportionally violated Palestinian rights. The new angle was that the HCJ acknowledged that Israel is legally authorised to build a separation fence to protect the lives and welfare of Israelis. It pointed out that the Judea and Samaria regions are held by the State of Israel by the power of belligerent occupation, according to the rules of international law, which further authorises the military commander of the region to build a separation fence for security reasons.

The HCJ's judgment does not, however, deal solely with the Alfe Menashe enclave. Dozens of pages are devoted to a factual, legal and academic analysis of the ICJ opinion, offering a competent and reasoned Israeli response to the ICJ's assertions. The ICJ opinion was an advisory paper, the Court stated, but should nonetheless be considered by the Court. The HCJ confronted the ICJ's every assertion, stating that, although the *Beit Surik* verdict and the ICJ opinion shared some views, they reached different conclusions, which the HCJ convincingly explained. The differences follow from the facts presented before the ICJ, which did not truly address the security-military considerations at

---

[55] HCJ 7957/04 *Mahmad Maraba v Israel's Prime Minister* (handed down on 15 September 2005).

play. The HCJ argued that the ICJ opinion referred predominantly to the violated Palestinian rights, while ignoring Israel's security justifications, which is why the ICJ's conclusion that the fence is illegal and conflicts with international law does not bind Israel's Supreme Court.

This judgment re-established and bolstered previous statements of the Court. The HCJ will continue to examine the route of the fence, making sure that the harm done to the welfare of local residents in each segment is minimal. The HCJ will examine every case for a proportional balance between security-military needs and the rights of the local population. Both international law and Israeli law require that every possible effort be made to ensure that injury to human rights is proportionate. Where construction of the fence demands that inhabitants be separated from their lands, access to these lands must be ensured so as to minimise damage to the greatest extent possible. In later appeals, the Court eventually discussed almost every segment of that fence, but most of the petitions against them were rejected after they were examined on their merits.

While the Israeli governments saw the security fence as no more than a physical, temporary barrier designed to block Palestinian terrorists, the Palestinians argued that it was a unilateral Israeli move to delineate permanent borderlines. More than a decade after its construction, the fence apparently resulted in the number of terrorist attacks dramatically declining, but the sense of security within Israel cannot be attributed exclusively to the fence, which serves as a means of separation. The security goal has been achieved through the combined efforts of all parties concerned: the government, the military, the intelligence services, and with the security coordination of the Palestinian police.

With the construction of the fence, Israel perhaps succeeded in establishing the concept of separation. This concept paved the way for broad national agreement on the creation of two states for two peoples. Still, the fence is a key source of Israel's international delegitimisation. In an article, Dr Dan Tirza, a retired army colonel and the IDF's chief architect of the security fence,[56] wrote:

> The fence created a conceptual and physical barrier between two neighboring peoples that have been entangled in conflict for a century but still hope to live in peace. I would have gladly done without the fence. Yet, we had no

---

[56] Col Dr Dan Tirza, in *Al-Monitor*, July 20102. See: http://www.al-monitor.com/pulse/originals/2012/al-monitor/israeli-security-fence-architect.html.

choice but to build it in order to protect our and our children's lives. I do hope the day will come when the threat of terror no longer casts its dark shadow over our lives and we will be able to live peacefully, safely and securely alongside our Palestinian neighbors; a day when there is no need for any fences or walls.

Targeted Pre-emptive Assassinations

'Targeted assassinations' or 'targeted pre-emptive killings' are the names the Israeli military has given to its long-standing mode of operation in which it targeted, attacked and killed terrorist leaders who were held responsible for the perpetration or planning of terror attacks against Israel's citizens. Around December 2000, the Israeli security forces started employing a tactic of 'eliminating' leading Palestinian militants, field commanders and infrastructure coordinators. Applied mainly in the context of the *Intifada*, this method was the Israeli reaction to 'escalating Palestinian violence', but often triggered further escalation and retaliatory Palestinian operations.

President Barak's verdict on an appeal filed against this method of targeted killings was the last he handed down before he retired in 2006. In it, the outgoing President quoted from a judgment he delivered several years earlier on GSS interrogation methods: 'We are fully aware of the fact that this verdict does not make dealing with this reality any easier. It is the fate of democracies that they may not approve of every means and cannot employ all the methods that their enemies use.'[57]

The verdict examined the legality of the targeted assassinations policy and outlined some rules for its implementation, but the petition against the practice was rejected. The decision neither authorises nor forbids the use of this tactic: 'It cannot be determined in advance that every targeted killing is prohibited according to customary international law.' The HCJ ordered that each case be examined in detail before the method is applied and that the military commander further consider alternatives and the expected damage. The use of targeted assassinations must be proportional, that is, based on the balance between military benefits and the expected damage they might cause to innocent civilians. In practice, however, the security forces had followed similar

[57] HCJ 769/02 *Public Committee against Torture v The Government of Israel* (handed down on 14 December 2006).

considerations even before that verdict was handed down. Targeted assassinations were not practised daily, but now their preceding considerations appear in a legal document. This document too was not written only for Israeli readers. Essentially, the targeted assassinations case resembles the separation fence case in nature, as the verdict on the former was also part of Israel's dialogue with the international community that closely monitors Israel's activities in the occupied territories. These 'security' verdicts explore the impossible situation faced by Israel when combatting terrorists who attack it and then find refuge among innocent civilians.[58]

It seems that, like many other security-related judgments delivered by him during his term, President Barak's last judicial document presents a sensitive statement of defence for Israel's constant war on terror. Sitting on and presiding over the vast majority of security-related cases presented before the HCJ, including the *security fence* ruling, Barak promoted the proportionality principle as a way of striking a balance between security needs and harm to human rights, stressed the need to avoid sweeping and generalising solutions that deny human rights, urging the authorities to examine each case by its unique criteria and merits, and established the principle that security considerations do not always take precedence. At the same time, these verdicts are mainly declaratory and do not in practice intervene in the military commanders' considerations.

In the 'targeted assassinations' case, the HCJ set several mandatory rules: assassinations must not be carried out if less harmful means can be employed and harm to innocent civilians must be avoided as much as possible. Such harm is only lawful if it meets the proportionality requirement, which means that Israel may not target terrorists if the expected collateral damage is too great. Here, as in other cases, Barak reiterated that democracies may not use every tool and certainly may not match the terrorists' methods: 'Democracies often fight with one hand tied behind their backs, but they will always prevail because guarding the rule of law and acknowledging individual rights are key elements of their security concepts. Observing those eventually bolsters their spirit and helps it overcome hardships.'[59]

---

[58] For additional reading, see Amnon Rubinstein and Yaniv Roznai, 'Human Shields in Modern Armed Conflicts: The Need for a Proportionate Proportionality' (2011) 22(1) *Stanford Law & Policy Review* 93.

[59] *Public Committee against Torture v The Government of Israel* (n 57), President Barak's verdict at [64].

The Court's judicial review of IDF activities in the occupied territories often reveals gaps between judicial rhetoric and the actual result. Arguably, this is an active approach de jure, but an abstention from de facto intervention. Although the HCJ was willing to discuss almost every petition filed against IDF operations in the territories, even in real time, and examined the security forces' authority to use various means and whether those means were proportionally employed, it approved of almost every method that the IDF employed in its war on terror and rejected most of the petitions. It must be stressed that the Supreme Court never endorsed the argument of 'security above all', nor did it accept charges that the violation of human rights is an Israeli policy.

CONCLUSION

The Supreme Court's significant contribution to the protection of human rights is perhaps a unique feature of Israel's constitution. Since the very early stages of the State of Israel, the Supreme Court has defended human rights and created what was to be known as the Bill of Judicial Rights. This comprises customary rights developed in case law which, by virtue of the principle of stare decisis, have transformed into binding legal norms in Israel. Human rights protection was recognised in the decisions of the Supreme Court long before these rights were explicitly mentioned in the basic laws. Following the constitutional revolution, and while the Knesset has failed to provide a charter of human rights, the Supreme Court stands out for its achievement both in the constitutionalisation of human rights and in expanding the scope of human rights protection in particular fields. Political silence in relation to these questions has been replaced by constitutional interpretation by the Court, allowing the recognition of new rights as part of Israel's incomplete constitution.

The war on terror and the ongoing conflict with the Palestinians have posed and still pose many difficult constitutional questions. Israel has struggled for its existence since its establishment, constantly living in a state of emergency. It is a Jewish and democratic state that consistently faces security threats. It has always acknowledged the need to strike a balance between conflicting needs and the interests of various nationalities and religions, between being the nation-state of the Jewish people and being a democracy, and between the desire to protect human rights and the need to provide security for all. Justice Rubinstein pointed out: 'We may not ignore the fact that Israel has not yet found comfort and peace. Indeed, it experienced relatively long periods of relative calm, but regrettably the winds of war never stopped blowing . . . Israel's situation was and still is sensitive and complicated, and in such a situation, the state authorities must not be left without the powers they need in emergency times.'[60]

FURTHER READING

Barak, Aharon, 'Foreword: A Judge on Judging: The Role of a Supreme Court in a Democracy' (2002) 116 *Harvard Law Review* 16.

Barak, Aharon, 'The Role of a Supreme Court in a Democracy, and the Fight against Terrorism', 2003, Faculty Scholarship Series, Paper 3693. Available at: http://digitalcommons.law.yale.edu/fss_papers/3693.

Barak, Aharon, *The Judge in a Democracy* (Princeton, Princeton University Press, 2006).

Barak, Aharon, *Proportionality: Constitutional Rights and their Limitations* (Cambridge, Cambridge University Press, 2012).

Barak-Erez, Daphne, 'Israel: The Security Barrier – Between International Law, Constitutional Law, and Domestic Judicial Review' (2006) 4 *International Journal of Constitutional Law* 540.

Bendor, Ariel, 'Justiciability of the Israeli Fight against Terrorism' (2007) 39 *George Washington International Law Review* 149.

Gavison, Ruth, 'The Controversy over Israel's Bill of Rights' (1985) 15 *Israel Yearbook on Human Rights* 113.

Gross, Aeyal, 'The Politics of Rights in Israeli Constitutional Law' (1998) 3 *Israel Studies* 80.

Gross, Emanuel, 'Fighting Terrorism with One Hand Tied Behind the Back: Delineating the Normative Framework for Conducting the Struggle against Terrorism within a Democratic Paradigm', ExpressO (2010). Available at: http://works.bepress.com/emanuel_gross/2.

Gross, Emanuel, 'Terrorism and the Law: Democracy in the War against Terrorism – The Israeli Experience' (2002) 35 *Loyola of Los Angeles Law Review* 1161.

Halperin-Kaddari, Ruth, *Women in Israel—A State of their Own* (Philadelphia, University of Pennsylvania Press, 2003).

---

[60] *Association for Civil Rights v The Knesset* (n 42), Justice Rubinstein's verdict at [11].

Hofnung, Menahem, *Democracy, Law and National Security in Israel* (London, Dartmouth Publishing, 1996).

Klein, Claude, 'On the Three Floors of a Legislative Building: Israel's Legal Arsenal in its Struggle against Terrorism' (2006) 27 *Cardozo Law Review* 2223.

Kretzmer, David, *The Occupation of Justice* (New York, SUNY Press, 2002).

Kretzmer, David, 'The Advisory Opinion: The Light Treatment of International Humanitarian Law' (2005) 99 *The American. Journal of International Law*. 88.

Orgad, Liav, 'Love and War: Family Migration in Time of National Emergency' (2008) 23 *Georgetown Immigration Law Journal*. 85.

Raday, Frances, 'On Equality – Judicial Profiles' (2001) 35 *Israel Law Review* 380.

Rubinstein, Amnon and Roznai, Yaniv, 'Human Shields in Modern Armed Conflicts: The Need for a Proportionate Proportionality' (2011) 22(1) *Stanford Law & Policy Review* 93. Available at: http://papers.ssrn.com/sol3/papers.cfm?abstract_id=1861161.

Saban, Ilan, 'Minority Rights in Deeply Divided Societies: A Framework for Analysis and the Case of the Arab-Palestinian Minority in Israel' (2004) 36 *New York University Journal of International Law and Politics* 885.

Shamgar, Meir, 'Legal Concepts and Problems of the Israeli Military Government: The Initial Stage' in Meir Shamgar (ed), *Military Government in the Territories Administered by Israel, 1967–1980: The Legal Aspects* (Jerusalem, The Harry Sacher Institute for Legislative Research and Comparative Law, The Hebrew University, 1982).

Conclusion:
The Future of the Israeli Constitution

THIS CONCLUDING CHAPTER focuses on the challenges that the Israeli constitution will likely face in the next few years. As we shall see, the constitutional questions that remain undecided and the compromises that would be required from the different groups in Israeli society – mainly from the Orthodox Jews and the Israeli Arabs – render the completion of the constitution a very difficult task.

A survey of the experience of other nations over time demonstrates that constitutions have been approved or established at critical historical junctures, in the aftermath of wars, after a revolution or upon the fall of an old regime and the rise of a new one. The foundation of Israel was perhaps the crucial moment for the adoption of a constitution and the newborn state actually planned to have a constitution, as was required by the Partition UN Resolution. The Declaration of Independence not only proclaimed the foundation of Israel as a Jewish state and promised equal rights to all its citizens, but also specified that Israel's governing bodies would be elected pursuant to the provisions of the new constitution enacted by the constituent assembly. However, the process of enacting a written constitution at the time of the State of Israel's establishment failed. In 1950, the Knesset decided, after a long debate, not to promulgate a constitution at that stage and instead to enact a series of basic laws that, when completed and finalised, would form Israel's constitution. The formation of the State of Israel launched its path among nations without a written constitution or a bill of rights, directly referring instead to the British tradition of parliamentary sovereignty. Over the years that followed, the Israeli Parliament introduced a dozen basic laws, but it never completed the task of drafting and approving a constitution. It was the

Supreme Court that stepped in and established the basic principles for the new state, as well as a solid base for the protection of human rights. In doing so, the Court cited the Declaration of Independence and its definition of Israel as both a Jewish and a democratic state. As we have seen throughout this book, the Supreme Court has played a special and crucial role in the development of Israel's constitutional law, primarily in the field of human rights.

The constitutional revolution of the 1990s and the Supreme Court's increased power of judicial review have prompted the emergence of a public debate in Israel over the adoption of a constitution. Several questions have been raised, some following Supreme Court decisions. In particular, these questions have concerned the nature of the body authorised to judicially review laws, whether to adopt a new formal constitution or to complete the existing basic laws, the process for adopting a new constitution and the values which would be incorporated in any such constitution. Any attempt to answer these questions in the future must take into account Israel's unique circumstances, the rifts in Israeli society and the political tradition, as well as the security problems and the ongoing conflict with the Palestinians.

Israeli Arab leaders are mainly in favour of the adoption of a constitution, but only one that abolishes the Jewish definition of the state and becomes the state of all its citizens. Therefore, entrenching a definition of the state as Jewish and arrangements such as those outlined in the Law of Return are strongly contested. A written constitution is also vigorously opposed by some Jewish groups, with the 'intra-Jewish' debate in Israeli society reflected in aspects of the debate concerning a codified constitution. Orthodox Jews are opposed to it. The compromise demanded of them is to accept a version of the constitution which is basically secular. A written constitution may be less favorable to them than the non-written status quo that has been in existence since the establishment of the state. Any constitution not based on *Torah* sources is likely to be unacceptable to them. On the other side of the spectrum, the Zionist religious factions are split between those who object to the process altogether and those who wish to entrench the Jewish nature of the state. For example, a recent political debate dealt with a bill proposal (led by the right-wing members of the Knesset) to enact Basic Law: Israel as the Nation-State of the Jewish People. This proposed bill primarily addresses the Jewish characteristics of Israel, stating that the State of Israel is the historical homeland of the Jewish people and that the right of national self-determination within Israel belongs exclusively to the Jewish people. The bill has arisen as a response not only to the political platforms of the Arab parties, which promoted the idea of Israel as the nation of all its citizens, but also as a response to what they argue is the problematic interpretation of the 'Jewish and democratic' principles by the Supreme Court in many cases.

It seems that the strong divisions in Israeli society serve to undermine the possible completion or enactment of a written constitution, without even referring to other challenges such as security, war and the occupied territories. Gavison argues that the more divided a society is, the greater the importance of a constitution to its political stability. However, the more divided a society is, the less likely it is to agree to a constitution. This is especially true for the 'substantive' parts of the constitution, such as the bills of rights and the basic principles.[1]

Adopting a constitution may also call for a redefinition of the relationship between the main branches of the state, as well as the balance between them. The debate over the appropriate electoral regime for Israel and the most desirable voting method to adopt is still high on the Israeli political and public agenda. Both right-wing parties and left-wing parties have been fervent advocates of different models. As a result, this is an unresolved issue that cuts across parties and religious groups.

Another reason for the incomplete constitution stems from the lack of agreement on the question of what kind of body should be responsible for constitutional interpretation. Since the *Bank Hamizrahi* case, with very few exceptions, Israel has actually experienced constitutional silence on the question of interpretation. As the Supreme Court put it: 'It seems that certain parts of the Knesset are displeased with the constitutional powers of this Court and fear that additional constitutional texts would further enhance its power.'[2] One option is to persist with a Supreme Court as the chief interpreter of the constitution. On the other hand, there is also support for the introduction of a special, constitutional court,[3] although this option is rarely raised. Jewish groups as well as Israeli Arab leaders seem reluctant to confer the power to deal

---

[1] Ruth Gavison, 'Constitutionalism and Political Reconstruction? Israel's Quest for a Constitution' (2003) 18(1) *International Sociology* 55.

[2] HCJ 4908/10 *MK Bar-On v The Knesset* (published by Nevo on 4 July 2011), para 4 of Justice Rubinstein's verdict.

[3] Claude Klein, 'A Constitutional Court: Things Aren't Really that Bad!' (2003) 19 *Mehkarei Mishpat* 497 (Hebrew).

with key issues to the judiciary, which is regarded by many political figures as a non-representative body identified with the secular liberal Jewish elite. The judicial approach to political questions is also disputed and, as is the case with respect to the electoral system, it is a matter of contention across parties and religious groups. Perhaps this explains why the project of completing the constitution has been almost forgotten as part of the platform of political parties in recent years. But, as we have seen, the political silence concerning the completion of the constitution has been replaced with a supplementary constitutionalisation undertaken by the Court. It appears that, over time, the Court's 'novel views' have become part of Israel's common law and their legitimacy is no longer questioned, even though certain cases have been severely criticised.

Looking towards the future, then, it will be apparent that the constitutional process in Israel faces many challenges. The first is to reach some kind of consensus across all the political parties regarding the rules of the constitutional game. Israel could benefit from a constitution, but as long as the fundamental political issues remain unresolved, it would be extremely difficult to complete the final stage of the constitutional enterprise and enact a constitution that will enjoy a broad legitimacy. As Gavison argues, the chances that 'regular politics' will generate a serious political change are very unlikely. Politicians need a serious emergency, a clear necessity or an unrelenting demand from their voters to initiate a change that will limit their own powers. These are hard to create within 'regular politics'.[4]

A far-reaching peace agreement between Israel and the Palestinians, and between Israel and the Arab world, may be the historical moment suitable for the enactment of a constitution. The establishment of borders may provide for this rare opportunity. But this is – for the moment – no more than wishful thinking. In its entire existence, Israel has not known a day free from a state of emergency and war. It has always been compelled to find a balance between the need to defend itself and the desire to protect human rights. As a consequence, a constitution must take into account Israel's existential struggle to survive. In one of the Supreme Court's judgments on Israel's state of emergency, Justice Elyakim Rubinstein summed up the situation well:

---

[4] Gavison (n 1).

Israel is a normal state that is also abnormal. It is normal in being an active democracy that protects basic rights – including free elections, freedom of speech, and the independence of the judiciary and the attorney general – fundamentally fulfilling its destiny as a Jewish and democratic state. It is abnormal because it is the only democracy under a constant threat of annihilation; because despite having peace treaties with Jordan and Egypt and certain political agreements with the Palestinians, its relations with its neighbors have not yet been properly arranged; and because the war on terrorism continues and will probably continue for the foreseeable future. We still may not rest under our vine and fig tree.[5]

Israel's constitutional history has demonstrated that the constitutional text is often less important than its interpretation by judges. Presently, in the wake of the constitutional revolution, the bulk of basic laws comprise, in effect, the major part of the current Israeli constitution. It is considered a 'constitution in the making', limited and still lacking many elements that characterise complete constitutions elsewhere. Its weakness lies not only in what it is lacking (namely, a complete chapter of human rights befitting a democracy and rules for the introduction of basic laws and their judicial review), but, most of all, its weakness lies in its ease of amendment for political and partisan reasons.

Any account of the Israeli constitution necessarily reflects the story of its society. Israel was formed as a Jewish and democratic state. It is a split nation, comprising diverse nationalities and religions, and so there exists a constant need for reconciliation between conflicting interests to maintain a nation-state of the Jewish people which is also committed to democracy. The future challenges for Israel's society, namely, defining minorities and protecting their rights, ending the state of belligerency and inwardly realising that all the political currents and nationalities must reach a compromise of coexistence, are all preconditions for the completion of the constitution.

---

[5] HCJ 3091/99 *Citizens' Rights Association v The Knesset* (published by Nevo on 8 May 2012).

Index